Life on the Other Border

The publisher and the University of California Press Foundation gratefully acknowledge the generous support of the Anne G. Lipow Endowment Fund in Social Justice and Human Rights.

Life on the Other Border

FARMWORKERS AND FOOD JUSTICE
IN VERMONT

Teresa M. Mares

UNIVERSITY OF CALIFORNIA PRESS

University of California Press, one of the most distinguished university presses in the United States, enriches lives around the world by advancing scholarship in the humanities, social sciences, and natural sciences. Its activities are supported by the UC Press Foundation and by philanthropic contributions from individuals and institutions. For more information, visit www.ucpress.edu.

University of California Press
Oakland, California

Earlier versions of material from the introduction appeared in *The SAGE Encyclopedia of Food Issues,* © 2015 SAGE Publishing.

Earlier versions of material from the introduction, chapter 1, and chapter 3 appeared in "Eating Far From Home: Latino/a Workers and Food Sovereignty in Rural Vermont," in *Food Across Borders,* edited by Matt Garcia, E. Melanie DuPuis, and Don Mitchell. © 2017 Rutgers University Press.

Library of Congress Cataloging-in-Publication Data

Names: Mares, Teresa M., 1978– author.
Title: Life on the other border : farmworkers and food justice in Vermont / Teresa M. Mares.
Description: Oakland, California : University of California Press, [2019] | Includes bibliographical references and index. |
Identifiers: LCCN 2018040134 (print) | LCCN 2018044141 (ebook) | ISBN 9780520968394 (ebook) | ISBN 9780520295728 (cloth : alk. paper) | ISBN 9780520295735 (pbk. : alk. paper)
Subjects: LCSH: Dairy workers—Vermont—Social conditions. | Foreign workers, Latin American—Vermont—Social conditions. | Agricultural laborers, Foreign—Vermont—Social conditions.
Classification: LCC HD8039.D32 (ebook) | LCC HD8039.D32 V455 2019 (print) | DDC 331.6/280743—dc23
LC record available at https://lccn.loc.gov/2018040134

Manufactured in the United States of America

28 27 26 25 24 23 22 21 20
10 9 8 7 6 5 4 3 2

This book is dedicated to my father David Mares and my daughter Evelyn. While the ends and beginnings of your lives did not intersect, I know that you would have loved each other deeply.

CONTENTS

TABLES AND ILLUSTRATIONS

MAP

TABLE

FIGURES

ACKNOWLEDGMENTS

As with any ethnographic endeavor, this book is the result of the collective and individual labor of dozens of people. First and foremost, I would like to thank the farmworkers who have shared their stories, experiences, and meals with me over the past seven years. Your resilience along *La Otra Frontera* has inspired me more than you could ever know. It is my hope that this book helps to make visible your struggles, your hopes, and your dreams. I came to Vermont knowing next to nothing about the dairy industry and the farmworkers who sustain it, and it is only because of your collective generosity and trust that I can now share your stories here.

To my colleague Naomi Wolcott-MacCausland: this book would have never been possible without your grounded guidance, support, and connections to the community. It has been an absolute honor to work with you as we have developed the Huertas project and as I have considered ways to piggyback my research on our gardening efforts. Your patience and commitment to others is astounding. Thanks also to the Huertas interns who have played double duty as research assistants for this project: Jessie Mazar, Claire Macon, and Elena Palermo. Your enthusiasm, energy, and commitment to social justice gives me hope that another world is indeed possible. You are the reason why I bring students into the field.

Thanks also to the many service providers and volunteers who sat down with me for interviews and shared the ways they support Vermont's farmworker community. Your assistance provided a vital dimension to this research, and your dedication to the well-being of others is deeply inspiring. In particular, Julia Doucet at The Open Door Clinic provided a much-needed space for me to do my research and form community connections.

In the early stages of developing this project and this book, I would have been lost without the support of my colleagues and mentors Amy Trubek and Luis Vivanco at the University of Vermont. You both campaigned for me way back in 2011, helped me to settle into life in Vermont, and have helped me at each critical juncture during my early academic career. Thank you for reading drafts of my book proposal and for championing my work for the last seven years. You have made UVM an intellectual home for me. Thank you also to all the members of UVM's Food Systems community who have been curious about and supportive of my research. Because of you all I never doubted the significance of this work.

The research underlying this book was supported at all stages by various departments and programs at the university. With funding support from the UVM Humanities Center, UVM Food Systems Planning Grant, The Graduate College REACH grant, the College of Arts and Sciences Joan Smith Faculty Research Award and Small Grants Program, and the Center for Research on Vermont's Frank M. Bryan Award, I gathered my data, hired my research assistants, and wrote this book. A junior leave and full-year sabbatical made this book a reality. I am incredibly fortunate to be employed by an university that supports the research efforts of its faculty in the ways that UVM does.

I owe a great debt to David Meek and Laura-Anne Minkoff-Zern who reviewed early drafts of the chapters for this book. To David in particular: this would have been an entirely different beast without your critical reading and excellent suggestions. Your feedback helped me to transform a rough assemblage of thoughts and arguments into a much more polished book.

To my dissertation advisors Rachel Chapman and Devon Peña, your guidance offered within the walls of Denny Hall continues to shape who I am as a researcher, writer, and teacher. You both provided me with a model for what an engaged decolonial academic should look like. I trust that you will read these pages and see your teachings intertwined with my words.

I am incredibly fortunate to have worked with the dynamic and supportive staff at the University of California Press to bring this book to fruition. To my editor Kate Marshall: I am thrilled beyond words that our initial conversations years ago have followed us to the publication of my first book. Your suggestions, questions, and attention to the nuances of publishing-while-pregnant are the reason that this book is being birthed at the time that it is. I look forward to many more years of working together. Bradley Depew, you were responsive and diligent beyond measure. You made the publishing process infinitely less intimidating and more transparent.

To Matt Garcia and Ellen Oxfeld, who provided in-depth readings of the full manuscript, your generous suggestions and questions were instrumental in bringing this project to its (tentative) conclusion. Thank you to Matt for also welcoming me into the Food Across Borders crew, where many of the seeds of this book were first planted.

To my compxs at Migrant Justice, thank you for your tireless work bringing dignity to the lives and labor of Vermont's farmworkers. I am humbled to stand alongside you all in *la lucha*. I am indebted to Brendan O'Neill and Marita Canedo for their reading of chapter 5 in particular and for their support of my research more generally. *¡Sí, se puede!*

For my family, spread from Colorado to Connecticut and New Hampshire, you are my backbone and my roots. The past few years have been a series of trials and celebrations, and I trust we are stronger because of it. To my mother, Joyce, and father, David, you provided all the love I needed to get to where I am today. Mom, you are the epitome of strength and care. Dad, I know you would have shown your copy of this book to everyone you know (and likely to strangers on the street) if you were still with us. To my siblings Jeff, Ted, and Liz: thank you for being older than me and always making the path forward a little easier. To my many nieces and nephews: I love you all. Judy Sauer, thank you for always asking me how the book was going and for producing such a wonderful son. Laura, you are my adopted family and I know that the next twenty years of our friendship will be as strong and secure as the last twenty.

Despite the frigid Vermont winters, I have found a warm home and growing family in this brave little state, and this is entirely because of the love and encouragement of Henry Sauer. You are my tireless cheerleader and I truly do not know where I would be without you. I cannot wait to see what adventures await us. To my furry muses Canela and Judge (and yes, even you, Simone): you provided excellent company during the long and furious days of writing and during the naps that interspersed them. And finally, to my sweet little Evelyn, thank you for choosing me as your mama.

Introduction

"That's the house that I am building! Those are the mango trees,
there are three of them! That's my little house!"

HUNCHED OVER A SMALL KITCHEN TABLE encircled by plastic lawn
chairs, Samuel and Hector zoomed in to the map of Jaltenango de la Paz I
had located using my smartphone. From a run-down single-wide trailer in
the northernmost part of Vermont, we gazed upon the street-view rendering
of their small village in the state of Chiapas, Mexico. Focusing in on the
house that Samuel was building with his earnings from *El Norte,* we could
see, in full color, the result of the remittances that he regularly sent home.
With these dollars-turned-pesos, he also sent his dreams of eventually returning and raising a family, surrounded by the region's coffee fields and Mayan
communities. Together, the three of us virtually strolled through the images
of village streets sent from more than three thousand miles away. We mar-
veled at the detailed images of homes and businesses, of people and of cars.
As we crossed each intersection, Samuel and Hector argued about what had
been built since each of them had made their long journeys north, and what
was no longer there. As time and space were flattened onto the glowing
screen, the connections between these two distinct locales came into sharp
relief, along with an understanding of how their food systems are intimately
intertwined. For Samuel and Hector, who have come to the United States to
work in Vermont's dairy industry, Jaltenango was both ever-present and a
million miles away, ripening mangoes and hungry Holsteins competing for
their labor, care, and attention.

Over the past twenty years, farmworkers like Samuel and Hector have moved to the picturesque rural countryside of Vermont to find work in the dairy industry. For some, this northern state is just the most recent stop in a long line of impermanent and unstable employment in the United States. For others, family networks have brought them directly to Vermont's rolling green hills and milking barns from their homes and fields in Mexico and Central America. Samuel, in his early forties, had migrated to the United States three times, previously working in landscaping and other seasonal jobs in South Carolina. Three years before we sat down for an interview at his kitchen table, he followed his brother to Vermont to secure the chance of year-round employment that the dairy industry promises. Samuel's nephew Hector, on the other hand, came directly from Chiapas just one year earlier to reunite with his mother, two U.S.-born brothers, and other members of his extended family. After paying off the debt he had accrued to pay for his crossing, he too planned to start saving for the family he hoped to have one day. For these two men, Vermont's often harsh climate stands in stark contrast to Jaltenango's lush green mountains. At first glance, their landscapes and agrarian economies could not be more different. However, what connects them is deep and complex: the political-economic interdependencies and migration networks that are inherent in the globalized industrial food system.

In *Life on the Other Border,* I unravel these interdependencies and follow these networks as I explore the intersections of structural vulnerability, food security, and the politics of visibility in the lives of migrant farmworkers in the northern borderlands of the United States. This book focuses on Latinx farmworkers who labor in Vermont's dairy industry, aiming to illuminate the complex and resilient ways these workers sustain themselves and their families as they simultaneously uphold the state's agricultural economy.[1] I argue throughout the following chapters that multiple forms of vulnerability and marginalization conspire to leave farmworkers like Samuel and Hector never fully satisfied with their sustenance or their living conditions, even as their labor contributes to the livelihoods of farmers and the well-being of consumers across the food chain. In these borderlands, anxiety and fear continue to shape the lives of migrant workers long after they have endured the trauma of crossing into the United States from Mexico. At the same time, Vermont's farmworkers are looking towards unprecedented possibilities for achieving food justice and food sovereignty, in large part because of worker-led grassroots organizing. This organizing builds upon decades of farmworker activism and labor movements, from the United Farm Workers (UFW) grape boycotts to more recent campaigns by the Coalition of Immokalee Workers (CIW). Although this ethnography is situated in Vermont, it is not a unique case. Across the U.S. food system—in the fields, slaughterhouses, fast-food kitchens, and canneries—it is the immigrant worker who feeds the nation. What is particular to this story is how the reality of Vermont's dairy sector rubs against—and is erased by—its carefully constructed image and branding.

Vermont is widely seen as an agrarian utopia where socially responsible brands like Ben & Jerry's and Cabot Creamery Cooperative have flourished. It is also a place where the local food movement has taken firm hold of the consumer imagination and purchasing power, as described by anthropologists Heather Paxson in her work on artisanal cheese in her ethnography *The Life of Cheese* (2012) and Amy Trubek in her work on *terroir* in *The Taste of Place* (2008). It is within this imagined agrarian utopia that migrant workers labor and live in the state's shadow economy to sustain industrialized food production while experiencing everyday discrimination and difficulty satisfying their most basic needs. In presenting a portrait of this shadow economy, *Life on the Other Border* examines how the broader movements for food justice and labor rights play out in an agricultural sector where systemic inequality is continually reproduced by the demands of an industrialized food system and the contradictions of racialized and misaligned agricultural and immigration policies. Of course, labor exploitation is not new to Vermont's food system, or any food system. Wherever food is harvested, cooked, served, or thrown away, there is someone working for too little and for too long. And, as food systems scholars have argued, this pattern of inequality does not follow a simple binary of local/organic = good and global/conventional = bad.[2] In the pages that follow, I continue with this project of demystifying and challenging these binaries in a place where the local is intimately bound with the global. A place where men like Samuel and Hector tirelessly work to produce dairy products bearing the wholesome Vermont brand, even as they are often sustained by foods with little cultural or nutritional value.

Building upon more than six years of community-based ethnographic research, *Life on the Other Border* explores the following interrelated questions: *What are the social, political, and economic factors that bring Latinx migrant dairy workers into the state of Vermont, and what factors shape their lives while here? How do Latinx migrant dairy workers access food and negotiate the reproductive labor associated with accessing and preparing foods within the household? How has the broader Vermont community responded to the presence and the needs of this workforce amidst an ever-changing political and social climate?* As I engage with these questions, I connect data gleaned through participant observation, food security surveys, and interviews with farmworkers and key stakeholders working with the farmworker community with an analysis of the broader structures that shape our food systems from the local to the transnational scale. Understanding the social, political, and economic dynamics that bring Latinx workers into Vermont and those that shape their living and working conditions once here is essential. It is essential because they are the cornerstone of an agricultural economy so marked by its proximity to an international border and particular racialized histories. This border is a place where insiders and outsiders are defined, where some bodies matter more than others, and where the labor of some food workers is visible and celebrated, while the labor of others is hidden and exploited.

BORDERING VISIBLE BODIES

In this book, I develop and engage with a framework of Bordering Visible Bodies, weaving together a diverse set of theoretical threads that allow me to investigate: (1) the border as a process—of bordering—and as a physical site of structural vulnerability, violence, and resilience; (2) the politics of visibility that are at play in Vermont's agricultural economy and working landscape; and (3) the embodied experiences of workers who have crossed borders and reside within them. I use this framework to contextualize and understand the food-related practices within migrant households, because they provide a critical vantage point for illuminating how the relationships between people and their basic needs move from intimate embodied experiences, through household and social reproduction, and outwards towards social and political institutions. As the editors of *Food Across Borders* remind us, "Food is a great way to understand what borders do: the bodily, societal, cultural, and territorial transformations that occur as physical sustenance flows across, or stops at, a boundary."[3]

There is an exceptionally rich body of literature on borders and borderlands, and in a post-9/11 world, borders and border-making are particularly salient as we theorize power relations, injustice, and in/exclusion. As we find ourselves in a moment of intensified focus on the U.S.-Mexico border and the demonization of those who cross over it, borders demand our attention. In my engagement with border theory—or better, border theories—I have been inspired by a line of transdisciplinary thinking that stretches from the recent work of Anssi Paasi to the canonical work of Gloria Anzaldúa. Anzaldúa, who pioneered—and queered—feminist borderlands scholarship, describes the borderlands as those spaces that are "physically present wherever two or more cultures edge each other, where people of different races occupy the same territory, where under, lower, middle and upper classes touch, where the space between two individuals shrinks with intimacy."[4] This view emphasizes that the borderlands are markers of difference and of closeness, of deterritorialization and reterritorialization, and of sovereignty of the nation-state and of individual bodies.[5] More than twenty years later, Paasi extends this line of thinking (though he fails to credit Anzaldúa) through his examination of borders as discursive and technical landscapes of control.[6] He argues that "borders should not be seen solely as phenomena located at the 'edges' of territories, but rather 'all over' territories, in innumerable societal practices and discourses."[7] Although Anzaldúa and Paasi both claim that borders permeate all social relations and discourses, they also emphasize that the discourses and practices of border-making are concentrated at physical boundaries, particularly those dividing nation-states.

Some border scholars have taken to using the term *bordering* to describe the inclusionary and exclusionary processes and practices of border-making. I have found this idea productive in better understanding the marginalization of farmworkers in Vermont. Johnson and his colleagues offer a useful definition of this concept:

> Bordering reflects politics in many ways. It is not only a politics of delimitation/classification, but also the politics of representation and identity that come into play. Bordering separates and brings together. Borders allow certain expressions of identity and memory to exist while blocking others. Respectively borders are open to contestations at the level of state and in everyday life.[8]

Within the scholarship on borders and migration, the bordering that unfolds at the U.S.-Mexico border has garnered much anthropological attention, with notable contributions coming from Ruth Behar (1993), Leo Chavez (1998), Jason de León (2015) and Seth Holmes (2013). While these scholars do not explicitly use the term "bordering," these books illustrate the depth that anthropology offers through their rigorous examinations of border violence and the complex ways that borders are enacted and embodied by Latin American migrants. These are significant and tragically beautiful pieces that have pushed my thinking in deep and productively uncomfortable ways.

And yet, *Life on the Other Border* offers something different. By extending northwards and drawing attention to a border region that has remained largely invisible in borderlands scholarship, I show how historically and socially contingent processes of bordering come to shape the minds and bodies of migrant workers in the food system. This bordering is inextricable from the politics of visibility that marks Latinx farmworkers in Vermont's dairy industry as the Other, as those who do not belong but whose bodies provide the invisible labor necessary for the state's agricultural economy to stay afloat. My analysis draws upon data collected both before and after the 2016 U.S. presidential election. In the pages that follow, I draw attention to this new political reality and how an increasingly hostile anti-immigrant discourse at the national level impacts the well-being of Vermont's farmworkers on the local level.

Often characterized as a "new" or "nontraditional" destination for Latinx migration, the increasing migration of workers from Mexico and other Latin American countries into Vermont's dairy industry began in the late 1990s, a period coinciding with an unprecedented scaling up of dairy production. The presence and everyday struggles of these workers are emblematic of the rapidly changing dynamics within Vermont's rural landscapes. Within these landscapes, the structural inequalities connected to race, ethnicity, and citizenship leave Latinx migrant workers simultaneously invisible in the workplace and hypervisible in public settings. This contradiction has significant implications for accessing basic needs like food, health care, and safe housing.[9] Although the academic treatment of the politics of visibility runs broadly across disciplines, my treatment of this topic is informed by a body of work that examines how (in)visibility is produced, denied, and struggled for and by immigrant bodies in specific spaces and places.

Whether the physical site is the U.S.-Mexico borderlands, downtown Nashville, farmworker housing projects in Oregon, the streets of Perry, Iowa, or in day labor sites in California, Latinx bodies continue to be marked as the Other.[10] This bordering of Latinx bodies has multiple motivations and outcomes: it is enacted as a defense of hegemonic whiteness; it reflects a deeply entrenched fear of "polluting" immigrant bodies; and it provides the terrain for struggles over visibility and recognition.[11] Licona and Maldonado point to the complex and often competing dimensions of visibility:

Within dominant populations, visibility is often experienced as positively coded. To be visible in community spaces means to be included, to have a voice that gets heard, to have access to institutions and resources. By contrast, in the present context of entrenched anti-immigrant hostility and heightened immigration enforcement, for Latin@s (immigrants and non-immigrants), visibility is often negatively coded: it often entails standing out as an 'unbelonging' presence, being the subject of surveillance and policeability, of criminalizing, pathologizing, and otherwise alienating discourses and practices.[12]

As I build upon and extend the scholarship on the politics of Latinx visibilities, I provide my own answer to the question raised by Monica J. Casper and Lisa Jean Moore: "What can account for the fact that certain bodies are hyper-exposed, brightly visible, and magnified, while others are hidden, missing, and vanished?"[13] By attending to the experiences of workers in our food system, my answer—in short—is that hierarchies and inequalities in agricultural labor reproduce and are reproduced by varying degrees of visibility. The invisibility of immigrant workers has material consequences—both for workers and the eventual consumers—and hiding the bodies and suffering of food workers is symbiotic with what Henry A. Giroux has termed the "biopolitics of disposability."[14] Indeed, as Sidney Mintz argued decades ago, the exploitation and invisibility of workers is not external to food production, but rather a precondition of it.[15]

For dairy workers in Vermont's border region, the international border manifests itself in everyday decisions about the risks of leaving the farm and becoming visible to U.S. Border Patrol versus exercising one's autonomy and right to mobility. For most, the risks of being detained and possibly deported do not outweigh the benefits of continued employment, resulting in a dependency on others for accessing food and medications, inequitable access to health care, and mental health consequences such as anxiety and depression. Throughout the years that I have studied migration in Vermont, the most common term that Latinx immigrants use to describe their experience has been *encerrado* (enclosed)—which refers to the feeling of being trapped behind the borders of the farms themselves. This term, *encerrado,* has appeared repeatedly in my conversations with Samuel and Hector, whose words opened this chapter, as well as in conversations with women like Sofía who faced surveillance from Border Patrol that discouraged her from attending prenatal appointments while she was pregnant with her second child. These forms of bordering, and the resulting feelings of being imprisoned and invisible, extend the violence and vulnerability produced at the national border all the way down to the borders around the farm that people confront on a daily basis.

The majority of Vermont, including more than 90 percent of the state's residents, falls within the one-hundred-mile expanse where Immigration and Customs Enforcement (ICE) officers have the authority to stop and search travelers without reasonable suspicion or a warrant.[16] The hypervisibility and assumed undocumented status of Latinx workers in this nontraditional destination of migration puts them at risk for compounding experiences of structural vulnerability and inadequate and irregular access to many basic needs and social connection. These anxieties tend to intensify the closer to the northern border one is living and working, because the concentration of active U.S. Border Patrol agents increases with closer proximity to Canada. While the one-hundred-mile expanse is indeed significant, the "primary operating domain" of Border Patrol is said to be within twenty-five miles of the Vermont-Canada border, meaning that most routine enforcement takes place within a much smaller region of the state. This primary operating domain encompasses three of the four border counties (Grand Isle, Franklin, and Orleans) that are home to a significant number of the state's dairy farms employing Latinx workers.

For farmworkers in rural areas of the state, a trip to the grocery store or to a doctor's appointment is cause for significant worry and fear. Merely speaking Spanish in public has been used as a cause for community members to call ICE officers. Indeed, just two weeks after arriving in Vermont, Hector was detained at a store when he was seen shopping for items for his little brother's birthday party. This set off a round of complicated and costly steps through immigration courts and detention centers, exacerbating the debt that he had already accumulated for his passage into the United States. At the time of writing, Hector is currently awaiting a final decision about what lies ahead for him, but for now he continues to work as so many food- and farmworkers do around the nation, plagued by feelings of anxiety and uncertainty.

There is yet another side to this politics of visibility. Since 2009, the living and working conditions of Latinx workers in Vermont's dairy industry have become more visible to the broader public. This increased visibility has followed a number of high-profile events and important farmworker-led organizing efforts for food justice that have challenged the erasure of Latinx farmworkers. These events include the death of a young Mexican farmworker while working with heavy farm machinery in late 2009, the detention of

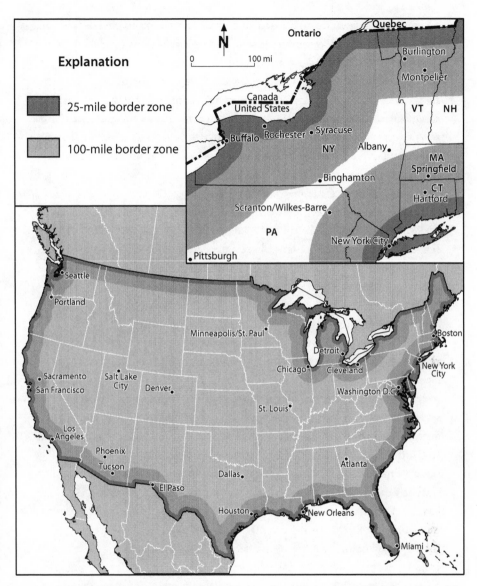

MAP 1. Map showing one-hundred-mile and twenty-five-mile border zones. Map prepared by Syracuse University Cartographic Laboratory and Map Shop. Reprinted with permission from Rutgers University Press.

farmworker activists and subsequent organizing around racial profiling within local and state law enforcement, and legislation approved in 2013 that grants driver's privilege cards to all residents, regardless of citizenship status. Most recently, farmworker activists involved with the organization Migrant Justice and their allies have campaigned to reconfigure the supply chain of some of Vermont's most well-known food corporations through the "Milk with Dignity" campaign. This campaign, which has attracted national attention, builds upon a successful model of worker-driven social responsibility pioneered by the Coalition of Immokalee Workers (CIW). Even with this growing visibility, Latinx migrants continue to experience a great deal of fear, isolation, and anxiety in their daily lives due to their status in Vermont as invisible workers in what some scholars have called a "carceral landscape".[17] For many workers, particularly those close to the border, Vermont's dairies resemble prisons where the line surrounding the farm becomes the most proximate border that may or may not be crossed.

Amidst these complicated dynamics, local politicians and dairy farmers have become more vocal about the industry's dependency on Latinx farmworkers and the need for policy reform. This dependency became especially poignant in September 2011, when two undocumented workers were detained after the car they were riding in was pulled over for speeding by state police near Middlesex, Vermont. One of these workers, Danilo Lopez, had become widely known throughout the state for his activism and criticism of the Secure Communities Program.[18] Both workers were subsequently transferred to Border Patrol authorities and detained. This event escalated later that same afternoon, when five local activists came to protest at the state police station near Middlesex, arguing that requesting documentation during a routine traffic stop was a clear violation of the recently passed policy of Bias-Free Policing. After forming a human blockade to stop the vehicle transporting the two detainees, three of the five activists were arrested for disorderly conduct, though they were all shortly released. Later that same evening, then Governor Peter Shumlin ordered an immediate internal investigation into the traffic stop.

This case took an interesting turn later that fall when Shumlin went on public record about his views on the presence of undocumented workers in the state. He asserted, "We have always had a policy in Vermont where we kind *of look the other way* as much as we can . . . I just want to make sure that's what we're doing" (emphasis mine). The governor then continued with a matter-of-fact observation that Vermont farms simply "can't survive without workers from outside America. It's just the way it is."[19] As might be expected, this statement set off a round of contentious debates and commentary on migrant labor that has not dissipated to this day, and any local coverage on farmworker issues is sure to produce a heated thread of commentary about the importance and the assumed illegality of these workers. More importantly though, this statement is also an explicit reinforcement of the conditions that keep migrant farmworkers invisible, reproducing the processes of bordering that keep their laboring bodies out of sight and, for many, out of mind.

A DISTINCTIVE RURAL PLACE?

Understanding the lives of migrant workers in Vermont's dairy industry demands that we consider the links between emigration from Latin America and the devastation of rural livelihoods following the implementation of neoliberal reforms such as the North American Free Trade Agreement (NAFTA). Neoliberalism is a political economic philosophy that asserts the primacy of the market in attending to human needs and well-being, and reorients the state towards the facilitation of market mechanisms.[20] The state often cedes its power through allowing corporate interests to advance this philosophy with the objective of increasing efficiency and allowing for the free flow of capital. NAFTA, as a state-backed trade agreement, aimed to facilitate the flow of capital and goods across the borders in North America. Following the passage of this agreement, scholars estimate that anywhere from 1.3 million to more than 2 million Mexican farmers were forced off their lands, pushed to the urban centers of Mexico as well as north of the U.S.-Mexico border to find work.[21] While much has been said about the dumping of U.S. corn on the Mexican market and consequent emigration, less attention has been paid to the political-economic histories and transnational impacts of the deregulation of Mexico's dairy industry amidst the increasing consolidation and concentration of the U.S. dairy industry. As with corn production, these neoliberal reforms were facilitated by NAFTA, an agreement that flooded Mexico with U.S. subsidized milk, often in powdered form.[22] And, as with corn, small-scale dairy farmers on both sides of the border have endured assaults to their livelihood and market volatility because of these reforms.[23] The U.S. Dairy Export Council, central in lobbying for these policies, comprises many dairy giants that operate in Vermont, including Dairy Farmers of America, Inc., Dairy Marketing Services, Dean Foods, and HP Hood.[24] These same players now profit from the labor of Latinx migrants who had little choice in their home countries other than to move in search of work.

As the U.S. state with the highest dependence upon a single commodity for agricultural revenue, Vermont has experienced significant shifts in the labor force that toils amidst the rolling hills and red barns that still dominate the pastoral working landscape.[25] According to the Vermont Dairy Promotion Council, Vermont currently sells more than 321 million gallons of milk each year, with 70 percent of agricultural sales coming from this single product. Approximately 80 percent of the state's farmland is dedicated to supporting dairy production, whether for dairy lots, for pasturing, or for growing feed crops. Dairy also accounts for six thousand to seven thousand jobs (more than any of the state's key private employers), providing $360 million in wages and salaries.[26] As of 2016, there are an estimated one thousand to twelve hundred Latinx migrant dairy workers in Vermont, and the vast majority—approximately 90 percent—of these workers are thought to be undocumented.[27]

The dairy industry has long been central to the state's agrarian image and this image is touted with great regularity in the marketing of the state's agricultural products and the celebration of its rural livelihoods. However, the role of farmworkers from Latin America in creating these products and maintaining the working landscape is rarely acknowledged. In many ways, this failure to acknowledge the contributions of Latinx workers in Vermont's dairy industry is similar to the historical and contemporary erasure of Mexican-origin agricultural workers that Mario Sifuentez describes in his book *Of Fields and Forests*.[28] As Sifuentez describes in his rich and deeply personal environmental and labor history of the supposed progressive "eco-topia" of the Pacific Northwest, it is often in these assumed "green" locales where immigrant and migrant workers remain the most invisible and marginalized. However, just as Sifuentez describes in his analysis of worker mobilization and the formation of the farmworker union *Pineros y Campesinos Unidos del Noroeste* (PCUN), Vermont's farmworkers are actively challenging this marginalization.

The erasure of farmworkers in Vermont is exemplified in the recent publication entitled *Milk Matters* cited previously. This sixteen-page publication prepared by the Vermont Dairy Promotion Council intends to illuminate the economic significance of dairy in the state but includes just one photo of a Latino farmworker and a mere two sentences about the "complex labor and immigration issues" that dairy farmers face. While the report is comprehensive in other ways, these kinds of representations render Latinx farmworkers and their labor largely invisible while upholding the image of Vermont as an idyllic and progressive state maintained only by the sweat and endurance of U.S.-born farmers. As scholars have shown, this image of Vermont's working landscape has been carefully produced alongside a long history of exclusionary politics and cultural boundaries based on race/ethnicity, social class, and national origin.[29] The struggles of Latinx farmworkers comprise the most recent chapter in the industry's history of hiring workers who will toil for substandard wages and in less-than-desirable conditions. Nevertheless, the discursive production of Vermont as a "distinctive rural place" steeped in Yankee values of hard work, modesty, and wholesomeness continues to circulate, drawing thousands of people into the state annually to engage in agritourism and to consume the state's bounty.

Once comprising primarily small-scale family farms, Vermont's dairy industry has been subjected to the same pressures of consolidation and concentration that pervade the U.S. food system as a whole. The image of the small family dairy farm that is invoked to sell the Vermont brand is now little more than a myth, since neoliberal policies and market volatility make small-scale dairy farming next to impossible. Over the past seventy-five years Vermont has lost more than 90 percent of its dairy farms. In the 1940s there were approximately eleven thousand dairy farms in the state; in early 2018 this dropped to fewer than seven hundred fifty.[30] Since the economic crash of 2008, Vermont's dairy farmers have faced unprecedented financial and environmental challenges, including high feed prices, unstable milk prices, and irregular weather patterns. This decline has spelled disaster for thousands of Vermont's dairy farmers, who, as of early 2018, earned roughly the same amount for fluid milk as they did in the late 1970s, even as the costs of production have multiplied. In February 2018, Agri-Mark, a Massachusetts-based cooperative that owns Cabot Creamery, sent their farmers a letter with information for suicide prevention hotlines along with their milk checks.[31]

Yet Vermont is currently producing milk at record levels, supporting trends that demand surpluses of fluid milk like the increased consumption of Greek-style yogurt and the manufacturing of whey protein, a by-product that is often more profitable than the cheese and yogurt from which it comes.[32] While a sizeable number of dairy farms (82 percent) have fewer than two hundred cows, economic conditions have pushed Vermont's dairy farms

FIGURE 1. Cows in Vermont morning mist. Photo by Jessie Mazar.

to become larger, with bigger herds to become more efficient and remain profitable, and to use more intensive milking technologies and schedules. The increased production of milk in the state, which comes at significant ecological and social costs, is directly facilitated by Latinx farmworkers who migrate in search of employment and the chance at a better life for their present and future families. This shift is reflective of national and international trends in the food system, where immigrant labor has become more central to production and profits, even if these workers are afforded little in the way of legal protections or the possibility of upward mobility.

The demographic changes that have occurred in Vermont over the past twenty years with increased migration from Latin America entail significant considerations with respect to the programs, agencies, and retail outlets that provide food, health care, and other basic needs to Vermont's residents. This book traces the impacts of these demographic shifts in a state that remains largely invisible in the scholarship of migration and borders. In neighboring New York State, the experiences of Latinx migrant workers living in rural areas have been examined from multiple angles.[33] These studies illuminate the lived realities that Latinx migrants face in a state where the federal border has become increasingly "Mexicanized" since 2001, amidst concerns of terrorism and lax surveillance.[34]

Like most agricultural sectors across the nation, the dairy industry in the state has grown increasingly industrialized since the 1950s. This industrialization has resulted in the consolidation of thousands of small family farms into a much smaller number of large farms. The technologies and labor practices associated with milking have also shifted to become more uniform, mechanized, and less amenable to small-scale family farming. Across the U.S. dairy industry, hiring Latinx workers has become more commonplace alongside the mounting ecological, technological, and financial challenges of farming, and Wisconsin, California, and upstate New York have seen similar demographic changes in the dairy workforce to those taking place in Vermont.[35] As of 2017, a significant number of Vermont's dairies employed migrant laborers, with 68 percent of Vermont's milk coming from farms that rely on immigrant workers (with a yearly sales of $320 million) and 43 percent of New England's milk supply coming from these farms.[36] Based on their study of Spanish-speaking workers on 293 dairies in New York, Vermont, and Pennsylvania, researchers predicted that within just a few years the majority of the dairy workforce in these states would be Spanish-speaking.[37] While Latinx workers in Vermont's dairies do not yet form a majority, their economic role in the industry remains significant.

FARMWORKER INJUSTICE GROWS IN EVERY FIELD

As U.S. food production has grown increasingly industrialized, the consolidation of small family farms into larger and often vertically-integrated farming operations has grown more commonplace. Since the end of World War II, these consolidation and industrialization processes have been spurred by a growing influence of large-scale agricultural corporations that now dominate most food production and distribution in the United States and abroad. Along with this consolidation, hiring laborers from off the farm has become the primary strategy of meeting the production needs of farming operations where labor needs exceed local labor availability. In Vermont, there is a particular dearth of local residents, especially younger individuals, available and willing to work the kinds of dairy jobs that immigrant laborers hold. Immigrant workers labor in nearly all sectors and scales of the food system, from the smallest family farms to the largest corporate food operations, from diversified farms to enormous dairy operations. In a nation where the food industry accounts for 13 percent of the total gross domestic product, the contribution of farmworkers is clearly significant to the nation's overall economic well-being.[38]

While Mexican workers have labored on U.S. farms since the drawing of the U.S.-Mexico border, the reliance on hiring farmworkers from outside the United States intensified much later with the institution of the Bracero program in 1942. Largely in response to labor shortages brought about by U.S. involvement in overseas wars, the Bracero program brought an estimated four million hired laborers from Mexico into the fields and farms north of the border. In response to concerns over labor abuses associated with the program, an increased presence of undocumented labor, and the growing significance of labor organizing by the National Farm Workers Association and the Agricultural Workers Organizing Committee, the program was officially ended in 1964. Since the end of the Bracero program, the United States has sought to manage the needs for guest workers through the H-2A Temporary Agricultural Worker program, though this too has been an inadequate and unsustainable solution, particularly within the dairy industry with its year-round labor needs.[39]

The growing reliance on nonfamily farm labor since the end of World War II has been significant. For instance, the percentage of hired and contract workers providing agricultural labor (measured in the percentage of hours) increased from 25.3 percent in 2003 to 41.0 percent in 2016 alone.[40] It is exceedingly difficult to pinpoint the total number of hired farmworkers laboring in the United States, given the off-the-books nature of many of these work arrangements. Additionally, given the increase of mechanization in the food system, the United States has experienced an overall decrease in the total number of farm laborers, so this proportional change is likely even more dramatic. According to the Bureau of Economic Analysis, the total number of wage and salary workers in crop, livestock, and related support activities was estimated at 1,344,000 in 2016, a figure that reflects a higher rate of growth in the number of contract workers compared to those hired directly.[41]

Given the high mobility and unauthorized status of many of these workers, it is not surprising that estimates of the number of foreign-born farmworkers are not consistent across sources. While the Southern Poverty Law Center estimates that roughly 62 percent of farmworkers in the United States are undocumented immigrants, NAWS data estimates that roughly half of all hired crop farmworkers lack official authorization to work in the country.[42] The top four nations sending undocumented farmworkers are Mexico, El Salvador, Guatemala, and Honduras.[43] From nations like these, both unauthorized and authorized farmworkers are pushed north by poverty, violence, political instability, food insecurity, and a lack of viable employment. Given the cultural diversity of farmworkers from Latin America, it is difficult to generalize about demographic factors and pre-migration experiences, but farmworkers tend to be less likely to speak English than other migrant laborers, and according to the National Center for Farmworker Health, the average level of completed education among farmworkers is the eighth grade.[44]

Despite these divergent data statistics, it is clear that a majority of these workers are male, with most estimates agreeing that only 18–28 percent of all hired farmworkers are female.[45] Many popular representations of farmworkers characterize them as seasonally employed and following various crop harvest cycles, but in reality, only about 12 percent of farmworkers work in this fashion.[46] Since the attacks of September 11 and the subsequent militarization of the U.S-Mexico border, foreign-born agricultural workers have become less likely to engage in circular migration to and from their home nations as they once were, because of the increasing risks of crossing the border.

Despite the significance of farmworkers in upholding the national agricultural economy, the economic conditions of farmworkers remain substandard. Seasonal farmworkers are often even more disadvantaged in the labor market than farmworkers who remain settled.[47] According to a recent report, only 13.5 percent of workers earn a livable wage across food sectors from production through retail, while for agriculture and nursery workers surveyed, this rate was 0 percent.[48] The poverty rate among farmworkers is much higher than average for salary and wage workers, and according to recent data, over three-fifths (61 percent) of the farmworker population lives below the poverty line.[49] Farmworkers are also particularly vulnerable to both wage theft and violations of minimum wage regulations. Based on surveys conducted by the Food Chain Workers Alliance, 92.9 percent of all workers experiencing wage theft were Latinx agricultural workers.[50] Research completed by the organization Migrant Justice has shown that Vermont's farmworkers are no exception, with 20 percent of workers surveyed reporting that their first paycheck was illegally withheld and 12 percent of workers reporting not being paid on time.[51]

Latinx farmworkers also disproportionately experience irregular and inconsistent work, with double the unemployment rates of all wage and salary workers.[52] On the flip side, farmworkers are also more likely to have schedules that exceed fifty hours per week, especially during peak agricultural seasons. Undocumented workers are unable to access federal and state-based programs for the poor, including SNAP benefits, housing assistance, disability and unemployment, Medicaid, or SSI. This is despite the fact that they pay billions into these federal programs annually.[53] Besides these inconsistencies and economic realities, farmworkers do not typically have access to unemployment insurance, workers' compensation, or disability benefits. This demonstrates how farmworkers often work in a "shadow economy" where they are vulnerable to the whims of unscrupulous employers, unable to assert their rights and, for all practical purposes, beyond the protection of labor laws that protect the rest of us from abuse, discrimination, and wage cheating in the workplace.[54] These lack of protections are particularly troubling given the hazardous working conditions that many farmworkers experience.

With the high number of undocumented workers on U.S. farms comes a preponderance of unsafe working conditions and labor abuses. Agricultural work is widely considered to be one of the most hazardous sectors of the economy, and safety and health concerns in the workplace are often exacerbated by unsafe and unhealthy living conditions. The occupational fatality rate for farmworkers was five times higher than the rate for any other worker in 2009.[55] Female farmworkers encounter these struggles in addition to even greater wage inequalities. And in many cases, they also experience sexual harassment and abuse. According to a recent study, as many as 80 percent of female farmworkers experience sexual violence; and they often fear reporting these crimes because of a generalized fear of police and other authorities.[56] The dairy industry is particularly unsafe given the size of milk cows and the hazardous working conditions produced by high levels of animal waste and mechanized equipment. The 2009 death of José Obeth Santiz-Cruz was a poignant and tragic reminder about these conditions, when he was strangled after his clothing got caught in a gutter cleaner.

Sadly, it is estimated that only one-tenth of farmworkers have health insurance.[57] This lack of protection is troubling given that a lack of adequate sanitation facilities, coupled with heavy exposure to pesticides and other agricultural chemicals, is a pressing and often deadly challenge confronting farmworkers. According to the Environmental Protection Agency, there are an estimated ten thousand to twenty thousand cases of diagnosed pesticide poisonings among farmworkers each year.[58] Prolonged pesticide exposure is linked to a wide range of illnesses and health conditions, including infertility and reproductive health problems, cancer, birth defects, skin problems, Parkinson's disease, and neurological damage.[59] In the dairy industry, exposure to the hazardous chemicals used to clean and sanitize milking equipment is a constant reality, and it is rare that employers and employees have clear and consistent lines of communication about their proper use and disposal.

Over my time conducting research in Vermont, I have repeatedly listened to stories of individuals migrating from Mexico to work in the dairy industry at ages as young as fourteen. These workers, often men, show the cumulative and embodied effects of their labor only a few years later, their bodies wracked with aches and pain. Yet children and youth receive fewer legal protections in agricultural work than in other sectors. For example, while workers in non-agricultural sectors must be eighteen to perform hazardous tasks in the workplace, the minimum age for workers in the agricultural sector is sixteen. The legal protections against child labor are certainly complicated by the lack of documentation status of many workers, leaving factors like age to be overlooked by employers in their hiring processes.

Forced labor is a persistent and troubling problem within the agricultural sector, and farmworkers are often vulnerable to physical and verbal abuse and threats of deportation if they do not follow strict orders from their employers. Since the late 1990s, cases of forced, indentured, and enslaved agricultural workers have made national headlines. Through the ongoing anti-slavery campaign led by the CIW, the enslavement and abuse of more than one thousand workers in Florida, Georgia, and the Carolinas have been investigated and prosecuted since 1997. While enslavement and forced labor have not been reported in Vermont's dairies, wage theft or delays in pay are commonly reported problems, leaving many workers vulnerable to the unreasonable demands of their employers to continue work without proper compensation.

Given these troubling conditions, it is necessary to highlight the discontinuities between legal protections and the actual experiences of farmworkers. Although there are state regulations designed to protect farmworkers, nearly all major federal labor laws that were passed during the New Deal under the administration of Franklin D. Roosevelt specifically exclude farmworkers. These exclusions, and their effects, should be seen as concrete forms of institutional racism. This is because they were largely motivated by concessions to southern congressmen firmly entrenched in the Jim Crow era who were invested in the ongoing exploitation of Black workers and other minorities working in agriculture.[60]

Laws that would be particularly helpful to farmworkers, including workers' compensation, mandatory breaks, and overtime pay regulations, do not apply to workers in this sector of the economy. Moreover, "under federal law, a farmworker may be fired for joining a labor union, and farm labor unions have no legal recourse to compel a company or agricultural employer to negotiate employment terms".[61] Although agricultural employers and farm labor contractors must abide by the Migrant and Seasonal Agricultural Worker Protection Act, this act does not cover some of the most pressing challenges that have been described above. It does, however, state that workers must be paid what and when they are due and that the terms and conditions of the employment must be disclosed. For undocumented workers there is little recourse to ensure that these standards are met.

HARVESTING A DIFFERENT PRODUCT: WHAT MAKES
DAIRY WORK UNIQUE

This book focuses on migrant farmworkers in Vermont's dairy industry because they face a set of everyday challenges distinct from workers in other sectors of the food system. At the same time, they are constrained by some of the very same structural inequalities that make food-related jobs some of the nation's most unsafe and underpaid. The year-round nature of milk production, in comparison to other sectors of farm labor, presents a different set of realities and limitations for those employed in the dairy industry. Unlike workers following seasonal schedules of planting and harvesting, migrant workers in this industry are excluded from federal seasonal work programs such as the H-2A visa program. This differential access to authorized work in the U.S. food industry is reflective of the deeper contradictions embedded within agri-food commodity chains, where immigrant workers are simultaneously indispensable and disposable. Organizations like the Food Chain Workers Alliance (FCWA) and CIW have documented and challenged these contradictions, drawing attention to the fact that food-related jobs, from production through disposal, are often filled by workers with limited access to the benefits and protections associated with U.S. citizenship. Vermont-based Migrant Justice, a farmworker-led organization that is a member of the FCWA, is working to challenge these inequities and bring greater agency and justice to the lives of dairy workers.

The vast majority of the research on farmworkers focuses on those working in seasonal agriculture. However, there are a few key studies that examine the experiences of migrant dairy workers in states such as New York and Wisconsin, and one study that attempts to take a global perspective.[62]

Together, these studies highlight the health concerns that dairy workers share, the ergonomic and other physical hazards that accompany this type of labor, and the rigid and racialized forms of occupational segregation that persist on dairy farms. Each underscores the fact that dairy work is one of the most, if not the most, dangerous agricultural occupations and that undocumented workers in this industry confront unique barriers that limit their access to health care, social networks, and dignified living and working conditions. As Kathleen Sexsmith demonstrates through her research in northern New York, dairy workers in close proximity to the U.S.-Canada border also experience greater chances of being detained and deported by Border Patrol and Immigration and Customs Enforcement personnel.[63]

Within Vermont, there is a small body of scholarship on farmworkers in the dairy industry. In their work surveying 120 Latinx workers in Vermont's dairy industry from 2009 and 2011, Baker and Chappelle found that a significant number of these workers, 93 percent of whom were male, experienced anxiety and depression linked to isolation and fear of immigration enforcement, in addition to the physical pain linked to hard manual labor.[64] About half of workers surveyed reported being in excellent or very good health, but overall, significant barriers prevented these workers from utilizing health services when it became necessary. These barriers included a fear of immigration enforcement, language barriers, and limited access to transportation. Although working primarily in milking barns, widely understood to be the hazardous part of dairy work, workers surveyed earned a median wage of $7.75 per hour. All were living on the farm where they worked, and most had housing and utilities provided. On Vermont's dairies, farmworker housing varies widely in quality, with some workers experiencing overcrowding and inadequate heat while others live in modest but safe and comfortable housing.

In a closely related study utilizing data from thirty-four semi-structured interviews with farmworkers, Wolcott-MacCausland found significant barriers to health-care access for workers located in border counties, which resulted in common practices of self-diagnosis and self-medication, as well as dependency upon employers and community members for decision making and access to health care. This study showed that medications were frequently requested from home countries, even if those medications were available over-the-counter in the United States, and that border proximity was a major factor in workers' decisions to request medications rather than search out local options. As Wolcott-MacCausland notes, these factors create "a circumstantial, complex, and inconsistent health care access system for the Latino dairy worker community."[65]

In an extended study of Vermont's landscapes, McCandless examines the experiences of farmworkers within the state's working dairy farms, paying particular attention to the spatial dynamics of their working and living conditions. Advancing the idea of the "carceral landscape," her study explores constraints that are produced by popular images of the countryside, industry practices, and local and federal law enforcement. Drawing upon participatory research methods, including in-depth interviews with farmworkers and participant observation at public events, McCandless argues that farmworkers experience "topologies of fear" that limit their experiences of Vermont's landscapes to the immediate surroundings of their workplaces, rather than the public spaces that the broader community utilizes and enjoys.[66]

This book builds upon these previous studies to show that while these topologies of fear still present formidable constraints to Vermont's farmworkers in their access to basic needs, recent changes and grassroots victories are opening up greater possibilities for achieving food justice and improved labor rights. These shifts are in large part worker-led, and Vermont's farmworkers are actively working in solidarity with other workers in the production sector to address farmworker struggles across the United States. While the state's farmworker community shares much in common with these other farmworkers, in the area of food security and food access, border proximity and the nature of dairy work present particular vulnerabilities as well as enduring forms of resilience.

IT'S NOT JUST ABOUT THE NUMBERS

Previous studies of farmworker food security have been conducted across multiple academic and applied fields, including medicine, nursing, geography, nutrition, and public health, and each offers compelling data gathered through a variety of tested quantitative instruments. Most notable among these instruments is the U.S. Department of Agriculture Household Food Security Survey Module (HFSSM). The HFSSM, which was developed through a collaborative effort led by the USDA and the National Center for Health Statistics, is the principal assessment tool utilized to measure food security in the United States. Since the widespread implementation of this survey module, public health and health policy researchers have made great strides in not only translating but also testing the linguistic relevance of this tool for Spanish-speaking households by conducting intensive focus groups to develop a rapid, well-formulated, and easily understandable instrument.[67]

As I set out to study the patterns of food access amongst Vermont's farmworkers, I expected to find rates of food insecurity as severe as those reported in previous studies of farmworker food access. Given what I knew about the isolated landscapes and demanding work schedules confronting these workers, I hypothesized that the incidence of food insecurity might be even higher for those sustaining the state's dairy industry. In order to compare data from Vermont with data collected in other states, I conducted one hundred surveys utilizing the HFSSM with help from two research assistants, Jessie Mazar and Naomi Wolcott-MacCausland, between June 2014 and April 2016. These surveys were conducted with farmworkers across Vermont. We aimed to oversample women, given the central role that women play in ensuring food security for their families. We conducted these surveys in the homes of farmworkers, in the waiting room of a clinic serving underinsured and uninsured clients, at annual visits of the Mexican consulate, and through field visits to dairy farms alongside doctors and medical students during an annual immunization clinic. Each survey was accompanied by a brief demographic survey to collect basic data on gender, age, educational background, income, and household composition. The full breakdown of these data is outlined in chapter 2.

In conducting these surveys, what I quickly realized is that because the HFSSM is designed as a rapid assessment of a household's food security, it inherently narrows the lived experience of food access to a series of predetermined choices and categories. Through multiple stages of questions that determine the severity of food security amongst adults in the household and amongst children, the HFSSM results in a score of "High or Marginal Food Security," "Low Food Security," or "Very Low Food Security," with parallel rankings for the food security rates of households with children. As this book will show, this survey instrument and the data it produces inherently flatten the complex negotiations and choices related to accessing food. Indeed, for workers supporting household economies on both sides of the border, the term *household* itself demands deeper inquiry.

These data provide a starting place to understand the complexities of food access for Vermont's farmworkers, though, as I will argue throughout this book, the strict quantitative methods used to measure food insecurity are inherently flawed. In most food security research, quantitative methods are hypervisible, yet they often render qualitative methods invisible, along with the more textured experiences and lived realities of food insecurity. In chapter 2 I argue that this methodological bias keeps much of farmworker food insecurity hidden. Through my field research, I have found additional problems with the HFSSM. In addition to the narrow categories that the HFSSM produces, and the trouble defining what constitutes a "household" for migrant workers with complex configurations of households and kinship, the HFSSM is also flawed because of its narrow focus on poverty as the underlying cause of food insecurity. To be certain, poverty is linked with food insecurity. However, it is only one factor among many that lead to inequitable food access for Vermont's farmworkers. Because of these methodological limitations, this book does not stop with quantitative measures but rather offers nuanced ethnographic insight from field research carried out from November of 2011 through October of 2017.

This ethnographic insight is gleaned from in-depth interviews with farmworkers and key stakeholders who are knowledgeable about the challenges that confront them, in addition to hundreds of hours of participant observation and analysis of primary and secondary data. Beginning in the summer of 2015 and wrapping up in the summer of 2017, I conducted thirty in-depth interviews with farmworkers and ten in-depth interviews with key stakeholders. Interviews with farmworkers were conducted entirely in Spanish and then translated into English, and interviews with key stakeholders were conducted almost entirely in English, except for one interview that was conducted in Spanish with Migrant Justice organizers. To conduct, transcribe, and analyze these interviews, I had the assistance of three research assistants: Jessie Mazar, Naomi Wolcott-MacCausland, and Claire Macon. All interviews were conducted after a process of verbal consent, recorded, and transcribed in full. Each transcript was then entered into Atlas TI for coding and analysis. The interviews with farmworkers were semi-structured. They focused primarily on food access but inevitably extended out into broader conversations about crossing into the United States and adjusting to life in Vermont, as well as the memories that people had of home and their future plans. Interviews with key stakeholders primarily focused on their experiences working with farmworkers, their organizational missions, and their observations about the network of providers in the state. Throughout this book, I use pseudonyms when referring to and quoting all interviewees.

The narratives of farmworkers are central to this book, though I complement these with the perspectives of key stakeholders working in the fields of public health, nutrition, and food security. There is no doubt that additional insights into my research questions could be gleaned from interviews with farm owners and those working with Border Patrol and ICE, along the lines of Laura Nader's (1972) call to "study up" the hierarchies of social power featured in her essay "Up the Anthropologist: Perspectives Gained from Studying Up." As I will discuss more in the conclusion, I have made a conscious decision to use the tools of critical ethnography to develop alliances and bonds of solidarity with those whose voices are typically unheard in the broader debates around immigration and food systems, even within the scholarship that focuses specifically on farmworkers. Through this stance, I attempt to answer Faye Harrison's call to stand on the side of struggle and transformation by illuminating examples of resiliency and autonomy within marginalized communities that are typically rendered invisible by those in power.[68]

In working with communities that are hidden and marginalized, trust is everything. This trust and my ongoing relationships with farmworkers have been facilitated through my volunteer work with two organizations: Huertas and Migrant Justice. Huertas is a food security project connected to University of Vermont (UVM) Extension's Bridges to Health Program that coordinates the planting and maintenance of kitchen gardens with farmworkers at the dairies where they live and work. Since 2011 I have codirected the Huertas project with Wolcott-MacCausland, and it has provided an important connection with the farmworker population and opportunities to conduct participant observation in farmworker homes, particularly those in Vermont's northern border counties. I have been involved with Migrant Justice in a number of ways since moving to Vermont in 2011. This has included volunteering at fundraising events, advising on research projects, participating in marches and rallies, and as of January 2017, serving as a member of the board of directors, or what Migrant Justice calls "La Junta de Apoyo." I describe my involvement with these two organizations in more detail in chapters 3 and 5, and I reflect upon what this involvement has taught me about the necessity and challenges of community-based research.

Ethnographic research methods have proven instrumental in understanding the daily lives of farmworkers; anthropologists in particular have offered important insights into their lives during and after the process of migration. Many of these studies have focused upon the well-being and health of those employed in seasonal agricultural production in states with a long history of migration from Latin America.[69] Together, these researchers highlight the structural vulnerabilities that leave Latinx migrant workers at risk for health disparities and decreased life chances. Structural vulnerability, as defined by anthropologists, is both a process through which the "vulnerability of an individual is produced by his or her location in a hierarchical social order and its diverse networks of power relationships and effects" and an analytical stance that examines "the forces that constrain decision-making, frame choices, and limit life options."[70] This book engages with the concept of structural vulnerability as an analytical stance to offer a fine-grained ethnographic analysis of how Latinx migrant workers sustain themselves and how these efforts are constrained by broader cultural, political, and economic forces. In this way, it builds upon and bridges a rich genealogy of work to offer a comparison of food access issues and structural vulnerabilities in non-traditional destinations of migration and amongst farmworkers employed in year-round production.

MIGRATING THROUGH THE CHAPTERS TO COME

At both the regional and national level, Vermont is at the forefront of food systems policy and advocacy. Its small size and tight social connections provide a distinctive field site for this study and for a broader inquiry into the interconnections among food, labor, citizenship, and migration. The discipline of anthropology has the potential to shape the nature of this inquiry, and Vermont presents a novel site for this project given the state's strong agricultural identity, its unique migration patterns and histories, and its proximity to federal border enforcement and security efforts. At the same time, the international movements connected to food and agriculture, and the associated scholarship, are demanding an unprecedented questioning into how food makes its way from farm to plate. In a food system riddled both with deep contradictions and exciting possibilities, this book examines the lives of workers who are working to put food on the table in a geographic region that remains severely understudied as a new destination of migration. As we face renewed hostilities towards immigrant communities and denials of their contributions to the United States, it is even more important to illuminate the impacts of migration on our fields and farms close to home and how those who uphold the working landscapes feed themselves and their families. This book travels through five central chapters to bring an examination of how Latinx migrant farmworkers negotiate daily life in

Vermont together with a critical analysis of the ever-changing dairy industry. In doing so, *Life on the Other Border* aims to highlight how new generative possibilities for building food and labor justice are emerging, with the potential to reshape both the broader movements for justice and the lives of agricultural workers across the food chain.

Chapter 1 continues with the framework of Bordering Visible Bodies through engaging with the scholarship on structural vulnerability and food security and bringing these concepts together in an examination of the multiple and often contradictory ways they manifest within a border region where Latin American migration is a relatively new phenomenon. The state of Vermont and its iconic working landscape are critically examined in this chapter, as I tease apart the racialized histories and the social and political policies that make dairy work an attractive option for recent migrants even as these histories and policies constrain their full integration into and access to the benefits of Vermont rural life.

Chapter 2 examines household food security practices among Latinx dairy workers in Vermont, revealing how both the terminology and methodology developed by the USDA to examine and quantify food security at the household level are inadequate for fully understanding the complexities of food access for migrant households. In this chapter, I pair quantitative food security survey data with demographic data and farmworker narratives about their efforts to feed their families, in order to illuminate the social, cultural, and political contexts in which migrant farmworkers access and prepare food.

In chapter 3, I pick up on the previous critique of food security to examine the potential for food sovereignty for Vermont's farmworkers who participate in Huertas, a kitchen gardening project that I have codirected since 2011. This chapter engages with and extends the framework of food sovereignty to reveal the resilience and agency that Huertas participants cultivate alongside the plants that hold deep cultural and nutritional meaning for them. Central to this chapter are farmworker stories of food and recipes from their home communities and their subsequent efforts to sustain these foodways through cultivating, harvesting, and cooking meals from their gardens in Vermont. In sharing these stories, I pay particular attention to the ways that these practices are gendered, extending an important line of anthropological inquiry into the importance of not only the right to food, but the right to feed others.

Chapter 4 draws upon key stakeholder interviews and ethnographic fieldwork to present the perspectives of those who provide food and other basic needs to the migrant farmworker community, even while working in a border region where surveillance from Border Patrol is a significant concern. Extending the framework of Bordering Visible Bodies, I argue that these service providers must negotiate a contradictory politics of visibility: they must ensure that their own efforts are visible to funders, employers, and larger state and federal agencies as they attempt to draw little attention to the presence of the undocumented farmworkers they serve. In sharing the experiences of service providers and the challenges they face, this chapter also works to disentangle the complex web of local, state, and federal policies that govern the distribution of food entitlements and how both the barriers and access to political citizenship are foregrounded in the distribution of these entitlements.

Chapter 5 situates the lives of farmworkers and recent farmworker organizing in the state of Vermont within renewed demands for change to our food system, responding to calls for scholars of the food movement to foreground issues of labor inequality and worker justice. In Vermont, farmworker-led organizing efforts have intensified since 2011, resulting in significant victories at the state level and greater visibility for the deplorable conditions in which many farmworkers work and live. In tracing these state-level victories and calls for change, this chapter shows how the farmworker campaigns led by Migrant Justice push against the too-neat categories outlined by food movement scholars.

This book concludes by pulling together the different threads of the book to rearticulate the intersections among structural vulnerability, food security, and resilience; underscoring how these themes animate and shape the lives of migrant dairy workers alongside the Other Border. Despite the very real inequalities that continue to dominate the lives of migrant workers, not only in Vermont's dairy sector but across the U.S. industrial food system, we also find ourselves in a moment where food is at the center of calls for change and greater equity. For this reason, *Life on the Other Border* ends on a cautiously optimistic note, underscoring the transformative potential of food activism that takes the lead from—and stands in solidarity with—the needs and priorities of those who feed the nation.

ONE

Vulnerability and Visibility in the Northern Borderlands

I live in an apartment attached to the barn. I used to only leave the apartment to go to the milking parlor to help my husband sometimes. I never went outside. I didn't see the sun.

SOFÍA

It's a constant fear. . . . I always think when I see a car get stopped in front of me . . . what would happen if that were me? What could I do? If a car follows you for a long time, you always are thinking that it could be *la migra*. And what happens if all of a sudden they turned on their lights? So I'm always watching to see which car is behind me. And before I wasn't afraid! I would go out as normal and I thought "Oh, here in Vermont? That won't happen!" But even though you might struggle against it . . . there are things that are too strong.

GABRIELA

THE RURAL LANDSCAPE SURROUNDING the large dairy farm where Sofía and her husband Santiago lived and worked for more than eight years could easily provide the background for a Vermont tourism postcard. Red barns and grazing Holsteins punctuate the rolling green hills, and narrow state highways transect the countryside in a haphazard patchwork. Fewer than two miles south of the federal border separating northern Vermont from southern Quebec, Sofía and her family have come to see this region as home, albeit an impermanent one. As I make my way north to pay them a visit on a warm September day following the first hard freeze of the year, the radio abruptly switches from English to French and Vermont Public Radio is replaced by the early nineties tunes that seem to dominate Quebecois pop stations. Just a few moments before I arrive at their door, my cell phone announces with the now-predictable tone that I am roaming internationally, despite the fact that I am still firmly within U.S. territory.

As my primary field site, the landscape of this northern region of Vermont has become deeply familiar to me. After years of driving through this area, I anticipate the bends in the road and the occasional roadside stand selling "farm-fresh" eggs and maple syrup on my way to the dairies where Latinx farmworkers work two, sometimes three shifts each day. The smell of manure that clings to the air and permeates my hair and clothing is a signal that I am in the field—both intellectually and physically. The sounds of the rough transition from paved highways to the ruts of well-worn dirt roads indicate an increasing separation from the small city where I live, write, and teach. Despite the astounding beauty of this rural landscape, I can no longer separate these bucolic sounds, sights, and smells from the violence I know is embedded in industrial milk production.

For Sofía and Santiago, this countryside holds an even more complex and intimate set of meanings. Through our many conversations spanning four years, I learned that it is a place of economic opportunity, of isolation and loneliness, and of frequent and perhaps unexpected conviviality with the family who owns the farm. It is a place of ugliness and fear, but also a place of joy, since it is where they started their young family next to the milking barn where Santiago worked upwards of 70 hours every week. And until 2015, when Sofía returned to Mexico with her two young children, it was a place where the risks and dangers of living in the borderlands were all too real. Every single day they lived in Vermont, Sofía and Santiago grappled with three distinct manifestations of the border. The first is the boundary that surrounds the farm, bordering their private home space from the public space where their ethnicity and language mark them as outsiders in this overwhelmingly white state. The second is the federal border that divides the United States from Canada just a few miles north, the proximity of which is never forgotten given the frequency of Border Patrol vehicles passing by the farm. The third is the border they crossed from Mexico into the United States, a boundary that separates their new life as a family from their previous one as two young adults in love—the former a life of poverty but greater freedom.

Over the many visits I paid to Santiago and Sofía, I never made it past the small ten-by-ten-foot room that functioned as kitchen, dining room, play room, and living room. Bathed in cold florescent lights and always accompanied by the chatter of *telenovelas* and rowdy Mexican talk shows, the room was always immaculately clean—an impressive feat given that it was a mere twenty feet from the milking barn. This room was separated from the filth, but not the smells, of the milking barn by a series of doors sealing off the farm's main office and a narrow hallway littered with manure-splattered muck boots and rain jackets. Off to the side of the hallway, there was a tiny bathroom adorned with bright pink Disney decorations, which I always found a bit too cheerful given the surroundings. I first met Sofía and Santiago in the summer of 2012, when their first child, Mia, was only about six months old. At this age, Mia was a bundle of chubby arms and legs, big brown eyes that always sparkled with mischief, and two tiny black pigtails sticking straight up in the air. As she grew, her bravery around giant bovines always impressed me, as did her mother's love and devotion.

In this small, multi-purpose room, Sofía dominated our conversations—gossiping about our shared acquaintances, cajoling me about when I would get married and have children, and often sharing a homemade lunch or strawberry ice cream in the same shade of Disney pink. On the days that we enjoyed ice cream, I could not help but wonder if the main ingredient had come from this farm, or any of the others I have come to know from the inside out. As I came to learn, this small room was a haven for Sofía and Santiago, cozier than the dark bedrooms that I could glimpse in the interior, despite its sterile lighting and utilitarian decor. It was a space that bell hooks might call a "home-place," offering their family somewhere to dwell and find familiarity. At the same time, this room functioned as a prison cell for Sofía and Santiago, who lived in continuous fear of the Border Patrol agents passing by the farm on a daily basis.

As a border state with an active presence of Immigration and Customs Enforcement personnel, many of the same fears, anxieties, and dangers that are endemic to the U.S.-Mexico border are reproduced in the state of Vermont. This brings with it embodied consequences for food security, diet-related health, and the mental well-being of migrant workers like Santiago and Sofía. In the post-9/11 era, scholars point to the ways that the U.S.-Canada border has become increasingly "Mexicanized" amidst concerns of terrorism and lax surveillance.[1] While the dangers of the U.S. northern and southern borderlands are distinct in how they impact the individuals and families who transgress and reside within them, significant and persistent patterns of structural vulnerability and violence pervade the everyday lives of Latinx migrant farmworkers in Vermont. For these workers, these forms of vulnerability and violence are inextricable from the ongoing fear and anxieties of living and working in a border region where one is invisible in the workplace yet hypervisible in public.

This chapter continues with the framework of Bordering Visible Bodies introduced in the previous chapter through illuminating and investigating how bordering plays out in the structural vulnerabilities and violence that migrant farmworkers experience in a region where migration from Latin America is a newer phenomenon than in most other U.S. states dependent on agriculture. In doing so, this chapter moves the fields of Latinx studies and border studies into a new geographic and social space that has remained largely invisible in these fields of scholarship. As I examine Vermont's iconic working landscape, I show how processes of racialization and labor exploitation exacerbated by the proximity of the border shape the experiences of Vermont's farmworkers in distinct ways. This lays the groundwork for the following chapters, which explore how Latinx migrant workers sustain themselves and how these efforts are constrained by broader cultural, political, and economic forces.

BORDER VIOLENCE AND VULNERABILITY

Throughout their journeys, individuals like Sofía and Santiago transgress, reside within, and are constrained by political and cultural borders that simultaneously act upon them and are remade by their presence. As a conceptual category tied to multidimensional and continuously shifting geographic and social spaces and processes, borders have long been an important area of scholarship across the humanities and social sciences. In an ever-globalizing world, contemporary border theory has to contend with a central question: Are we moving toward a borderless world, characterized by flows and networks, or, are new forms of nationalism and xenophobia reinforcing territorial lines and often-violent defenses of state sovereignty? As Anssi Paasi argues, this is in reality a "both, and" question rather than an either-or dilemma.[2]

Calling for new approaches to studying borders in a dynamic world, Paasi emphasizes that we must explore how territoriality works in practice, rather than seeking to build a universal border theory. This demands that we examine not only the geographically specific and physical divisions of territories but also the processes of bordering that are intensified at these divisions and inevitably extend outwards to other geographies and inwards to the bodies and minds of border-crossers and border-dwellers. Tracing the development of border theory, Paasi states,

One important step has been the abandonment of the view of borders as mere lines and the notion of their location solely as the "edges" of spaces. This has helped to challenge strictly territorial approaches and to advance alternative spatial imaginations which suggest that the key issues are not the "lines" or "edges" themselves, or not even the events and processes occurring in these contexts but nonmobile and mobile social practices and discourses where borders—as processes, sets of sociocultural practices, symbols, institutions, and networks—are produced, reproduced, and transcended.[3]

The U.S.-Mexico border has long been a key sociospatial location for the study of borders. We owe a great debt to Gloria Anzaldúa for her work blurring these theoretical imperatives long before Paasi called for it. Yet as crucial as it is to examine the dividing line between the U.S. and Mexico for individuals like Sofía and Santiago who migrate between these two nations, I make the case in this chapter and those that follow that we must extend our analysis to the violent forms of bordering that follow these same individuals into other borderlands.

In the post-9/11 era, social scientists have been particularly active in pushing borderlands scholarship forward, engaging in dynamic conversations about how to best utilize the strengths of ethnography and other anthropological methods in a period when the borders of the nation-state are becoming more porous for the movement of capital and more impervious to the movement of people. The most relevant of these works to my own study are those that examine the violent forms of bordering that are unleashed against migrants—before, during, and long after the border crossing. Two scholars in particular, Seth Holmes and Jason de León, are recognized for their work in illustrating the contemporary forms of violence and suffering that persists along the U.S.-Mexico border and continue to shape the lives of migrants as they move across the United States. As I have considered the ways that crossing the southern borderlands and laboring in the northern borderlands shape the daily lives of migrant workers in Vermont, their analyses have proven useful as a starting point for my own work.

Both Holmes and De León draw upon theories of structural violence to examine the risks and dangers confronting immigrants making their way north to the United States. Their studies of violence build upon and extend the work of anthropologists including Paul Farmer (2005) and Nancy Scheper-Hughes (1992), who have engaged ethnographic methods in their efforts to demystify the social inequalities that pervade everyday life and decrease the life chances of the poor. While definitions of structural violence abound, I always find it useful to return to the following articulation by Paul Farmer, who describes structural violence as a

> broad rubric that includes a host of offenses against human dignity: extreme and relative poverty, social inequalities ranging from racism to gender inequality, and the more spectacular forms of violence that are uncontestedly [sic] human rights abuses, some of them punishment for efforts to escape structural violence.[4]

In Farmer's view, human suffering is structured by historic and economic factors that conspire to constrain agency. As both Holmes and De León show, long histories of poverty, systemic racism and classism, and dispossession of land and other natural resources are the foundations of the structural violence that both impels people to migrate from Latin America and shapes their lived realities in the United States.

In his ethnography *Fresh Fruit, Broken Bodies: Migrant Farmworkers in the United States,* Seth Holmes offers a window into the lives of migrant farmworkers in U.S. agriculture. Through bringing his readers from Oaxaca, Mexico, across the U.S-Mexico border, and into the states of California and Washington, Holmes traces the transnational circuits of people that sustain large-scale berry farms and other sectors of industrial agriculture. As a trained physician, Holmes details the forms of structural violence and suffering that the Triqui (an indigenous group from Oaxaca) endure in both Mexico and the United States, and how the medical establishment largely fails them in both nations.

While the book's opening sequence of migration, detention, and eventual release is attention-grabbing, for me it is Holmes's analysis of how violence against mostly poor indigenous migrants is naturalized, normalized, and internalized that is the most instructive. With a nod to Paul Farmer's work but also to Bourdieu's theories of symbolic violence, Holmes examines how violence is enacted on the migrant body, underscoring how the industrial food system is quite literally built upon the backs of immigrants. Pointing to both the rampant racism in rural farming regions and the "subtle complicity of the dominated," Holmes lays out how symbolic violence, or the "naturalization, including internalization, of social asymmetries," enables the manifestation and embodiment of structural violence in premature death, sickness, and severe economic inequalities.[5] He demonstrates with ethnographic detail how classed, raced, and gendered bodies located at different positions along the "ethnicity-citizenship hierarchy" are socially determined to be more or less worthy of respect, health care, and ultimately, living. The browner that body is, the more indigenous, or the extent to which a person is female determines how they are subjected to and experience violence.

In *The Land of Open Graves: Living and Dying on the Migrant Trail,* Jason de León presents an examination of border violence through his analysis of the suffering that persists in the deserts of Arizona and northern Mexico as migrants make their way north to the United States. Shedding light on the human consequences of immigration and border policies, De León's work draws attention to the material remains and narrative traces of border crossings. As he opens his book, De León critiques the "immigration pornography" that sensationalizes and ultimately dehumanizes those who attempt to cross the border. This kind of sensationalistic journalism does little to illuminate the daily realities of life on the border and how border crossing has, because of the systematic destabilization and impoverishment of Mexico, become normalized rather than exceptional.

In critiquing the shallowness of sensationalism, De León points to the power of ethnography to provide deeper, more historically grounded narratives that better represent immigrants as complex individuals. What is particularly powerful about his analysis is the framework he engages, namely Callon and Law's theory of the *hybrid collectif.* As he synthesizes it, this theory postulates that "people and objects don't act in isolation, but instead have complex relationships at different movements across time and space that sometimes create things or make things happen. It is these relationships that 'perform agency,' not isolated humans or solitary objects".[6] This ecological approach draws attention to the natural and cultural environments that migrants encounter in the borderlands, but also to the policies that have pushed migrants into increasingly dangerous paths while crossing the border.

De León's work has been instructive for me in considering how the northern borderlands of the United States are a space where violence is made possible because of a particular confluence of racialized histories, patterns of migratory labor, and pressures from an industrial model of food production that has come to dominate Vermont's dairy industry. While the lush green hills of Vermont couldn't seem any more distinct from the barren, harsh Sonoran desert, both regions produce a landscape where migrants are subjected to exclusion, entrapment, and fear. These processes of violence are enabled by what De León calls a "fundamental socioeconomic conundrum," which comes down to "the United States' need for cheap labor that can easily be controlled with the threat of deportation and the duplicitous stance that we don't want undocumented laborers in this country".[7] As I show throughout this book, Vermont dairy workers are stuck within this conundrum, leaving them vulnerable to both to border violence and to the many violences endemic to the industrial food system.

The ethnographies that Holmes and De León offer are important contributions to migration literature. However, even though their books are rich in detail and theoretically groundbreaking, the experiences of women are largely missing from their work. De León acknowledges this absence early on in his book, stating "As a Latino researcher, I had significantly more access to men than women, at least during the phases of ethnographic work that took place on the northern Mexico border."[8] He underscores that women face particular vulnerabilities to gender-based violence when crossing the border. Holmes does not offer a similar disclaimer of how his gender influenced the choices he made about his field research, and a critical analysis of gendered violence is largely missing from his work, though he does point to ways that the "fault lines of power" are exacerbated in the field by overt and covert forms of sexism, such as not promoting women to supervisory positions. While I accept that the gender of a researcher impacts one's access to research participants and the relationships that develop in the field, I am not content to limit my analysis to either men or women. Instead, my aim in this chapter and those that follow is to amplify the experiences of individuals across the gender spectrum so that we may consider more deeply how suffering is embodied and gendered and how the surveillance of the northern border complicates the suffering and vulnerability that migrants experience. In order to tip the scale of borderlands and violence scholarship a bit more evenly, this chapter focuses primarily upon the experiences of women before continuing on in later chapters to consider the experiences of the broader community.

While the concept of structural violence has found a firm place within anthropological scholarship, the concept of structural vulnerability has made a more recent appearance. Even so, it has become particularly useful within the field of critical medical anthropology. James Quesada and his colleagues (2011) define structural vulnerability as both a process through which the "vulnerability of an individual is produced by his or her location in a hierarchical social order and its diverse networks of power relationships and effects" and an analytical stance that examines "the forces that constrain decision-making, frame choices, and limit life options."[9] In many ways, structural violence and structural vulnerability are interdependent ideas and processes. Structural vulnerability allows us to understand the structural relationships of power and inequality that make a person or community vulnerable to violence. Structural violence, then, is the cumulative effect of those vulnerabilities.

What structural violence does not allow us to consider is how people remain resilient to vulnerability or how they confront, resist, or work to overturn the systems of power that act upon them. In some ways, a narrow focus on structural violence can result in a disavowal or a misrecognition of the agency that all people exercise against the constraints of their social positioning. In the chapters that follow, I highlight how resiliency is found in the food-related activism and daily practices of Vermont's migrant dairy workers. As I show, these illustrations of resiliency and vulnerability are inseparable from the particularities and peculiarities of the state of Vermont and its dairy industry.

"THERE'S NO MEXICANS IN VERMONT!"

When I am asked to present my research to audiences in Vermont, I often open up my talk by sharing a story that illustrates the politics of visibility that render the presence and contributions of Latinx farmworkers invisible. During my very first visit to the state in 2011, as I was interviewing for the faculty position I now hold at the University of Vermont, I was tasked with delivering what those of us in academia call a "job talk." Always the source of much anxiety, a job talk is your chance to dazzle your future colleagues and students, giving them a sense of your research accomplishments to date and your plans to establish a long and productive intellectual career—all in forty-five minutes or so, typically while wearing an uncomfortable suit. As my previous doctoral fieldwork was rooted in Seattle, I knew I had to convince this crowd that Vermont was the place for me, and that I could effectively make the transition from studying the role of Latinx immigrants in urban food systems to the rural systems that predominate in a state of roughly 625,000 residents. So I did my research, combing through all of the online materials I could find on Latinx migration to the state, mostly finding news articles and the website of an emerging group called the Vermont Migrant Farmworker Solidarity Project (now called Migrant Justice). In the last few minutes of my job talk, I presented the seeds of the study that is the basis of this book. I explained to the audience that if I found myself fortunate enough to be employed at UVM, I would extend my previous interests on immigrant food security and foodways to the migrant community that labors in the state's industrial dairy sector.

When I finished presenting, I breathed a sigh of relief and turned to the question-and-answer section, optimistic that I had effectively made the case that I was the best candidate for the job. After I fielded a few questions about my Seattle research, a student raised his hand and asked, "Wait, what are you going to do in Vermont? There's no Mexicans in Vermont!" As I later learned, this student was not simply testing my composure. Rather, he was an advanced undergraduate student who, like so many Vermonters, was unaware of the presence, let alone the contributions, of the state's farmworkers. While my immediate response to his question was flustered and ultimately may have embarrassed him (and myself), I have come to understand that his lack of awareness is not at all unique for the state's students, let alone the broader Vermont community. Students and acquaintances born and raised in Vermont regularly tell me that they had no clue that the large dairy farms they had grown accustomed to seeing on their drive to school or work employ farmworkers from Latin America. Indeed, their presence is almost entirely erased from the representations of the rural landscape that are effectively marketed both inside and outside the state, drawing thousands of agritourists to sample the artisanal cheese, maple syrup, and craft beer that is produced within the state's boundaries. While the public awareness of the role of the state's dairy farmworkers has certainly grown over the years since my first visit in 2011, there remains a generalized erasure of these workers, their lives prior to migration, and how they contribute to the state's agricultural economy.

An enduring contradiction of industrial dairy production is seen in these kinds of erasures amidst a growing dependence on exploiting immigrant communities of color to produce a food long associated with "white social dominance." In examining the promotion of milk as a cure for bodily and social illness in the early 1900s, Melanie DuPuis notes, "milk became not only one of the reasons for Northern European white racial superiority but also a way to pass that superiority onto other races and ethnicities."[10] While today's industrial dairies share little in common with the "cow and milkmaid" pastoral representations circulating during earlier times, the values of purity and wholesomeness that are still invoked to sell milk products belie the racialized labor systems that leave workers vulnerable to abuse and the political and economic conditions that make small-scale dairy farming next to impossible. The racialized labor patterns embedded within Vermont's dairy sector and the assumed undocumented status of Latinx workers in the industry leave them at risk for compounding structural vulnerabilities and inequitable access to many basic needs.

To fully understand Vermont's contemporary border dynamics, it is essential to situate them within the historical and strategic production of the state's rural countryside. As Clare Hinrichs has highlighted, the production of Vermont's countryside has long been mired in a history of bordering based on hierarchies of race/ethnicity, social class, and national origin. The promotion of the state as a "distinctive rural place" steeped in Yankee values of hard work, modesty, and wholesomeness has been carefully geared toward select groups of outsiders, particularly those with economic capital they might infuse into the rural economy.[11] These outsiders have primarily included white New Englanders who might visit the state to establish a second home or small business, to ski or otherwise recreate in the wilderness, or to consume the state's specialty agricultural products (namely maple and dairy). Decidedly absent from this welcome embrace has been groups "of foreign stock," including French Canadians coming south across the border from Quebec in search of greater economic opportunity. While the state's Quebecois influence is now celebrated, in part because of the dependence upon tourist revenue from visiting Canadians, a newfound marginalization of "foreign" newcomers has come to rest squarely upon the backs of Latinx workers who have crossed the U.S.-Mexico border to work on the state's dairy farms.

If we return to the quote made by then Governor Peter Shumlin that I discussed in the introductory chapter, another dimension of this carefully produced erasure becomes more clear, and perhaps even more insidious. In stating, "We have always had a policy in Vermont where *we kind of look the other way as much as we can* . . . I just want to make sure that's what we're doing" (emphasis mine), we must ask what else the former governor is implicitly encouraging us to look away from.[12] Should we be looking away from the wage theft that these workers commonly experience and the fact they do not receive overtime pay? Should we avert our eyes from the substandard housing that many farmworkers and their families live in, and the dangerous working conditions they encounter in milking barns while working with animals that weigh upwards of thirteen hundred pounds? Or should we ignore the fear and anxiety that shapes their daily lives even as they engage in everyday activities such as visiting the doctor or going grocery shopping? I believe that one way to combat these erasures is to engage the strengths of critical ethnography to challenge the politics of visibility that erases who these workers are and what they contribute to the state.

As is the case in farms and fields across the United States, getting an exact count of the number of migrant workers in Vermont is next to impossible. Given the high mobility of this workforce, between farms and between states, the estimates for foreign-born workers in Vermont's dairy industry vary across sources. Sofía and Santiago are a rare case, as they only worked and lived at one farm during their time in Vermont. Gabriela, whose narrative follows, is more typical, because she and her family have worked on multiple farms, constantly in search of better working and living conditions. According to the Vermont Migrant Education Program, the population as of 2016 ranged between one thousand and twelve hundred, with women comprising only about 10 percent of that estimate, or approximately one hundred women living in the state. However, the farmworker-led organization Migrant Justice estimates that the population is closer to fifteen hundred, and in the past has given counts as high as two thousand. It is of course difficult to count individuals who are trying to remain under the radar, and as I have seen through my years of fieldwork, the economic instability that many farmworkers experience often results in last-minute decisions to move to other farms or other states. Moreover, to borrow a term from Nicholas de Genova, there is a "regime of deportability" at play that keeps undocumented farmworkers fearful of entering public spaces, forcing them deeper and deeper into the shadows.[13] As I discuss later in this chapter, an increasing hostility towards immigrants following the election of Donald Trump and a ramping up of detentions in the state has only exacerbated these fears.

The data on Vermont's farmworkers comes from a variety of sources: UVM Extension's Bridges to Health Program, The Open Door Clinic, Migrant Justice, and faculty and student researchers affiliated with UVM. Given the methodological difficulties of studying a highly mobile and hidden population, it should come as no surprise that these efforts to understand the demographic composition and experiences of the state's farmworkers are all necessarily incomplete. Each of these entities has its own particular channel of access to the farmworker community and different motivations for collecting data. Here, I attempt to pull these sources together to paint as comprehensive a picture as possible.

It is difficult to generalize the cultural and livelihood backgrounds that farmworkers bring with them into the state. Indeed, it is critical to recognize the cultural diversity of the farmworker population, so as to not homogenize or flatten their experiences, a point echoing the argument that Seth Holmes advances through his analysis of the ethnoracial hierarchies at play in the berry fields of Washington State. The population of Vermont's migrant farmworkers is ethnically and culturally diverse, yet there are evident demographic patterns connected to the general well-being of the farmworker community and the shared constraints they experience. Much of what we know about the demographics of Vermont's farmworkers comes from the academic and applied research focusing on health care.[14]

Based on the most recent data compiled by Bridges to Health (at my request), for 489 individuals who enrolled in their services during 2012–2017, the two highest sending countries were Mexico (88%) and Guatemala (10%). Within Mexico, the three most common states of origin were Chiapas (51%), Tabasco (23%) and Veracruz (9%).The gender imbalance of the population is clear, with 88 percent identifying as male. The factors underlying language barriers are also evident, with only 3 percent of the sample speaking English and 5 percent speaking an indigenous language as their first language. The sample was mostly young (60% under the age of 30, with most between 20 and 29 years of age) and single (40%), and 49 percent had less than a ninth-grade education. Only 3 percent of this group had health insurance, and only 4 percent had a driver's license.[15] While this data represents only a subset of the total population of the state's migrant farmworkers, it is relatively large sample and provides a good sense of the demographic background that workers bring with them into the state.

Migrant Justice is the state's leading organization working for the rights of farmworkers. Their work has brought greater visibility to the substandard living and working conditions that many farmworkers face. Originally named the Vermont Farmworker Solidarity Project, Migrant Justice was formed in 2009 after the death of a young farmworker while working on a dairy farm. In 2014 Migrant Justice designed and conducted a survey with 172 farmworkers in the state, which to date is the largest survey completed with Vermont's farmworkers outside of those conducted by health providers. Migrant Justice embarked upon this project to better inform and support their campaigns, particularly the Milk With Dignity campaign.

In June of 2014 I was asked by staff at the organization to review a draft of the survey from a "methodological perspective," but was not involved in any of the data collection or analysis, though I was asked to review the results before they were made publicly available.[16] The surveys were conducted by farmworker leaders on farms, at consulate visits, and at other worker gatherings, and the organization has regularly shared survey results at their events and rallies, through social media, and in interviews with local and national press outlets. The following findings are reported on the Migrant Justice website:

> 40% receive less than VT minimum wage; 40% don't have a day off (ever); 30% have had a work related injury or illness; 32% say they aren't treated equally as US born co-workers; 26% don't receive a pay stub; 29% regularly work 7 (or more) hours without a break to eat, 20% have their first paycheck(s) illegally withheld; 20% don't have access to a bathroom or clean water in their workplace; 9% say they have been verbally abused by their employer; 16% have to sleep on the living room sofa due to overcrowded housing; 15% have insufficient heat; 19% have worked for more than 2 years at their farm without a pay raise; 16% have less than 8 hours (in a row) to sleep due to work schedules.[17]

These figures document a number of pressing issues that Vermont's farmworkers encounter in both their workplaces and in their homes, which are usually provided by their employer. For Migrant Justice, these figures also demonstrate the need for their organizing work in the state, which has largely taken shape through campaigns for state policies and the development of the Milk With Dignity code of conduct. I will describe these campaigns in more detail in chapter 5.

Although the population of farmworkers in Vermont is relatively small and the number of dairy farms is also in a continuous decline, it is also difficult and perhaps counterproductive to generalize the relationships between farmworkers and farm owners within the dairy industry. While the power dynamics between farmers and farmworkers are necessarily borne out of imbalances of power and privilege, it must be acknowledged that farmers themselves are also caught in a cycle where their productive work is continually devalued by the globalized market economy, where pressures from corporate consolidation and failed agricultural policies are ever present. These pressures do not and should not excuse the well-documented cases of worker abuse and the significant concerns of ongoing exploitation. Further, as Margaret Gray observed through her work with Hudson Valley farmworkers in New York State, paternalism or what she calls "the price of proximity" is also rampant on Vermont's dairy farms given the close working relationships between farmworkers and farm owners and the politics of invisibility that keep them hidden. With this level of workplace intimacy, Gray defines the "price of proximity" as the consequences of those relationships, specifically the "paternalistic power disparities between workers and farmers and a labor regime that serves to deter collective action."[18] As I describe below, these power disparities are exacerbated by the fears and anxieties that Vermont's farmworkers experience as they live and work in the northern borderlands.

ENCERRADO

As we saw in the opening vignette to this chapter, the boundary surrounding the dairy farm is the most proximate of the dividing lines that borders farmworkers into the margins. It marks the separation between the milking barn, where one's labor is simultaneously invisible and indispensable, and the public spaces where one's body is hypervisible and vulnerable to surveillance and deportation. These tensions between invisibility and hypervisibility echo the points that have been raised in a recent body of work examining the politics of visibility for Latinx immigrants in the United States. Drawing attention to the "social production of Latin@ visibilities and invisibilities," Licona and Maldonado explore how "borders within" are reproduced in rural areas of the United States, particularly within nontraditional destinations of immigration.[19] Linking this politics of visibility to the "regime of deportability," discussed previously, Licona and Maldonado assert

> We suggest that the regime of deportability is implicated in the production of hyper/visibilities and hyper/invisibilities as it, at once, calls migrants out from the shadows (in a spectacle of detention practices and raids) and forces them back into the shadows by entrenching notions of illegality and practices of surveillance and policeability while society continues to rely heavily on (unauthorized) immigrant labor.[20]

This politics of visibility is manifested as immigrants employ invisibility as a tactic, crafting alternative routes to keep out of sight as they go about their daily lives in Perry, Iowa. Here is a clear illustration of the ways that bordering becomes embodied, even in an interior state hundreds of miles from the physical border. As I describe here, the bordering and invisibility that Vermont's farmworkers experience reflect similar patterns, yet is compounded by their proximity to the U.S.-Canada border.

Throughout my years of researching food access issues within Vermont's farmworker community, there is one term farmworkers use more than any other to characterize their experience in Vermont: *encerrado*. This term translates into a number of English descriptors: confined ... trapped ... bounded ... enclosed. In all cases, this term is laden with sadness, frustration, and pain. It is used to describe the isolation that farmworkers and their families experience in Vermont, an assumed agricultural utopia. This sense of being *encerrado* is amplified by the hegemonic whiteness of rural Vermont and is perpetuated by the ever-present fears and anxieties of residing in a border region where their livelihood is in the hands of Border Patrol. Within agricultural regions, hegemonic whiteness, or more specifically, the reproduction of whiteness, is enabled by the exclusion and marginalization of nonwhite bodies.[21] In his examination of California's labor camps, Don Mitchell characterizes this as the "social and spatial relations of agricultural labor reproduction" that perpetuate a "normalized geography of farmworker invisibility."[22]

For migrant farmworkers in the dairy industry, the milking barn is an extension of their home—a place where they remain out of sight and, therefore, as safe as possible in this often unforgiving landscape. Their invisibility and uninterrupted labor are critical for the continued operation of the dairy farm; because of this, the fear of Border Patrol is often shared by the farm owners and managers. To date there have been few raids on dairy farms in the state, and most detentions occur when farmworkers leave their homes or places of work. For those who do not work outside the home, mostly women caring for young children, the home is the only place with a sense of tentative safety. Still, the fear of being seen is as visible as the flattened cardboard boxes and cartoon-character printed bedsheets that block the windows of farmworker homes and the quickness of the sprint from the front door to a rare waiting car. As I describe here, these fears have only intensified following the 2016 U.S. presidential election. In this section, I focus in on the experiences of two young mothers I first met when their children were infants, extending the analysis that opened this chapter through the vignettes about Sofía and her family. For both Paula and Gabriela, their experiences before and after the election, shared through in-depth interviews, reveal this sense of being *encerrado* and how it impacts them as women and mothers who experience the embodied effects of bordering and invisibility.

Sharing a run-down double-wide trailer with four others, including her young daughter, her spouse, and two other farmworkers, Paula lives further south than Sofía from the Canadian border but still well within the region regularly patrolled by *la migra*. In a 2015 interview with my research assistant Jessie Mazar, Paula shared her experiences living in Vermont since she first arrived to the state in 2011 at the age of sixteen, as well as reflections on her life in Mexico. Coming from a rural part of the southern state of Chiapas (or as she measured it, two to three hours from the nearest McDonald's), Paula explained, "When I was in Mexico I had no idea that Vermont even existed, and I know a lot of people who will ask me where do you live? I say in Vermont and they do not even know!" Like many women, Paula learned about the economic possibilities in Vermont from her spouse, who had previously lived in Vermont and worked in the dairy industry. When she decided to cross the border into the United States, she suspected that she might be pregnant, because she and her partner, Felipe, were not using birth control. Fearing that others in her community would gossip about her pregnancy and relationship with Felipe, she decided to leave to escape judgement and reproach from her family, even though she knew she would be putting herself and her potential baby at risk as she migrated north. As she remembered during the interview, it was a very difficult crossing, but not as difficult as others in her family had experienced. It turned out that she was not yet expecting but soon became pregnant with her daughter Isabella after arriving to Vermont to live with Felipe and some of his relatives.

Even before Paula met Felipe, the idea of moving to the United States, and specifically to Vermont, to find work was already a familiar one for her family. She shared, "My father has already come here thirteen times, and from these thirteen *la migración* has grabbed him like two or three times. But he almost always makes it." This cycle of attempting to cross and being apprehended echoes the cat-and-mouse game that De León problematizes in his description of border enforcement activities. Of the ten or so successful crossings made by her father, he had worked in Vermont's dairy industry for two separate periods. Despite the fact that he "almost always makes it," during one of these attempts Paula's father found himself lost in the desert and nearly lost his life. She shared the story with Jessie, even as it pained her.

> And once when he came, they got lost in the desert and they stayed twenty-two days without food and my *papi* was dying and they did not know where to go. And they [*the coyotes*] gave him a pill, and they drank a bit of water that they could find. They were on foot. It's so difficult not to have anything to drink or eat and he thought he was going to die. And there was a girl from our community that got lost in the desert. He [her father] got lost about five years ago, and about six months later he appeared. He got lost because he did not know where to go. But now he is back. But I didn't suffer like this.

His experiences echo the risks documented by De León in his work, but like so many stories of migration, this painful story was not shared with Paula in detail before she made her own trip north. Instead, her father and Felipe only shared with her the promise of *el norte*. Paula reflected with a sense of frustration and sadness, "If they tell you one thing, they might talk about how it was momentarily difficult to cross, but then they say 'oh . . . now I'm in the United States and it's so easy.' So you start saying, '*Papi*, send me this and that, and send me money.' But now, I can see the suffering, working at night when there is snow everywhere, all of the work. But before, he would send me money and I would not think about the suffering he was going through."

When she arrived in Vermont, Paula was taken aback by the rural landscape and the limited transportation options she encountered. As a very social person, she has found it exceptionally frustrating to remain stuck in her home, leaving her unable to visit friends and family as often as she would like. The driver's licensing bill that went into effect in 2014, just one year prior to her interview, had little impact on Paula's comfort in leaving her home on her own terms. She shared that Felipe wanted to get his license and purchase a car but felt that it would not be all that helpful, since they "cannot really go anywhere because we are afraid of immigration." This fear of being seen was particularly acute when she had the rare chance to visit friends and family on other farms, leaving her reluctant to leave her home even though she loved to get out of her home and socialize, particularly with other mothers. However, she did not feel as much fear when she went to the grocery store, perhaps because she was usually accompanied by the wife of Felipe's boss and the trips were short and direct.

Almost two years after Jessie's interview with Paula, in the spring of 2017, I returned to her home with another research assistant, Claire Macon, to get a sense of how Paula was faring after the 2016 presidential election. When I asked her if she still went to the grocery store, she responded

> Well, we weren't going because of the new president. We have been really afraid and we didn't want to leave for the fear of the police detaining us or migration, well we don't know which. And we said to the wife of the boss, my daughter's father told her that we can't go anymore because we can't risk them taking me from my daughter. So a lot of things are different now. And she said it's okay, that she would go and buy the food, but one time she went and didn't bring everything I needed."

Feeling caught in a bind because of this incomplete favor, Paula decided to accompany the boss's wife and do her own shopping again, though she now does so with a high level of anxiety. She conceded that she felt less fearful in her immediate community than in either Burlington or in a neighboring county where her brother works: "And well, I go here close by but I don't want to go to Burlington or other places . . . before I would go to visit my brothers-in-law in Swanton, but now I don't go because of the fear . . . because I am really afraid." Prior to the election, I never heard research participants express fear over visiting Burlington, which is Vermont's most ethnically and racially diverse urban area. However, a series of arrests of three farmworker activists within Burlington's city limits had left the broader community on edge, as Paula explained

> Well in Swanton I haven't heard of them grabbing anyone. But it could happen because it's close to the border and there's always *la migra* near there. In Burlington just recently they held three people and Burlington is the place where I never thought this could happen, and even less with ICE! I go to Burlington and for me it was the safest city. Well I *went* . . . but now no, I'm too afraid.

This newfound fear of Burlington demonstrates how bordering works to keep people invisible and isolated, but also demonstrates the widespread network of communication that exists among farmworkers on Vermont's dairy farms. Through Facebook, WhatsApp messages, and text messaging, farmworkers are keeping one another updated about the changing political and cultural climate in Vermont and minimizing their time spent outside the home when their fears and anxieties are heightened.

Nevertheless, the well-being of her daughter, Isabella, often overrides Paula's concerns about being visible in public spaces. When I asked her if she felt that people were making different decisions about going to the doctor and getting other care because of the increased fear they experienced after the 2016 election, she responded in depth:

> Well now, I don't know, because there are people I've talked to that say they're leaving for Mexico or going to places like New York but I don't know . . . I am afraid, but not so much as to not go to the doctor. Well, no, because she [Isabella] has to go to the doctor. The doctor needs to know how she is because she is her doctor! I go to her visits; we go to the school because at school the police wouldn't take me. And I go there and to the farmer's house . . . I was thinking of leaving the third of April, of this month . . . but it has already passed. But I was thinking about this because everyone was saying, "they're going to do this, they're going to do that, they're going to take your child and you won't see her," and my mom was saying, "well, come back, don't lose your daughter just because you want to be there." But now I'm a little

calmer, and not doing as much to prepare to leave because I have had meetings with lawyers from Mexico and lawyers from here and now I have more ideas to not lose my daughter because it could happen.

Both Paula and her family in Mexico were fearful that she would become separated from Isabella. She shared angrily, "If I was here alone, I wouldn't care if they took me and detained me and deported me to Mexico. I would go to Mexico with no problem. But it's with my daughter that I am afraid."

Because of this fear, Paula had consulted with lawyers who helped her to fill out temporary guardianship paperwork that would ensure that Isabella was cared for in the event that she was detained by Border Patrol. In the case of an extended detention, the agreement dictated that the guardian would take her daughter to Mexico. She felt "happier" and more "confident" after the paperwork was completed, but the confidence did not entirely make her feel comfortable when she left her home. Paula shared that her fears came and went in the months following the election, but that certain events reminded her that not all Vermonters welcomed her. I asked her directly about whether she experienced fear because of other community members, and she responded

Well, the truth is now not as much, but after Donald Trump won I didn't want to go to the store. I was shaking with fear and I was so worried someone would look badly at me because I thought, this person will call *la migra*. I felt like they all hated me and they didn't want me in the store. But there are a lot of good people, people who greet me and smile. But there are people that look at you badly, like with disapproval and it makes me afraid, like when they look like that I am afraid. Until recently I thought: well, I'm not going to the store because migration is going to come. But they won't go to your work. Now it scares me to see a police car, before it didn't scare me to see a car because they were just passing by. But now, yes, it is scary. I'm afraid for everything.

These newfound fears and uncertainties have become embodied in ongoing stress and anxiety and have made it so that Paula feels even more out of place in Vermont, even as she is growing more and more distant from life back home.

I first met Gabriela when I volunteered to drive her and her two infant daughters to a local farmworker meeting, and I was immediately impressed by her energy and commitment to the farmworker community. Several farmworker organizers in the area had recommended that I interview her for this project, but I soon learned that Gabriela was not yet eighteen years old, leaving me unable to interview her because of the guidelines of my Human Subjects research protocol. Although Gabriela was a mother of two and was navigating very adult responsibilities starting with her decision to migrate to the United States, I had to wait for the chance to interview her.

It would be nearly two years after our first meeting until we sat down to discuss her experiences as a young migrant mother living in Vermont. Late one fall afternoon, I visited the small trailer that Gabriela shared with her husband and two daughters, just down the road from the dairy farm where her husband Mateo worked twelve hours per day, seven days a week. In this first interview, we discussed her life in Mexico, her experiences becoming a mother and dealing with postpartum depression, and her efforts to earn a small income by cooking Mexican dishes and delivering them to the farmworkers in her area.

Learning about Vermont from her father, who had worked on the state's dairy farms for twelve years, Gabriela briefly lived in North Carolina but soon was drawn to what she describes as the "tranquil, calm" lifestyle of Vermont. Following in the footsteps of her father, Gabriela milked cows until shortly before the birth of her daughters. Milking cows is a job that is typically reserved for men, though I have found that women often find their way into this employment before having children, or if they are able to find care for their children during their shifts. Gabriela reflected upon this work:

> To be a woman here in Vermont, a migrant, it's difficult because there aren't as many opportunities to work in places where you would like to work, like in a restaurant as in other places. There isn't anything for us, so there isn't anything else left for you except to work in a dairy farm, even if you don't want to because it's really difficult. Oh God . . . it's like really hard work, even for men. You have to work like twelve hours and it's really too much work. When I worked there, it was like I was drugged when I finally had a chance to sleep. I have never felt as tired as that. Because it was so hard and so much work, sometimes I worked twelve hours as well. And it was hard.

Now that she is a mother, finding work that accommodates her schedule is even more difficult. She explained, "And now that I'm a mom, it's still even more complicated, much more complicated. I have to look for somebody and then pay them so that the girls can be taken care of, so I can work. But it costs a lot to find someone to care for them, so I end up paying half of what I earn for them to be cared for."

Gabriela is one of only two women I have met who has obtained a driver's privilege card, and with this card she experiences a degree of freedom to move around the county, unlike most other migrant workers. Part of this freedom is due to her living further south from the constant surveillance of the border than women like Paula or Sofía, but part is also due to a seemingly inherent sense of bravery and resistance to the forces that would push her into the shadows. This bravery has become more focused since the birth of her children, and at the time of our interview she was studying English and preparing to start a program to earn her GED. Following that, she hoped to attend college, with the goal of becoming a legal advocate for immigrants. She stated firmly, "I have a lot of will to keep going. I never thought I would have stopped studying, and it was a big gap, from when I came and where I was and with the girls. But I still have a lot of will and I want to keep studying." Demonstrating a remarkable level of resilience and tenacity, Gabriela hopes to one day become an immigration lawyer to help people who have faced similar struggles as she and her family have.

Given that our interview took place just a few short weeks before the 2016 presidential election and because I knew Gabriela would have plenty to say on the matter, I decided a follow-up interview was in order. Accompanied by my research assistant Claire, I returned to Gabriela's home in May 2017 to continue our conversations. During this visit, her daughters were not napping as they were during my previous visit, instead bouncing from all four walls, dancing and singing along with the dozens of cartoon videos saved to their mother's tablet. Their joyful chatter provided a jarring backdrop for the very serious conversation the three of us had about the new uncertainties and fears that Gabriela and her family were experiencing post-election. Unlike the first interview when her voice was infused with enthusiasm, Gabriela was much more subdued and serious. We asked her for her thoughts on the matter of the election and she shared:

> Well, when I learned he was the president I was really sad, I was crying. Because I didn't know what was going to happen to us. At first it was like "What's going to happen to us? Is he going to deport us and discriminate against us?" And I still think that same thing, that I don't know what is going to happen with us. The truth is that things have changed a lot, before there was much more tranquility in the community, we were a lot more calm. We didn't have as much fear about leaving or to go and do things, and now it's different because we feel much more fear, now the people . . . are more . . . like they feel like they have the right to discriminate against you. This had never happened to me, but it happened to me the other day in Middlebury with this guy.

When we asked her to share what happened, Gabriela continued:

> I was paying for our insurance, and I left and I was going to my car and he was talking to me and I thought he needed something so I left very nicely to go see if he needed something. Then it struck me that he was only saying things about Trump and he asked me "Do you have papers?" And I said "You can't ask me that question!" and so he said "Oh so you don't have papers?" Then he started to laugh at me. And he said things about Trump, about the president, so I got in my car angrily and I left. And nothing like this had ever happened to me! I was scared and I felt like I was being attacked, so I just left. When I got back home I asked myself "Why does it have to be like this?"

Having never personally felt this kind of hostility from those in her community, Gabriela was now much more nervous about leaving her home, even to do such routine tasks like paying for her insurance or going grocery shopping. In this instance we see a clear case of the interpersonal forms of bordering that seem to have become more acceptable and virulent following the 2016 presidential election.

As for Paula, the fear was particularly acute when Gabriela considered the possibility of being separated from her children. She explained:

> This is the most difficult part for us it's because we are a family. So to separate us from them, this is so painful. Because they [the politicians] don't think about how this would affect the children and the parents to be separated. This is so so ugly. And for me, at first I intended to be really strong and not think too much, but the next moment I'll watch the television and I'll start to cry because I felt like "This can't be." It made me so depressed to think about it . . . and the girls' father, he feels the same.

In this quote, we can see clearly how the political shifts at the national level are embodied through assaults to the mental well-being of migrants who contend with the pressures of caring for their children in a time of extreme uncertainty.

As millions of people experienced on the day following the election, Gabriela was shocked when she woke up to the results.

> And when I woke up in the morning Mateo was crying, and he told me "Donald Trump won" and I was like "What?!" and he said "Yes, he is the new president" and I was just like "It can't be" and he said "Yes" and I said "What is going to happen with so many people? With all of us? We are many and he hates all of us." I don't know, it made me really sad and I got up without

any joy. Like I wanted to cry. And on the television they were talking about the new president and I just said, "it can't be!" I had to cook that day and I was very weighed down but I said, "Ok at the end of the day, we have always struggled because everything has always been difficult for us." So I thought: Ok, all of these Mexicans are here working on these farms even though this president doesn't want it, the people will keep working and will keep getting up every morning. So, this gave me a little hope.

And yet, even with this glimmer of hope, the concern for her children still was amplified, leaving her unsure about whether it would be better to return to Mexico.

But with everything that is happening now, I just don't know. I haven't been able to think about it fully, if I want the girls to stay here after everything that has happened. Because now the discrimination is an everyday topic, and it's becoming more normal. And when the girls go to school I don't want for them to feel like they are less than the other kids. . . . I have thought that for kids this can be really difficult, being a kid can be difficult and sometimes kids are really cruel. With saying things, even if they don't mean what they say they just say it. And I don't know how to handle things with the girls. . . . It's something that Mateo and I have talked about, if we want to stay here. Well, he wants them to stay here because they were born here and so they're American. In our country there isn't a lot of opportunity for them to study, and we want for them to study and accomplish many things and in Mexico, well that's really difficult. Despite everything here, there it is much more difficult for them, we don't want to expose them to new dangers in Mexico.

For both Gabriela and Paula—two young mothers with dreams of a better life for themselves and unlimited opportunities for their children—the intensified fears and renewed anxieties following the election impose on their minds and bodies new and insidious forms of bordering. This leaves both women feeling increasing vulnerable to an ever-changing political and social climate, even when they are in their communities, where they once felt relatively safe being visible in public.

THE TRUMP EFFECT

Writing this chapter just months after the inauguration of Donald Trump was exceedingly difficult, given that the sociopolitical machine of immigration policy and border enforcement is ever shifting and churning under our feet. As soon as I think I have a handle on these changes, a new proposal for how to enact further violence against immigrants and refugees is unveiled. This climate of uncertainty has certainly brought with it a constant sense of malaise to the writing process, but more importantly, it has generated a source of heightened fear and anxiety within the everyday lives of Vermont's farmworkers. As much as I might like to ignore the anti-immigrant rhetoric that seems to be escalating on a daily basis, this is impossible given how much this rhetoric, and the proposed policy changes, impact the well-being of migrant farmworkers in the state. One day we hear that Mexico will "pay for the wall," the next we hear the bizarre proposition that solar panels on top of the wall will generate the revenue needed for its construction. Demonstrating his ability to prognosticate, Jason de León reminds us in his 2015 book that a border wall is not the solution to undocumented migration, even as it repeatedly punctuates political discourse: "Despite the evidence that the border wall is no match for catapults, car jacks, and other forms of human ingenuity, the United States can't seem to shake the fixation that building more of it will somehow fix our country's economic and social problems. Politicians are well aware of this fixation and routinely use it to their advantage".[23] Throughout the last U.S. presidential campaign and election, we saw this fixation at work, whipping the newest iteration of anti-immigrant hatred into a frothy mess of bordering that is unlikely to subside anytime soon. This sentiment reaches from the southern border all the way up to the northern borderlands, following the path of the migrant trail that sometimes ends in the Vermont milking barn.

Characterizing individuals like those who toil in Vermont's dairies as "bad hombres," and stating:

> When Mexico sends its people, they're not sending their best. They're not sending you. They're not sending you. They're sending people that have lots of problems, and they're bringing those problems with us. They're bringing drugs. They're bringing crime. They're rapists. And some, I assume, are good people.[24]

there is little doubt that the forty-fifth president is both shaping and reflecting the damaging negative stereotypes that many U.S. residents hold about Mexicans. Even in blue-state Vermont, where left-leaning politicians like Senators Patrick Leahy and Bernie Sanders find a firm footing for their progressive platforms, the Republican agenda is embraced in the very same border counties that depend on Mexican farmworkers for the revenues generated by the dairy industry. Following Donald Trump's election and subsequent inauguration, multiple media outlets in Vermont have covered the impacts of this latest political cycle on the vitality of the state's dairy farms, noting that some of the same dairy owners who are now expressing concern about labor shortages are the same ones who voted for Trump.[25]

As the narratives shared in this chapter reveal, life in Vermont prior to the election was not easy, and there has long been a concern amongst farmworkers about being seen in public. Yet the tenor of the conversations about the fear and anxiety that migrant workers experience has certainly intensified following the election. This has altered the ethnographic process in ways that I couldn't have or, perhaps, refused to anticipate. Prior to the election, I was fairly confident that I was nearing completion with data collection, reaching the "saturation point" that ethnographers refer to when interview data begins to yield few new insights. I thought I had a pretty good handle on the forms of vulnerability and violence that impeded access to basic needs for farmworkers and their families, and I was ready to hang up my field hat in exchange for my writing hat for at least a few months. Even in the era of mass deportations that were carried out under the two terms of Obama's presidency, there was at least a sense of "Hope" that things wouldn't get much worse for immigrants trying to earn a living in the United States, particularly for those who were anything but "bad hombres." However, ethnography, particularly research on politically charged issues, is anything but predictable, and so I decided to return to several of my key research participants, including Paula and Gabriela, to see how they were faring after the election. Throughout the remainder of this book, I will continue to bring in the insights I gained through these follow-up interviews, but only one thing remains certain as I write this just a few months into the new presidency: it remains to be seen just how low the pits of xenophobia and historical amnesia might go.

TWO

More than Money

EXTENDING THE MEANINGS AND METHODOLOGIES
OF FARMWORKER FOOD SECURITY

*It was different, because for breakfast we would walk to the market
to buy vegetables and meat, and then in our home we would eat
beans, beans, beans! Those that our family had grown, in the
morning and the afternoon. When we planted them, we would
plant enough for the entire year . . . enough to eat and to plant
for the next year.*

NATALIA

What is a typical food? Well, beans more than anything. You can
eat beans with pretty much anything. We are used to eating that
in Mexico. In Mexico, in the villages you eat beans, vegetables, rice,
pastas, vegetables we grow, or what we get from the fields. But,
because there is not a lot of money to buy meat and there are more
opportunities to buy vegetables, you barely eat meat in Mexico,
and here, no. Here we almost always have to buy chicken, beef, and
fish, but not a lot of fish because it is hard to find fresh fish here.

ALMA

LIVING WITH FOOD INSECURITY ON
BOTH SIDES OF THE BORDER

On a rainy spring day in 2014, my research assistant and I arrived at the door of
Natalia's single-wide trailer that sits alongside a two-lane state highway in
Franklin County, Vermont. The plywood steps up to the front door were in
even worse shape than at my last visit, and the mud and manure that the rains
carried from the nearby fields had made them especially treacherous to climb.
As we waited for the door to open, the bedsheet covering the front window was
pulled to the side and the large brown eyes of a young girl peered out at us,
revealing a brief moment of surprise before she raised a tiny hand in an excited

wave. These eyes belonged to Martina, Natalia's daughter, and after a few minutes, Natalia opened the door and welcomed us inside. Over the three previous years I had gotten to know Natalia's family through birthday parties, gardening days, and gatherings held to celebrate the harvest season for the Huertas project. We were visiting her that cold spring morning to discuss what she hoped to plant that summer, the first summer in her new home, and to begin our in-depth interviews on food access within Vermont's farmworker households.

From our earlier conversations, I knew that food security was no simple matter for Natalia and her family. Coming from a small village in the southern state of Chiapas, Natalia is one of the few Mexican mothers who has found regular work in Vermont's dairy industry, and she often reminds me that finding work, not starting a family, was her original goal and purpose for moving to Vermont in 2009. However, upon meeting her husband Nicolás after arriving in this small northern state, her plans soon changed. About two years later, Martina was born. As a working mother, Natalia contributes in equal ways to her household economy even while raising Martina within a very different rural environment than the one she left behind in Mexico. Explaining her decision to migrate at the age of 16 simply, "Because there in Mexico, there is no work for women, only the men work in corn and beans," Natalia has created a new life in Vermont, though it is a life where insecurity and irregularity continue to shape her access to basic needs. Even with these challenges, she describes this northern state as "beautiful" and "tranquil," explaining with a sense of longing that the countryside reminds her of home.

This was my first visit to Natalia's new home, a small but tidy trailer where she, Nicolás, and Martina are kept company by a constant stream of Spanish cartoons and *telenovelas* that are piped into the home via satellite. The home is full of toys and a jumbled assortment of older pieces of furniture that, like the front steps, have seen better days. Pictures of Martina adorn the walls of the living room and the refrigerator, and elementary English worksheets are pinned up as a constant reminder to Martina, who is already more bilingual than her parents. Working seven days per week, Natalia and Nicolás spend what little free time they have doting on their daughter, preparing home-cooked meals, and on rare occasions, visiting with family members, including her niece, Alma. Until late 2015, Alma lived on a different farm within the same northern Vermont county. Despite the fact that Alma is her niece, Natalia is actually a few years younger than her. This reversal of kinship positions was a common theme of jokes when they were able to find the time to see one another.

Over the years that Alma lived in Vermont, she too found work in the dairy industry, though her schedule and earnings were more sporadic than Natalia's—in part because of the fluctuating needs of the farm where she worked, but also because of her husband's opposition to her working outside the home. Alma's four children are separated not only by significant age differences, but also by their nation of birth. For most of the time Alma lived and worked in the United States, her two older children, a son and a daughter, remained in Mexico. Both children were born in Alma's home village in Chiapas and raised primarily by her mother, while Alma worked first in California, then in South Carolina, and finally in Vermont. For her two younger children born in the United States, Vermont was the only home they had known. In a 2015 interview, Alma explained that her decision to move to Vermont was largely motivated by her concern for her children's education: "It is very difficult there [in Mexico], in terms of the economy. After I had my two children, my daughter and my other son, I wanted them to keep studying and they were only in secondary school. My daughter is the youngest, but over there, there is no good work, and they pay very little." The sacrifices that Alma has made are not unique for migrant workers; it is this deep concern for their families that has motivated the majority of Vermont's farmworkers to move north.

What unites Alma and Natalia, beyond their bonds of kinship, is their shared love for gardening, their love of Mexican food, and more than anything else, their deep love of their families. Unfortunately, while living in northern Vermont, they also shared continual anxiety about leaving their homes given their proximity to the U.S.-Canada border, long histories of being exploited in food-related work, and ongoing difficulties in accessing basic needs. For these two women, poverty has followed them from the rural countryside of Chiapas to the rural countryside of Vermont, shaping their hopes, dreams, and aspirations. The bordering that they experience as women of color, as undocumented immigrants, and as exploited workers in the food system intersect and determine the choices they can make, and at the same time, provide the foundation for their struggle and resiliency.

In the pages that follow, I share the stories of workers like Alma and Natalia as I explore the multivalence of food security for migrant farmworkers who are currently upholding Vermont's agricultural economy. For many farmworkers and other workers along the food chain, food insecurity is a persistent, lingering problem. This points not only to a serious case of injustice, but a fundamental contradiction: those who put food on our tables are disproportionately experiencing food insecurity in their own homes. Yet as researchers have long argued, the very meaning of food security, the alternative terms to describe it, and the best way to measure it remain points of contention, especially cross-culturally.[1] For migrant workers and their families who seek to sustain culturally meaningful foodways from home, the realities of living and working in Vermont's borderlands present significant challenges to achieving food security on their own terms.

In this chapter, I argue that food security is an inadequate and overly simplistic concept that cannot fully encompass the discourses and practices that migrant workers engage in as they work to feed their families, who more often than not, reside on both sides of the border. Moreover, the assumptions underlying how we define and measure food insecurity in the United States keep the food insecurities that farmworkers experience largely invisible. For workers who are supporting household economies in the United States and Mexico, the idea of a household itself specifically demands a deeper inquiry.

Through examining the household food security practices of Vermont's migrant farmworkers, I show how the standardized questionnaires developed by the U.S. Department of Agriculture (USDA) to quantify and categorize food security are inadequate for fully understanding the complexities of food access for these households. I simultaneously present and question food security data collected through administering the USDA Household Food Security Survey Module (HFSSM) with one hundred Latinx farmworkers in Vermont. However, in making the case for the promise of deep ethnographic research, this chapter also draws upon extended interviews with farmworkers in Vermont's dairy industry to examine how migration to the United States is typically predicated upon food insecurity linked to historical patterns of poverty and dispossession in Latin America. Indeed, for many farmworkers who toil in the state's milking barns, food insecurity and hunger were the driving forces leading them to cross the border and seek work in the United States. The border, in all of its physical, economic, and affective dimensions, continues to shape the realities of Vermont's farmworkers long after their treacherous crossings across the southern desert.

FEEDING THE NATION BUT NOT BEING FED

As the world's population approaches seven-and-a-half billion people, a confounding and violent contradiction persists within the global food system: while there is enough food produced to feed everyone in the world, millions continue to go hungry.[2] This is not just a problem in impoverished nations; every year, food insecurity statistics reveal the startling disparities in food access that persist in the United States. In this country, where up to 40 percent of food that is grown, processed, and transported goes to waste, millions of households experience food insecurity. The most recent figures collected by USDA researchers show that 12.3 percent of people in the United States experienced food insecurity at some point in 2016, with nearly 4.9 percent experiencing "very low food security." For "Hispanic" households, the incidence of food insecurity in this same year was 18.5 percent, with 5.8 percent experiencing very low food security.[3]

The problems confronting our food system are cause for great concern, but numbers alone do not explain how access to healthy and culturally relevant food has become unequally distributed across lines of race, class, gender, ability, and national origin. Numbers alone do not account for the embodied and emotional consequences of going without meaningful food. They do not capture the stress and anxieties that families experience with dwindling food supplies, the careful stretching of meals with inexpensive but often unhealthy ingredients, or the fear of going grocery shopping if one is undocumented. Further, because rates of food insecurity in the United States both mirror and reinforce other patterns of structural inequality that persist in this country, disparities in food access are especially damaging to communities of color, the working class, and immigrant populations.

Recently, anthropologists have contributed to engaged scholarship on these issues through investigating how Latinx households and communities negotiate inequitable food access and changing dietary practices. These studies have focused on both U.S. citizens and noncitizens, revealing important findings on how Latinos/as with differential access to citizenship cope with changing and insufficient food supplies after moving to the United States.[4] Anthropologists have also offered important insights into the lives of farmworkers during and after the process of migration, focusing mostly upon the well-being and health of those employed in seasonal agricultural production in states with a long history of Latinx migration.[5] Together, these studies highlight the structural vulnerabilities that leave Latinx migrant workers at risk for health disparities and decreased life chances. Yet scholars have not explored the intersection of food insecurity and structural vulnerability within farmworker populations, even though it has proven to be a fruitful line of theoretical inquiry in studies of non-farmworker communities and families.

In *The Unending Hunger,* Megan Carney (2015) describes *la lucha diaria* (the daily struggle) of migrant women in Santa Barbara County, California, as they work to feed their families. She uses deep ethnography to make a series of sophisticated claims about food security as a biopolitical project. In doing so, she sheds light on the daily struggles that Latinas face as they negotiate the responsibilities of feeding their families with navigating the private food sector and food-based entitlements. This daily struggle is also seen in the lives of Vermont's migrant farmworkers. This chapter builds upon Carney's work by examining how food security plays out in a nontraditional destination of migration and for entire families involved in food production. This moves Carney's cogent structural analysis to a more comprehensive view of how women *and* men navigate food access during the process of migration and settlement.

Outside of anthropology, scholars have worked to document the severity of food insecurity and other inequalities in food access among farmworkers.[6] Collectively, these studies reveal that the incidence of food insecurity among farmworkers is as high as three to four times the national average, with a disproportionate number of households experiencing "very low food security with hunger." These reported numbers are not only higher than the national average, but also higher than the average for "Hispanic" households in the U.S. (*Hispanic* being the identifier used by the USDA and most other federal agencies). It is important to note that all of these studies have been conducted with seasonal farmworkers, who often have to migrate multiple times each year and are often paid through piece-rate arrangements. To date, there are no studies on food insecurity for farmworkers who labor year-round in the dairy industry. This book represents the first attempt to investigate food insecurity amongst farmworkers in New England.

Of the studies on seasonal farmworker food security, four in particular have provided relevant methodological and theoretical models for my own research. Brown and Getz (2011) base their analysis of farmworker food insecurity in central California upon data gathered through the Fresno Farmworker Security Assessment, paying particular attention to the factors that produce hunger. Of the 454 respondents, 45 percent were food insecure, including 11 percent experiencing food insecurity with hunger. Their piece is instructive, because it views hunger and food insecurity not as natural phenomena but rather as products of systematic inequalities. In another piece based upon this same data set, Wirth and colleagues (2007) add further depth to these findings, demonstrating that the prevalence of hunger was lower in the summer months and that overall, factors that were associated with food security included income, documentation status, migration status, accompaniment status (whether someone was living with a spouse and/or children), and the utilization of food stamps.[7]

Kresge and Eastman (2010) report findings from surveys of migrant workers in California's Salinas Valley on food security issues, vegetable and fruit consumption, and expressed interest in growing their own food and obtaining nutrition education. This study found that 66 percent of migrant farmworkers were food insecure, 39 percent had used food stamps, and 37 percent were already growing fruits or vegetables. Of those who were not growing their own food, 71 percent were interested in doing so. This study is significant because it goes beyond quantitative measures of food insecurity to identify the strategies that farmworker households engage in to access food and the desire to pursue alternative strategies in accessing and preparing foods.[8]

Minkoff-Zern (2014) argues against the assumption that dietary health issues result from a lack of knowledge about procuring and preparing healthy foods. Based upon ethnographic work with indigenous Oaxacans in the Northern Central Coast of California, she claims that food assistance providers tend to ignore both the nutritional and agricultural knowledge held by farmworkers and larger systemic issues that limit farmworkers' access to food, including structural racism and classism. This study is helpful for unpacking the structural inequalities that are embedded and perpetuated within the food system and illuminating the diverse knowledge systems that migrants bring with them into the United States.[9]

Finally, guided by an ecological framework, Sano and colleagues (2011) examine how low-income rural Latinx immigrant families attempt to meet their food needs, describing both their successes and failures. The study found that a higher incidence of food security was associated with higher incomes, better financial management skills, legal documentation status, stable employment, available social support, and access to health insurance and home ownership. The ecological model that the study employs is useful in its description of the various systems that the mothers participate in to feed their families—ranging from microsystemic factors within the household to macrosystemic factors like federal laws and policies. In this way, this study is instructive in connecting an analysis of household food access with a systems-oriented approach.[10]

A key difference between my research and these previous studies is that Vermont presents an entirely different geographic and social context from areas like California that have long histories of Latinx migration. These different contexts entail differences in the scale and scope of resource provisioning, social networks, and food access. For Vermont's farmworkers, fear of border enforcement, unforgiving work schedules, and a rural environment bereft of transportation options and culturally appropriate food options produce a system of vulnerabilities where food access is often compromised. As I will show, these particular forms of bordering and the limitations of food security metrics reproduce the invisibility of both farmworker bodies and the food insecurities that they face.

MEASURING THE IMMEASURABLE? ASSESSING
DAIRY WORKER FOOD INSECURITY WITH THE
(QUANTITATIVE) TOOLS AT HAND

The U.S. HFSSM, which was developed through a collaborative effort led by the USDA and the National Center for Health Statistics, is the principal assessment tool utilized to measure food security in the United States. This tool provides the foundational data for how we understand the severity and distribution of food insecurity, including the previously cited studies of farmworker food security. Since the widespread implementation of this survey module, public health and health policy researchers have made great strides in not only translating but also testing the linguistic relevance of this tool for Spanish-speaking households through conducting intensive focus groups to develop a well-formulated and easily understandable instrument.[11] The first phase of my study was devoted to collecting baseline data on the incidence of food insecurity among migrant farmworkers in Vermont utilizing the standardized HFSSM translated into Spanish. However, as my data reveals, the cultural relevance of the survey module is not always clear for immigrant households and other socially marginalized groups.

The HFSSM was designed to capture respondents' perceptions of four domains of food security: anxiety about a household's food supply, perceptions about the inadequacy of the quantity or quality of that supply, reduced adult food intake, and reduced child food intake.[12] Because the HFSSM is designed as a rapid assessment of a household's food security, it inherently narrows the lived experience of food access to a series of predetermined choices and narrow categories. Through multiple stages of questions that determine the severity of food security amongst adults in the household and amongst children, the HFSSM results in a score ranging from "High or Marginal Food Security" to "Low Food Security" and "Very Low Food Security," with parallel rankings for the food security rates of households with children.[13] Although the HFSSM provides a quick quantitative measurement of a household's food security, its emphasis on quantitative yes/no and multiple-choice questions, such as the number of times meals were skipped or replaced with low-cost food, does not capture the qualitative dimensions or lived experiences connected to food security.

Drawing upon long-term ethnographic work with Inuit communities in the Canadian Arctic, Elspeth Ready (2016) shares important findings about the poor fit of the HFSSM model for indigenous communities who engage in mixed economies, where traditional hunting and gathering is complemented by foods purchased within the formal economy. Ready argues that "we need to do a better job of evaluating how etic concepts such as food insecurity relate to the lived experience of food insecure people."[14] As I saw in my research, few participants could relate to the concept of food security in our conversations, and I found using this term in the field was often clunky and overly technocratic. Rather, when asking about food access issues, interviewees much preferred to use the term *hunger* or talked about the abundance and quality of food in more descriptive terms, sharing stories like the vignettes that opened this chapter.

This important matter of the cultural relevance of food security measurement tools is also examined in the work of Jennifer Coates and colleagues. In their analysis of twenty-two food security scales and related ethnographies in fifteen different countries, these researchers question the possibility of a common core of household food insecurity that transcends the boundaries of culture that could be used as the basis of a measurement tool. While suggesting that there are shared domains in food security in these cross-cultural studies (including uncertainty/worry about food, inadequate food quality, insufficient food quantity), the authors argue that the "US HFSSM (and therefore translations of the US HFSSM) does not adequately represent all potentially important domains and subdomains of the food insecurity experience."[15] Although the HFSSM might not work for all communities at all points in time, the authors suggest that we do not need to reinvent the wheel when redesigning culturally appropriate food security measurement tools but rather build upon these shared domains.

Despite the inadequacies of the USDA survey module, I chose to employ it in my study to establish baseline data of farmworker food insecurity in

Vermont, so that we may compare food insecurity amongst year-round farm-workers with their seasonal worker counterparts and with state and national averages. The plight of dairy workers has only recently begun to attract attention from activists and scholars, whereas the working and living conditions of farmworkers in other sectors, deplorable as they often are, have long been scrutinized. Researchers based in Vermont have examined the physical and mental health of Latinx migrant workers in the state, documenting the significant barriers to health care access and the patterns of self-medication that result from these barriers.[16] However, despite the obvious connections between food access and health, prior to my research there were no data on the rates of food insecurity among Vermont's migrant dairy workers. In fact, there are no data on farmworker food insecurity available for any of the New England states, in spite of the important role that migrant workers have come to play not only in the dairy industry, but also in vegetable production, berry harvesting, and orchard operations.

Over the course of twenty-two months, from June 2014 until April 2016, my research assistants Jessie Mazar, Naomi Wolcott-MacCausland, and I conducted one hundred surveys using the HFSSM with Latinx migrant farmworkers or their spouses/partners. These surveys were accompanied by a brief demographic survey, which asked for the participant's age, gender, ethnicity/race, county of residence, annual household income, the number of adults and children in the household, primary language spoken in the home, highest level of formal education, and a section on the food programs that the individual had utilized. We conducted these surveys in a variety of locations, including farmworker homes, during semi-annual visits of the mobile Mexican consulate held in Plainfield and Middlebury, in the waiting room of the Open Door Clinic in both Vergennes and Middlebury, and alongside doctors from Little Rivers Healthcare doing field visits in the state's central counties. Conducting these surveys in a variety of places allowed us to connect with farmworkers living and working in multiple counties, though our sample was concentrated primarily in Franklin and Addison, the two counties with the highest numbers of migrant farmworkers.

Although we used a standardized tool, the surveys ranged in length from approximately five minutes to upward of thirty minutes. The differences in duration resulted from my intent to capture any additional commentary that the participants wished to share, both about their household food security as well as the measurement tool itself. Additionally, given the structure of the survey, the fewer challenges accessing food a respondent reported, the fewer

TABLE I Demographic Characteristics of Survey Respondents, n = 100

Average Age	30.8
Range in Age	18–63
Gender of Respondent	Man: n = 75
	Woman: n = 25
Country of Origin	Belize: n = 1
	Guatemala: n = 3
	Mexico: n = 96
Annual Income	Less than $20,000: n = 10
	$20,000–30,000: n = 66
	$30,000–50,000: n = 19
	$50,000–75,000: n = 2
	Don't Know: n = 3
Highest Level of Education Completed	Primary (Primaria): n = 36
	Secondary (Secundaria): n = 44
	Preparatory (Preparatorio): n = 15
	Some University: n = 1
	Technical University (Técnica): n = 2
	Declined to Answer: n = 2
Average Number in Household	4.35
Range in Household Size	1–12
Average Number of Children (under 18) in Household	.43
Range in Number of Children in Household	0–4
Primary Language Spoken in Home	Spanish: n = 98
	Mam: n = 1
	English: n = 1

questions were asked. Surveys that lasted longer were typically associated with the households with children under the age of eighteen living in the home.

Given the small percentage of migrant farmworkers living with children in Vermont, the data on child food insecurity shows an oversampling of families with children. The secondary screening questions for households with children were administered with 25 percent of the sample, which reflects my intent to oversample women. My preliminary research prior to beginning the surveys demonstrated that the presence of women and children has definitive impacts on the variety and quality of foods that are consumed within migrant households and the social relationships and practices that accompany eating. These differences are particularly evident if children meet eligibility requirements for federal food benefits like those coordinated by SNAP (Supplemental Nutrition Assistance Program) and

WIC (Women, Infants and Children). The variances that exist between households made up entirely of foreign-born individuals and those with U.S.-born members were of particular interest to me, due to the different food-related entitlements available to these families. In the total sample of survey participants, we connected with both individuals and families who were active with the Huertas project, and those who were not involved. To some degree, conducting the surveys with farmworkers not active with the project allowed us to share information about the project and identify future participants.

After completing the surveys, all data from the demographic survey and the HFSSM were entered into a spreadsheet for analysis, and the field notes on any additional commentary were transcribed and included in a separate column associated with the participant. Our surveys revealed that overall, 18 percent of households surveyed were food insecure, with 4 percent experiencing "very low food security." Seen another way, these data reveal that 82 percent of households surveyed reported that they were food secure. This compares to the 2016 Vermont average food insecurity of 10.1 percent and the U.S. national average of 12.5 percent.[17] Compared to the other studies of farmworker food security that have reported food insecurity rates as high as four times the national average, it would seem that farmworkers in Vermont's dairy industry are faring much better than their counterparts in other sectors and other regions. However, what these numbers do not capture are the complex negotiations that farmworkers engage in as they access food in an environment that produces significant anxiety and fear.

While these data point to important and troubling disparities in food access confronting the state's farmworkers, these figures are not nearly as severe as previous studies on farmworker food insecurity have reported in other parts of the country. It would appear at first glance that my presumptions about the severity of food insecurity were fortunately false, and that Vermont's farmworkers were having an easier time accessing food than their seasonal counterparts. However, in looking closer at these figures at the county level, the geographic dimensions of food security come into sharper relief. Franklin and Addison Counties rank as the two areas with the highest number of dairy farms employing migrant workers, with Franklin located along the U.S.-Canada border and Addison in the central part of the state. In comparing survey data from these two areas, the incidence of food insecurity is just over 18.2 percent in Franklin County, and 15.7 percent in Addison County. This demonstrates that border proximity leads to difficulties in accessing basic needs, not only in terms of the health-care barriers noted above but also in terms of food access.

However, my experience in conducting these surveys reveals that unless paired with qualitative and demographic information, the survey module results in little more than a group of quantitative assessments that fail to illuminate the social, cultural, and political contexts in which households access and prepare food. In addition to the narrow focus on available cash reserves, the survey module pays little attention to the cultural relevance of foods that households have access to, the time they must spend on securing food, or how they define families and households. In the next section, I turn to the narrative data that reveals a more nuanced understanding of food security and the negotiations that households engage to access food on their own terms.

TELLING THE STORIES OF FOOD INSECURITY WHEN NUMBERS FALL SHORT

As described in the previous chapter, the anxiety and fear that Vermont farmworkers experience is largely shaped by the proximity of the spaces where they live and work to the federal border. Both Alma and Natalia found work within the twenty-five-mile expanse along the border known as the "primary operating domain" for ICE personnel. Neither woman possesses a driver's privilege card, and their access to food, health care, and other basic necessities is necessarily and almost entirely mitigated by third-party actors. These actors include farm owners and managers who provide groceries using poorly translated lists of foods, unscrupulous pizza delivery men charging a premium for their services, and a patchwork of entrepreneurial men and women who bring Mexican goods in large vans from locations as distant as Boston and New Jersey. Alma and Natalia are not alone in this regard; for the majority of families and individuals that I have met in the northern counties, this is the daily reality of accessing food. For workers further south, even just one hour of distance from the border often means less anxiety about leaving the home. For example, in Addison County, farmworkers and their spouses are increasingly obtaining driver's privilege cards for themselves or rides from other farmworkers who are now driving legally. However, as Gabriela's narrative in the previous chapter revealed, these dynamics have rapidly changed since the 2016 presidential election.

Despite the lengths they must go to as they secure food for their families, neither Alma nor Natalia is categorized as food insecure according to the results of the HFSSM. Indeed, for Vermont's farmworkers, the HFSSM merely offers a superficial categorization of food insecurity, rather than a more nuanced understanding of the lived experience of being without food. Even more problematic for Vermont's farmworkers is the exclusive emphasis it places on the linkage between access to money and the presence or absence of food security. While there are very real economic challenges confronting farmworkers in the state—Natalia, for example, experienced illegal pay withholding at her previous job—dairy workers receive relatively higher wages as compared to seasonal farmworkers in other agricultural sectors. Yet both women have described the significant challenges they experience in providing culturally familiar foods to their families, particularly foods that are fresh and obtained through dignified and fair means.

Given the inadequacies of the HFSSM, I aimed to enrich findings from the household food security surveys with interview data that more deeply examines the qualitative aspects of accessing food amidst migration and settlement. Collecting in-depth interview data has proven essential in previous studies of food access strategies among Latinx farmworkers, particularly among women, and allows for a better understanding of the broader context through which farmworkers define and address food needs and preferences.[18] One significant finding of my qualitative research is the continuation of, yet differentiation between, the food insecurities that migrant workers confronted in their countries of origin and the insecurities they experience in Vermont. As I will show in the following narratives, these factors, and the risks that workers face as they cross into the United States, are indeed gendered. In sharing more about Alma and Natalia's experiences, but also through sharing the narratives of Andrés, Josefina, and Martín, these gendered dynamics will become more evident. Despite the differences in their experiences, what they share is how severe poverty, unemployment, and the need to provide for their children have led these individuals to come to the United States in search of economic opportunities. For many, Vermont is only the most recent stop within a long pattern of migration, more often than not following other employment in the agri-food sector.

Returning to the experiences of Natalia, whose story opened this chapter, we see a clear case where laboring in Vermont's dairy industry followed a longer history of agricultural work—paid and unpaid, in the United States and in Mexico. Natalia first migrated to Kentucky with her brother at the age of 16, staying only four months before returning home. Later, she returned with a different brother and her nephew, moving even further north. Recalling these experiences, Natalia described, "The first time I came, I went to Kentucky, to a packaging plant for computers. And afterwards, I came to New York to work in the fields. There we worked in vegetable production—strawberries, corn, all kinds, cherry, apple, cauliflower, broccoli, everything." Her labor in the industrial food system was a complete contrast to the more localized food system she had grown up with in rural Chiapas. There, Natalia and her family grew many of the foods that they ate, beans included, and as a child she even hunted for some of her food using a slingshot.

> Yes, in Mexico we would get animals from the mountain. We would catch *las palomas* (doves) but bigger, called *pascha*, almost like a chicken. And turkeys too! And we would eat them. The *ardillas* (squirrels), they would be up in the trees, like a cat. They are here in Vermont as well. Here they are quite small, but there they were bigger. We would eat these animals and we would fish.

In these brief accounts, we see a diversity of food access strategies, ranging from subsistence farming, to foraging, to working for wages. Looking deeper, these strategies also reflect multiple dimensions of autonomy, power, and control.

Even while experiencing significant poverty in Mexico, Natalia's family was much more intimately connected with the sourcing of their foods, a set of relationships that Amartya Sen would characterize as direct entitlements.[19] In Vermont, Natalia's connection to food ranged from direct, seen in the gardens that she tended at the various farms where she had worked, to indirect, as her family had to depend on others for most of the food they consumed. Living and working on several dairy farms in rural Franklin County and in upstate New York, Natalia and her family did not regularly do their own grocery shopping. This fact did not change even after her husband obtained his driver's privilege card, because they only felt safe enough to drive the half mile to the dairy where they worked. Instead, they prepared a translated grocery list to send with their bosses, who would go grocery shopping every two weeks. Natalia admitted that it was difficult to communicate with their bosses about what they needed given the language barriers, and that other factors, especially issues with fair pay, also complicated this relationship of dependency.

These relationships of worker-employee paternalism echo the conditions that Margaret Gray described for migrant workers in the Hudson Valley of

New York.[20] During our 2014 interview, Natalia explained that she was much happier at the dairy where they currently worked, stating, "Yes, we like it a lot! The farm owner is very nice, since we arrived she has been very dependable. She pays on time and everything!" She contrasted this with the farm that she had recently left, "We had problems on the other farm. It was a lot of work. The pay was irregular and we would work ten-hour shifts. And the other one in New York, the hours were okay but the boss would only pay four dollars an hour because of my daughter. And here, it's different, they pay well." She continued, "At the other farm we would have to borrow money or go in debt in order to have food. And now that farm is asking that we return because they have not found other workers." In these words, the structural vulnerabilities that confront Natalia and her husband as undocumented workers are starkly evident. Low pay, unpredictable pay, late pay—all of these labor abuses result in significant problems in food access for Natalia's household. Nevertheless, Natalia's household was classified by the HFSSM as food secure, albeit marginally so.

The dependency on the boss for grocery shopping is mitigated somewhat by the purchases that Natalia and Nicolás make directly from the off-the-books delivery drivers that come to their home with Mexican products. Arriving once a month but, as Natalia notes, only if they have placed an order that exceeds one hundred dollars, these delivery drivers bring a number of goods right to their front door. Natalia purchases items from both of the two men who regularly circulate throughout rural Vermont in vehicles filled with Mexican products. Natalia explained that these products include Maseca tortilla mix, powdered milk, cookies, fresh *nopal* cactus leaves, frozen banana leaves and dried corn husks to cook tamales, prepared foods (including tamales and burritos), in addition to nonfood items like piñatas, such as the Hello Kitty piñata that had recently adorned Martina's birthday party. These delivery drivers source these goods from as far away as Massachusetts and New York State. Natalia explained that these items tended to be fairly expensive but were worth it, because they could not be found in Vermont's stores.

An additional source of food for Natalia's household came from the biweekly WIC deliveries that came directly to the home. As I will discuss in a later chapter, household WIC delivery was replaced in 2016 by an EBT system that required mothers to obtain their food benefits from a grocery store. These deliveries were important for Natalia's household because of the consistent quantity of milk they received, saving Natalia and her husband considerable money on this key staple food. Receiving milk through a federal entitlement program while working upwards of seventy hours producing this same product is a startling example of the contradictions built into the industrial food system. Rather than receiving a small portion of the product they were helping to produce, Natalia and Nicolás instead had this same product delivered to their home after it had made its way through a complicated supply chain.

The kitchen garden that Natalia tended through the Huertas project brought her the most direct and immediate control over the food that entered her home. In the winter months, access to fresh fruits and vegetables was considerably more difficult for Natalia's family, and she explained that they typically finished consuming these well before their boss's next shopping trip. However, in the summer months, when their garden was in full production, Natalia was able to harvest the items she needed when she planned to cook them, saving them considerable money on fresh produce. She explained, "When we have a garden we do not buy anything that we need to buy in the winter. It is a lot! All that we have to buy is sugar, soap, and salt. The rest can come from what we grow." While Natalia is likely overstating the amount of food that she can obtain from her garden—I have seen during my summer visits that plenty of items from the grocery store and the delivery services are still consumed—the connection and autonomy that is derived from growing her own food is clearly important, not only economically but for Natalia's feelings of self-sufficiency.

Prior to arriving in Vermont, both Natalia and Alma worked in other states, including restaurant work in California, cutting tobacco in Kentucky, and harvesting fruit and vegetables in New York. But unlike the single young men that make up the majority of Vermont's foreign-born workforce, these women have had to balance reproductive work in their homes, particularly child rearing, with their obligations in the workplace. Alma learned about the work opportunities in Vermont's dairy industry from Natalia while she and her husband were struggling to find consistent employment in South Carolina. She recalled, "She was the one who told me that there was work for men here, and we did not have work there in South Carolina. We were desperate to pay bills and rent since it was a very expensive city. You have to pay for water, for light, and for car insurance, because you need a car to get around and to get to work." Given the distance between South Carolina and Vermont, Alma and her family first attempted to relocate to Kentucky, where she and her husband worked cutting tobacco for two months. Unable to make ends meet with the two hundred dollars they were each paid weekly, and hoping to find better housing conditions for their family, Alma and her family soon decided to venture on the longer road north to Vermont.

At the time of our interview, Alma's family had lived and worked on two different dairy farms, though they moved one more time before she returned to Chiapas with her two youngest sons in late 2015 after grappling with the deaths of close family members. The realities she faced in this northern state were very different than what she expected, explaining, "I thought I would be able to leave the house, to go find work, that I could go out and find work for myself. I thought it would be easier. But no. It's been difficult, because I have not had work here. But I want to be able to work, to make my own money." The economic instability that Alma's family faced in Vermont was an extension of the poverty she experienced in Mexico and presented significant barriers to accessing food and other basic needs. Just prior to our interview, Alma had been let go from a job where she had cared for calves for about five months. Her firing was the result of a large transition on the farm where robotic milking machines were installed to replace much of the manual labor. She reflected on this transition with a sense of frustration and sadness, "But since they put the machines, they don't need us. They have machines now, they do it on their own. The *patrón* [boss] wakes up early to get the milk, they are very practical, these machines." However practical these machines were for the dairy operation, this switch to mechanization meant devastation for Alma's household economy and an injury to Alma's feelings of self-sufficiency.

As for Natalia, Alma's garden served as the most immediate and localized source of her family's food. Over the years that I witnessed its growth, I also witnessed a growth in Alma's confidence and connection to her family. While her husband and son were reluctant to eat vegetables and preferred less healthy options, Alma found a way to sneak them into all of her meals out of concern for their health and well-being. The connection between food and family was enduring for her, even while living thousands of miles away from her two older children and her extended family. Although she had not worked in her family's garden in Chiapas, she recalled the foods that her father tended fondly.

It wasn't a big garden. They grew radishes, cilantro, and there's an herb called *mostaza* (mustard). Turnips and *chipilín* (a leguminous plant grown for its greens). Yes, my father had a *milpa,* with beans, and *chipilín*. There are other veggies that are really delicious but they have thorns. To cook it, you can take them out and then you can cook them like spinach. I think it only grows in

Chiapas. Like the *tomates de árbol* (tree tomatoes, also called *tamarillo)*, they are very big trees that grow very tall, and the tomatoes have a very thick skin, and at harvest time, you can eat it raw. *Tomate de árbol.* That's what I ate in Chiapas where I lived.

While Alma only began growing her own food after becoming connected to the Huertas project, she brought to these efforts a serious love of food and a voracious curiosity about how to expand the options she had available for cooking and providing for her family.

Alma is a skilled and passionate cook and had learned how to prepare full meals at a very young age when she was employed as a domestic worker for wealthy families in her community. When she was asked whether the foods she cooked for these families were similar to those she enjoyed in her family's home, she replied:

No, it was very different, because in the people's houses where I worked they could really buy what they wanted, and in my house we could not. We were poor, we had to work to be able to buy food and what we could—the most typical food was *frijoles,* nothing else, and tortillas, that was what we made to make do with. Because we could not buy anything else, eggs only sometimes! But every day we ate beans, vegetables, because sometimes we grew vegetables, but we could not buy them. But the ladies I worked for could because they had a lot of money. They could buy vegetables, and anything they wanted. And that's where I learned to cook because they could cook and eat what they wanted.

Alma also reflected upon the differences between accessing food in Mexico and in the United States, stating, "Well, I have to think about what I have here, because if I don't have things, now that I can't go to the store whenever, I have to cook with what I have.... In Mexico there are many stores nearby, so if we need something, we go to buy it, but here no. Here I have to buy for fifteen days' worth, and if we run out of ingredients, I have to do what I can.... Here we can buy the food that we want. The problem is that we cannot leave." In this recollection, we clearly see the bordering that encourages her to remain invisible in her home. While Alma and her husband regularly enjoyed meals that reminded them of home as they worked in Vermont, the lengths to which they had to go to access food through third-party providers and the premium they had to pay for their food present entirely different food access challenges compared to the poverty they experienced in Mexico.

As was the case for nearly all of the farmworkers I interviewed, Alma and her husband did not do their own grocery shopping; instead they received a delivery of groceries once every three weeks or so. Additionally, she received WIC benefits for her youngest son, and found the milk and cheese they delivered particularly useful, despite living fewer than a hundred feet from the milking barn where her husband worked. She admitted that the groceries they purchased rarely lasted the full three weeks, and as noted previously, she did not feel safe leaving her home. She and her husband prepared the grocery lists for the boss using dictionaries and other translational aides, but she found this process difficult and did not always receive what she was hoping for from the store. Although her husband played a role in preparing the grocery lists, Alma was the only cook in the home, where her brother also resided and shared in household expenses. She noted, "Since everyone else is working, I am here, doing everything! Preparing the food, making the tortillas, cleaning the house, washing the clothing, putting away the clothing and the games, and attending to my children." Even when Alma was able to find employment outside of the home, the reproductive labor responsibilities she shouldered within the household were not diminished.

Like Natalia, Alma found a sense of autonomy and control in growing a portion of her own food, and she found particular joy in harvesting vegetables to use for traditional meals from her home state of Chiapas. With her U.S.-born sons not yet attending school, these items were one of the principal connections to their family's cultural heritage. Although they usually preferred the pizza and submarine sandwiches that were sometimes delivered to their home when Alma did not have the time or resources for a full home-cooked meal, Alma found a sense of pride in feeding her sons some of the foods that she once prepared for the wealthier families in her village using her and her husband's earnings.

In his early fifties at the time of our interview, Andrés was born in the same village in Chiapas as Alma and Natalia, and he had known Natalia since she was a young girl. While they were only distant relatives, Natalia called him *tío* (uncle) as a term of endearment and respect. Andrés arrived in Vermont in 2011 after many years of working in U.S. agriculture and other service sector jobs. His life prior to finding year-round work in Vermont's dairy industry was one of constant movement. First arriving to the United States in 1994, Andrés followed a path of circular migration for seven years, crossing the U.S-Mexico border with regularity and relative ease. After 2001, he remained in the United States because of the increased risk and cost associated with crossing this increasingly militarized border. For the next ten years, Andrés migrated to find seasonal jobs in the fields of Georgia, Florida,

New York, Virginia, and finally, Kentucky. He supplemented this agricultural work with other forms of labor when needed, but struggled constantly with unpredictable and inadequate pay, as well as ever-increasing competition for the few jobs that were available. He learned of the work opportunities available in Vermont's dairy industry through Natalia's brother. Drawn to the promise of year-round employment, he made his way further north.

As a single father of a teenaged son, Andrés had to balance duties of reproductive labor with his labor as a farmworker, and his son Emilio had moved with him through all of these states. A devoted provider and friend to his son, Andrés milks cows for upwards of seventy hours per week to provide for both their basic needs and for the consumer goods that Emilio desires. Having endured the economic challenges of seasonal labor, Andrés was proud of his work in Vermont and what he could provide for his son, explaining in a 2015 interview:

> Yes, here I work every day and all year, it's beautiful, and it's nice. I got a permanent job here, and it's good. Because my son tells me things like, "Papa, I want a pair of shoes because I want to play," or something like that—so I tell him to put it on the list. Sometimes he asks me for a shirt of a certain color and I say "Ok, my son." So, I have to work—I don't want to say no because I can't pay, because I don't have work.

While Andrés is the sole wage earner in the household, the relationship between Andrés and his son is one of interdependence. Especially as he has grown older, Emilio has played a central role in household decision making because of his ability to speak both English and Spanish.

Every week, Emilio prepares a shopping list for Andrés's boss, combining both the household necessities that Andrés requires to prepare their meals at home and items that Emilio likes to take to school with him. As Emilio has grown older, he has grown increasingly health-conscious, and over the years that I have known him, he morphed from a round-faced, chubby child to a slim, athletic adolescent with the trendiest haircuts. Emilio's role in preparing the shopping lists determined not only the quantities of food that entered the house, but also their nutritional content. Andrés was not at all opposed to this power that Emilio exerted in the household, stating:

> Yes, because when we got here, he was a bit heavier, so he said that we were not going to eat a lot of meat—and that we were going to eat vegetables. So, there are things about the foods I prepare that he does not like. And there are things that he wants that I don't really like. So, we see what everyone likes,

like chicken. I love to eat it, and cook it in the pan, with rice or with a pasta. And that's what I like, but sometimes he doesn't like it.

These differing perspectives on what constitutes a healthy or desirable meal might result in more household tension if Andrés was not earning enough to provide for their differing tastes.

In addition to the groceries that are purchased by Andrés's employer, another key source of food for his household is the entrepreneurial delivery service that comes directly to the farm. Every few weeks, a rather nondescript delivery vehicle comes from New York, packed full of Mexican ingredients, prepared foods, and other household items. Andrés shared that he purchases several items from this informal delivery service, including frozen products like seafood and prepared enchiladas, *menudo,* and *pozole,* dried beans, chilies, and herbs, packaged crackers, and fresh avocadoes and bread. Describing this delivery truck as a "little store," Andrés explained that for the most part, prices for these products were pretty similar to store prices, though the specialty goods and prepared foods were often a bit more expensive. However, the familiarity of these foods makes them worth the price, and the convenience factor of the prepared foods is certainly attractive to Andrés given his heavy work schedule.

While Andrés and Emilio have found their routine in accessing foods, things were not always as easy for them. When they first moved to Vermont, Andrés was struck by the differences between the conditions of the state and those in Kentucky. He was particularly concerned about how the rural isolation would affect Emilio.

> And when kids move here it's a little difficult. Because I thought, "how will we do this?" Because they told us how we could not leave here, that going to the store was dangerous because of the law. And we were coming from Kentucky where there are a lot of stores very close by, so when I was tired and didn't want to prepare food, I would just go out and eat with my son. But coming here, it was a bit more difficult, and given that my son already knew English, I asked him to ask how we were going to get our food. And they told him to make a list of things we want and he would get it for us. So, that's how we started. The first days, we had very little, but now, everything is good. Now we are used to how it is here. We cannot leave, but what we want to eat, we send out for it, and he brings it all for us.

Despite the complex avenues that Andrés and Emilio have to engage in accessing food, they are characterized as having "high food security" by the

HFSSM. Here, we see again the failure of this survey instrument in accounting for the complexities of household food security. We also can observe how the bordering processes that unfold in Vermont's rural landscape result in spatialized limits to the autonomy that Andrés and his son can exercise over their consumption choices, compared to the more urban landscape in Kentucky.

Martín's experiences living and working in Vermont were more typical for the men within the state's farmworker community, but he resisted gendered norms in some important ways. As a forty-year-old husband and father of five, Martín moved to Vermont to earn money to support his family from afar, living at times alone and at times with male coworkers. Talking with his children on the phone twice each day, he is constantly reminded of the importance of his earnings, even as it pains him to be so far away from his children. Over a meal of tamales that Martín had prepared in anticipation of our visit, my colleague Naomi and I interviewed him about his experiences accessing food and other basic needs. As he was contemplating his return home, Martín shared memories of his home in Tabasco and stories of his life in Vermont. At the time of our interview, he had been working in Vermont for a total of four years, three of which were spent at the dairy where he currently worked. He had returned home for just one month during this time. Vermont is the only state where Martín had found employment, and he expressed a sincere appreciation for the tranquil nature of the rural region where he lived. However, he looked forward to returning home and reuniting with his wife, children, and extended family.

Martín is from a region of Tabasco rich in cacao cultivation, and alongside his family, he had previously worked in the fields where they grew cacao, watermelon, and other produce for sale. When I asked whether Martín felt that hunger was a common problem in his community, he responded that it was not a problem given the bounty of agricultural production, but that growing certain crops for sale, particularly cacao, was often prioritized over using the land for subsistence farming. Coming from a rural area, Martín was accustomed to the freshest of ingredients, and he explained that this was one of the things he missed most about Mexican foods. Even though he could find things that approximated the ingredients from his homeland, he felt the taste was completely different from the fresher items back home.

Unlike many of his male colleagues, Martín loved to cook. The tamales that we enjoyed that day were his specialty, rich with tender black beans and a mild salsa, and wrapped using aluminum foil instead of the more traditional banana leaves that are difficult and often prohibitively expensive to obtain. During his time in Vermont, he frequently cooked for community events and for everyone who visited his home. He saw cooking as a way to support others, and was bothered by what he perceived to be a fault of Mexican men, explaining, "The majority of Tabasco is very *machista,* they [the men] do not like to cook or to help in anything. To them it is bad to clean the house, to do laundry. But here you do it out of necessity. If not, who will do it?" Learning to cook from his father to support his wife as she raised five children, Martín's family challenged many of the gendered norms in their community. However, he did concede that his brothers, some of whom worked in the United States, were perfectly happy to let women take on the majority of the reproductive labor when returning to Mexico. Referring to his brothers, he explained, "But the others don't help. Here they do. But there they don't! They let the woman do everything. They come back to the home when everything is ready. They want to be served even! And she will clean up after them too!" Over the many visits I made to Martín's home in connection with the Huertas project, I was always prevented from raising a finger to help prepare or clean up after a meal, with Martín always explaining that it was his pleasure to host.

During the time Martín worked in Vermont, the way that he went about purchasing food had changed significantly, from being dependent upon his boss for groceries to doing his grocery shopping on a weekly basis with this same boss. The reason for this change is significant, and it has everything to do with Martín being detained by immigration enforcement several months prior to sitting down for our interview. Late one evening after work, Martín's boss was driving him home after his second shift, and both were pulled over by a local policeman for the expired registration and broken lights on his boss's truck. Upon seeing Martín in the vehicle, the police called ICE officers, and shortly after, they arrived to question Martín. He remembered:

> They took me from the truck and handcuffed me and the immigration told me—since they speak Spanish—they asked me if I knew that they were going to deport me and I said, that, yes, I knew that I was illegal, and that they were going to deport me. And I asked if they could just let me take out my important things from the house, or if my boss could go get my things. Since I knew that they were going to deport me. And they said, "Yes."

When returning to his home to gather his things, Martín was fearful that the two men he shared the trailer with, farmworkers from the neighboring farm, would likewise be detained. His fears turned out to be a reality. Along with Emmanuel and Gabriel, Martín was processed through a local immigration office and then sent to Boston for a hearing at the immigration court.

After their hearing, the three men were permitted to return to work, receiving another court date a year later, which Martín was unsure about attending given the cost of the lawyer and his desire to return home, though he imagined that it would be after the scheduled court date. His roommate Emmanuel had already returned to his home state of Guerrero, and Gabriel was contemplating his return as well. While this incident is revealing about the complexity of immigration enforcement and the realistic fear that it entails for farmworkers on a daily basis, it also shows how, once detained, farmworkers like Martín often experience a new freedom of movement. Given that Martín cannot be detained again before his next court date, he is now much freer to move about the rural landscape. In fact, he jokingly refers to his court papers, saying *"Ahora, tengo mis papeles,"* (now, I have my papers)—the same phrase that would be used if he had obtained either a green card or official permission to be in the United States.

Following these events, Martín could now do his own grocery shopping, a change that he felt had changed his diet significantly, because it allowed him to exercise more choice over what he consumes. He explained, "It is different because before the boss would bring us everything and sometimes they would bring us things that we do not eat, mostly because they would think we would like these things, but no. . . . Sometimes they would bring us fried beans. They were flavorful, we are just not used to it coming in cans." While Martín experienced a new feeling of freedom, his boss was still fearful of encountering ICE. He shared:

> Well that is the nice thing about going out whenever you want to. Without problems. Although the boss does not like us going out too much because of fear. He says he doesn't want this because he says I could have all sorts of problems. Like they will arrest me and I won't be able to work anymore, which is the only thing he is really interested in. But it was good, on the one hand, because we can leave, but what is not good is that starting in November, I will have to be very careful because if they catch me they will throw me in jail. So, that is what I am thinking that come November I will not leave to go to the store and will I have to buy everything like I did before.

Despite having enough money to purchase the foods he prefers, Martín's ability to go to the grocery store to make his own choices over what he eats is time limited. The ability to procure food with cultural meaning and without fear are crucial elements of food security that the HFSSM does not capture, and in Martín's case, we can see how important this is for fostering well-being and a connection to home.

Alma and Natalia are exceptional women in many regards, and the fact that they have found employment on Vermont's dairy farms is noteworthy given that most of this work is reserved for men like Andrés and Martín. For most of the Mexican and Guatemalan women who have migrated to the state, finding work outside the home is exceedingly difficult. Yet all of the women I have interviewed have expressed a desire for paid work, whether or not they have been successful in finding it. Given the challenges of finding jobs, particularly given citizenship barriers, many women have relied upon their creativity and entrepreneurial skills to earn income for their families, often through informal catering and food delivery microbusinesses. Josefina, a mother of three in her mid thirties, has become widely known in her local community for her cooking skills, and her small home-based catering business brings in much-needed income for her family's needs. While Martín cooks for pleasure, Josefina does it to earn an income. At the same time, her work provides a taste of home—an important dimension of food security—to the men purchasing the ready-to-eat meals of tamales, tacos, enchiladas, and chicken with mole sauce that she delivers to a handful of workers on nearby farms. Drawing upon her formal education in marketing and nearly five years of building social connections in the state, Josefina's business has a loyal following. At times, she has also been able to complement the sales of her food with paid instruction of cooking classes at local community centers and universities.

Having previously lived for eight years in a small city in North Carolina, making multiple visits to New York City while her sister was living there, Josefina much preferred the rural nature of Vermont. She particularly enjoyed living in an agriculturally rich county, explaining, "I like everything about Vermont. I like the nature, the country, how free and open it is. There are many things that I like here. I love to harvest fruit. Yesterday we went to harvest strawberries. And after that there are the cherries and the apples, and the sweet corn. All year we are harvesting things." This direct connection to the farms around her is facilitated by the fact that Josefina has an out-of-state driver's license and a reliable vehicle, unlike most of the women I have met. This allows her to visit Middlebury, the closest town, for events at her daughters' school and for the exercise classes that she attends to help manage her type 2 diabetes. She also feels more freedom given that she lives further away from the U.S.-Canada border; for most of the time she was in this community, the presence of ICE patrols was limited.

Unlike Natalia and Alma, Josefina does her own grocery shopping, often visiting multiple stores based on their sales and the availability of certain foods. The comfortable salary and regular raises that her husband earns allow her to be flexible with her purchases of food and other items. She understands that things would be different if she lived further north, and she empathizes with the farmworker families who live in Franklin County. She supplements these groceries with the WIC deliveries that she receives for her youngest child and purchases from the same mobile delivery drivers described above. When her sister was living in New York City, she also received regular deliveries of Mexican ingredients from the *tiendas* her sister frequented in Queens. Josefina also maintained a garden for the two years prior to our interview, after moving to a trailer where they have considerable space around their home. While it is not a large garden, she grows *epazote,* lemongrass, garlic, *hierbabuena,* chamomile, and rue. These items are all used to add a flavor of home to the dishes of grocery store ingredients, meals that she both enjoys within her home and sells as part of her business.

Josefina first learned to cook from her father, who had worked in a Mexican restaurant in North Carolina for five years. Reproducing his recipes for homemade chorizo, *carnitas,* and tacos *al pastor,* Josefina continues to rely upon her father's knowledge, calling him when she is in need of a new recipe or culinary advice. She is the primary cook in her household, feeding herself, her husband, and their three children, in addition to the six to eight workers on other farms for whom she cooks at any given time. Her husband, Gregorio, often contributes the milk he obtains from the dairy farm where he works to the family's supplies. While some employers allow their employees to take milk home, this is not universally the case, as seen in the cases of Alma and Natalia. With this milk, Josefina and Gregorio prepare *queso fresco* (freshly made cheese), to top the tacos, enchiladas, and tostadas that I have enjoyed on multiple occasions during our visits. During these visits to Josefina's home, I have been impressed by the number of people who are circulating through their home, with Josefina acting as a charismatic and welcoming host to friends, students, other farmworkers, social service providers, and the visitors from multiple local churches whom she refers to as her "bible teachers." Gregorio's friends and coworkers also stop by their home with regularity, at times exchanging money for a home-cooked meal, or sometimes bartering herbs and vegetables from the gardens they grow at their own homes.

Despite its importance for her household economy, the income that Josefina has earned through her home-based business has fluctuated over the years in connection with the obligations to care for her children. She reflected upon these changes in a 2016 interview:

> Well, I am not selling now like before. Before, I sold a lot more to the farms, when I first came to Vermont. But it has been five years now. And with my children I did not have any other option for work, only selling Mexican food. They wanted tamales, *mole, pozole,* tortillas, tacos. All of the foods that they know and missed. Because here in Vermont there is not a place where you can go to buy *comida Mexicana* (Mexican food).

Given both her cooking skills and the dearth of authentic Mexican food in Vermont, Josefina had attracted a clientele of both male farmworkers and individuals of higher socioeconomic status who pay her to cater large events. This recognition was a source of pride and excitement for her: "Yes, sometimes I cook for events when people ask me to cook something. Most recently I was asked by a teacher to cook something for a graduation. Her kids had graduated and I made her tacos, empanadas, and *chicharoncitos* (a snack of fried pork skins). I cooked for 150 people, Americans!" Yet it is clearly the case that these foods have different meanings for these different groups of clients. While for these "Americans" the meals likely represent an exciting opportunity to try "ethnic" foods, for the farmworkers she serves, these meals instead reproduce a sense of place and allow for a connection to their foodways. These connections are central to a more nuanced and comprehensive understanding of food security, which includes an attention to the accessibility of culturally familiar foods.

FOOD INSECURITY CROSSES ALL BORDERS

For Vermont's farmworkers who produce food that is core not only to the profitability of the state's dairy farms but also to the food security of millions, inequality in food access is just one marker of broader inequalities that go beyond the U.S.-Mexico border. These narratives reveal how different configurations of household structure, productive and reproductive labor obligations, and experiences of isolation and fear along the U.S.-Canada border shape food security at the household level, beyond what quantitative methods can measure. For these individuals, migrating to the United States was a way to ensure the food security of their families and thus is an important dimension of care work, or what Sobal terms "foodwork."[21] Whether their children are living in the United States or thousands of miles away, each day these parents spend working in Vermont means that their children remain fed, housed, clothed, and provided with school supplies. Their work also feeds the rest of us, giving us the milk we add to our coffee, the ice cream that we enjoy after dinner, and the cheese that we grate on top of our Americanized tacos. However, their daily struggles and food insecurities remain largely invisible as they are pushed further into the shadows of the industrialized food system.

The structural vulnerabilities that these individuals must navigate on a daily basis impact what ends up on their plate, as well as the well-being of their families back at home. For Natalia, Andrés, and Martín, working sixty to seventy hours per week with demanding milking schedules leaves few extended periods of time to shop for food and cook meals as they might wish, let alone properly rest and recuperate. Despite this, we see resiliency as they hold on to their foodways and thus their identities, whether it is in their gardens they cultivate or the pot filled with foil-wrapped tamales. On the other hand, Josefina's work as a small-scale caterer helps others to eat foods that remind them of home, and Alma does what she can in a difficult environment with the earnings provided by her husband and her occasional wages. These households were categorized by the HFSSM as being food secure, except for Josefina's, a surprise given that she lives furthest from the border and is the only one with a driver's privilege card. She is also the only one of the five who came to the United States from an urban environment and has a considerable degree of formal education, perhaps experiencing the greatest change in her food environment and access to basic needs.

All of these five individuals must balance a set of often-competing demands between providing for their families at home and providing for their Vermont-based households. The remittances that each sends back to Mexico surely have an impact on what they can purchase for their immediate needs, but no complaints were raised in any of these interviews. Instead, working in these northern borderlands was seen as an obligation, a duty to fulfill, a sacrifice for the future. These lived experiences cannot be captured on a standardized survey and remind us of the limitations of conceptualizing and measuring food security in narrow economic terms. Given what numbers do not capture, it is crucial that our understanding of food security within marginalized communities goes beyond the realm of quantifiable data so that we may demystify the structural vulnerabilities that pervade our current food system and work for real solutions and opportunities for justice in our food system. In the next chapter I will draw attention to not only the multidimensional meaning of food security but also the possibility of cultivating food sovereignty in farmworker gardens.

_____

THREE

Cultivating Food Sovereignty Where There Are Few Choices

I have always worked with the land. I have always liked being a campesino.

EMMANUEL

The garden gives us balance. What we harvest from the garden is healthier for me and my kids, my whole family because it is fresher. My children also help in the garden with preparing the soil, learning how to plant. And maybe in the future, they will continue doing it.

GLORIA

IT WAS A GORGEOUS, LATE AUGUST MORNING. As I made my way north along I-89, I was surprised to find that the trees were already beginning to change into the Technicolor show for which Vermont is well known. Less than one hour by car from Burlington, this region appeared further advanced into autumn, and the yellows and reds of the sugar maples intensified with each mile I drove closer to the border. It was 2012 and this was the end of my first full summer living in Vermont. It was also my first summer as Huertas codirector, though both the project's name and this volunteer title had only recently become formalized. Jessie Mazar, the first student intern we had hired for Huertas, was along for the ride. We shared a sense of nervous excitement for the day of field visits we had planned to check in on the progress of the farmworker gardens that had been planted a few months prior. Before we set out for the day, our colleague Naomi had warned us, half-jokingly, that we would need to make sure the car was empty to carry all of the produce that would be given to us as we made our rounds. This warning turned out to be a justified promise, as we soon found ourselves the lucky recipients of pounds of produce. Most of this produce came from the hands and the garden of Emmanuel.

After we knocked at the front door of his single-wide trailer, Emmanuel quickly welcomed us into the small two-bedroom mobile home that he shared with two other farmworkers. The front living room clearly doubled as a bedroom. As we entered what was ostensibly a shared space, one of Emmanuel' housemates jumped up from the twin bed where he had been dozing, giving us a shy *"Buenos días"* before heading to the bathroom at the far end of the trailer. Before we had a chance to remove our shoes, a customary show of respect (and necessary given the never-ending quantities of manure and mud that surround farmworker housing), Emmanuel pushed into our arms three gallon-sized bags of frozen wild black raspberries that he had picked from the surrounding hills in anticipation of our visit. As it was my first visit to his home, I could not help but glance around as he did so, resting my eyes first on the phone numbers tacked to the kitchen cabinets. The numbers included those for several of the delivery drivers who brought Mexican products door to door (including, I assumed, the stacks of tortillas and bags of Maseca I spied on the counter), as well as the number for Migrant Justice's *Teleayuda* hotline, which is available to farmworkers like Emmanuel and his housemates for support and reporting work-related complaints. In scanning the remainder of the room, the delicious smells emanating from a large pot finally brought my visual investigation to the stove. Seeing my raised eyebrows, Emmanuel shared in a joking tone, *"Sí, comemos bien!"* (Yes, we eat well!)

He scooted us through the trailer and out the back door, bags in hand. We were stunned to see the vibrant, intercropped garden that spanned almost the full length of the trailer. We were even more taken aback when we learned that the space in which we were standing was just one of four gardens that Emmanuel tended around the property, all while working fifty to sixty hours per week milking cows. In these gardens, Emmanuel was putting into practice both the decades of knowledge he had gained as a farmworker and the traditional ecological knowledge he inherited within and from the fields that his family had tended for generations in Mexico. The garden just behind his home represented a polyculture of complementary crops, leaving enough space for flowers and medicinal herbs. The gardens that he tended in the more distant fields were almost uniform in comparison, vast spaces where only a few crops were cultivated. His favorite crop for these gardens was butternut squash, grown both for its edible flowers and for the eventual fruit that he would use to make the sweet dessert of *calabazas en tacha* (candied pumpkin).

FIGURE 2. Gifts from Emmanuel. Photo by Jessie Mazar.

As Jessie and I chatted with Emmanuel over the next hour of our visit, we followed him along the rows of the smaller polycultural garden as he proceeded to fill plastic grocery sacks of tomatoes, ground cherries, herbs, winter squash, corn, and zucchini that he insisted we take home. Given Naomi's earlier warning, we were not surprised by the gesture, but rather the sheer abundance of his generosity. As Emmanuel filled bag after bag, he joked that these gifts would ensure that we would return soon to visit with him. As I came to learn in later visits, he also shared this produce, which he regularly called "gifts from the earth," with his housemates, the health outreach volunteers from Bridges to Health, a few neighbors, and the wife of the farm owner for whom he worked (in fact, she was quite jealous of his garden). He was even known to package up produce to send through the mail to his children living in the eastern and southeastern United States. The *moras,* or black raspberries, that he had picked for us also found themselves into the kitchen of a health access volunteer he had befriended and were fermented into the berry wine that he and his housemates enjoyed alongside the bottles of Corona that marked the rare times of rest and conviviality. These gifts, as most gifts do, helped to sustain the social relationships that Emmanuel greatly enjoyed. Along with the edible gifts that he bestowed to me, he shared some of the most animated stories I have heard in my years as an ethnographer.

In his gardens, Emmanuel was cultivating not only a sense of place through foods that reminded him of home but also a sense of autonomy and sovereignty over what sustained him. It was one of the few places in these northern borderlands where he felt like he truly belonged, even after working in the United States for more than forty years of his life, and in Vermont's dairy industry for nearly thirteen of those years. In most academic and activist literature, food sovereignty has been primarily conceptualized as an all-encompassing movement with the end goal of rebuilding locally controlled and oriented food systems, rather than a set of everyday practices and choices that individuals and families make over the food that sustains them. Drawing upon insights gained from my work with Huertas and from my ethnographic research with farmworkers like Emmanuel, this chapter argues that food sovereignty can and should operate at both levels, and that the household—or garden—is a crucial space where food sovereignty might emerge. In making this argument, I follow on Amy Trauger's attention to how food sovereignty mobilizes oppositional power from the margins, often in "small but significant acts of defiance."[1]

Through weaving together narratives from Huertas gardeners and reflections from one of the long-term volunteers for the project, this chapter illuminates the glimmers of food sovereignty that have sustained gardeners as they labor in an agricultural economy where they are separated both from the products of their labor and the foodways rooted in their countries of origin. These glimmers of food sovereignty are deeply intertwined with the processes of bordering that, while producing exclusion and marginality, also create spaces of resilience and cross-cultural connection. Central to this chapter are farmworker stories of food and recipes from their home communities, as well as their subsequent efforts to sustain these foodways through cultivating, harvesting, and cooking meals from their gardens in Vermont. In sharing these stories, I demonstrate how isolation, fear of border enforcement, and anxieties around leaving the home combine to both create marginal spaces through which migrant workers reformulate ideas of meaningful food and reveal the layered and often contested dimensions of food sovereignty.

GROWING A PROJECT FROM SEED

At first glance, Huertas might seem like an unlikely project. Planting vegetable gardens with farmworkers who often labor more than seventy hours per week in a place where snow sometimes falls in late May and as early as mid September does not exactly seem like a recipe for success. Add to the mix a shoestring budget and no full-time paid coordinator, and the dozens of gardens Huertas helps to plant each year might seem rather miraculous. Huertas, which supports migrant farmworkers in planting home kitchen gardens, is a project of the University of Vermont Extension's Bridges to Health (BTH) Program. As the codirector of the project, I often find myself surprised by our successes—especially when considering the very real and ever-shifting environmental, social, and financial challenges that constrain our work. Yet for every difficulty we encounter, it is in these gardens where I have borne witness to countless examples of hope and resilience. The success of Huertas is the product of the deep connection between farmworkers and the gardens they cultivate, combined with the energy and commitment of the dozens of volunteers, interns, and donors who support the project each year.

The project began informally in 2010 when a community volunteer gave BTH Coordinator Naomi Wolcott-MacCausland extra seeds and plant starts to distribute to farmworkers with the hope that these plants would help to improve access to more localized and culturally appropriate sources of food. After I moved to Vermont in 2011, I soon met Naomi, given our shared research and advocacy interests. Together, we have guided the project to where it is today. I initially engaged with Huertas as a way to become more deeply aware of the food access issues that Vermont's farmworkers encounter, so that I could guide my research in an applied and community-based manner. Since then, my faculty position at a land grant institution has also allowed me to leverage university resources to strengthen our work and create spaces where farmworkers and student volunteers and interns can find common ground, despite the chasms of cultural difference that separate them. Since the project's inception, Huertas has worked on approximately fifty of Vermont's dairy farms with families and individuals from both rural and urban regions of Mexico and Guatemala, prioritizing the cultivation of culturally familiar varieties of herbs, vegetables, and fruits.

Depending on the number of interested farmworker households each year, Huertas has helped to build and maintain gardens on as few as twenty-one dairy farms and as many as forty-four. The gardens, which are collaboratively designed and planted, range in size from a few square feet to hundreds of square feet of growing space, providing varying amounts of food for farmworker families and those with whom they share extra produce. The multiple gardens grown by Emmanuel occupied what was clearly the largest of the

FIGURE 3. Early spring planting. Photo by Naomi Wolcott-MacCausland.

spaces cultivated with the support of the project. Farmworkers who participate in Huertas are primarily identified through ongoing outreach coordinated by BTH; they have expressed interest in growing some of their own
food after learning about the project from BTH staff or other farmworkers
in the community. For instance, it has become increasingly common for
Huertas participants to share pictures of their garden on social media and
through smartphone messaging applications, which are crucial in the communication networks between farmworkers. There are no minimum standards for program participation, and Huertas serves a diverse group of households, ranging from groups of men sharing cramped living quarters to nuclear
families with young children. However, given what we know about the
impact of border proximity on access to basic needs, we prioritize working
with dairy farms in the border counties. We also have observed that households with children seem to grow more deeply connected with the project, a
connection I will elaborate upon later in this chapter.

The majority of farmworkers with whom Huertas collaborates are geographically isolated, and most do not have access to personal transportation, much less
public, while living thousands of miles away from family and friends. Moreover,
as discussed in previous chapters, farmworkers—particularly those living near
the international border—are fearful of being visible in public spaces, making
traditional community gardening approaches next to impossible. By connecting
farmworkers with volunteers, materials, and the permission from the dairy owners to plant these gardens within this set of constraints, Huertas aims to address
the disparities in access to nutritious food while simultaneously bridging the

FIGURE 4. Epazote harvest. Photo by Claire Macon.

barriers of social isolation that are sustained and reproduced in this type of working landscape. On the farms where Huertas is active, all of the farm owners are supportive of the project, though this support ranges from a simple granting of permission to utilize a small plot of land to helping to prepare the soil and adding compost enriched by manure generated by the herd.

Beginning in 2012, we realized that the project would be more effective if farmworkers could select the exact varieties of plants and quantities they would like to grow, rather than selecting from a random assortment of surplus seeds and seedlings. In our effort to learn about and prioritize the cultural preferences of the dairy workers with whom we work, our project team initiates conversations with participants early in the season, usually with several inches of snow still on the ground, to gain a better understanding of the preferred selection of vegetables and herbs for each participating household. These vegetables range from the everyday staples easily found in U.S. grocery stores, like lettuce, tomatoes, carrots, and onions, to culturally familiar herbs like *papalo, chepil, chipilin, pepicha, epazote, hierbabuena*, and several varieties of *chiles* (including *poblano, miracielo, jalapeño, habanero*, and *serrano*) used in preparing various Mexican dishes. While some of the herbs and chilies may be found in some of Vermont's cooperatives and specialty grocery stores, they are next to impossible to locate in either fresh or dried form in any chain grocery store. Based on the preliminary list, we solicit the generous support of local plant nurseries and farmers who have provided greenhouse space, seeds, and transplants for the gardens. Several of the gardeners also plant their own seeds that they saved from previous years or those they have brought or have had sent from home.[2]

It is important to note that the majority of gardens are located on land owned by the employing dairy farmers, due to the fact that the majority of Latinx farmworkers are living on the farms where they work or in nearby housing provided by their employers. Unlike most community gardening initiatives, the community aspect of Huertas is fostered by the social relationships between volunteers and members of farmworker households, rather than the social ties facilitated by the shared use of space. In examining community gardening efforts around the country, it seems that Huertas is unique in this regard. Most of the volunteers and interns involved with the project are university students, though supportive neighbors living in rural Vermont have also been heavily involved. Volunteers are matched with gardeners to do three outreach visits: the early survey visit, plot planning and preparation in the late spring, and a planting day in the early summer. However, several of these partnerships have extended past these visits, resulting in regular visits and shared meals between farmworkers and project volunteers. For our intern Emily in particular, close friendships have formed through her work with Huertas, and she remains connected to several families despite moving out of the area and on to other employment.

Since becoming involved in the project, I have regularly visited with Huertas participants during each season, often alongside my research assistants and Huertas interns. During the peak harvest periods, we have set aside several full days to visit participants to gain a better understanding of what has worked well and what we might consider doing differently the following year. These visits, while having a clear applied component for the project's development, have also provided important ethnographic insights and have allowed me to refine my research directions and goals. As seen in the opening vignette to this chapter, the most important outcome of these visits is learning more about the role that these gardens play for farmworkers like Emmanuel, in basic terms of access to food but more importantly in terms of sovereignty, choice, and autonomy. After providing some brief context about the concept of food sovereignty, I will transition to sharing narratives of some of the farmworkers involved with Huertas: what I have learned about their relationships with their gardening spaces, the experience of migration, and the food that sustains them. Through these narratives, I will draw attention to the potential of food sovereignty that Huertas provides as well as the limitations of the project.

IMMIGRANT GARDENS AS FERTILE GROUND FOR
FOOD SOVEREIGNTY

In my previous work, I have written about the ways that gardens can serve as an important source of sustenance and the maintenance of cultural identities, especially in the midst of migration and settlement.[3] This point echoes other authors who have demonstrated how gardens enable immigrants to protect their cultural and culinary heritage in the face of assimilatory forces and xenophobia. In her book *The Earth Knows My Name,* Patricia Klindienst observes that garden metaphors have long been used to describe the migration experience, particularly in metaphors of being uprooted or transplanted. She proposes to reverse the metaphor, to focus on the immigrant as a gardener rather than an uprooted plant—"a person who shapes the world rather than simply being shaped by it."[4] In a related vein, my colleague Devon Peña and I have referred to this intentional grounding of identity in place as "autotopography."[5] Through presenting beautifully descriptive case studies of U.S. ethnic and immigrant gardeners, Klindienst illustrates this process of autotopography and demonstrates how food carries with it a deep repository of cultural memory. In her case studies, we see how food, as a material substance, fulfills many hungers—physical, spiritual, and cultural. She argues that "to garden is to claim a portion of American soil as their symbolic home, even when they can never hope to own any land."[6] This claim to land is something that unfolds in nearly every garden grown through Huertas, even amongst individuals and families who do not envision the United States as their permanent home.

Although Klindienst does not use the term food sovereignty to describe the relationships between immigrant gardeners and the foods and spaces they cultivate, I would argue that this concept is useful for both understanding these relationships and locating them within structural considerations of agency and resilience. Although Huertas started as a food security project, as the project has grown and changed we have become increasingly guided by and committed to a food sovereignty framework. The promise of a food sovereignty framework stems from its bottom-up perspective that demands a deeper conversation about rights, control, and choice. In her 2017 book, Amy Trauger asserts that food sovereignty is

> a struggle that emerges from the margins by and on behalf of the poor, the hungry, and the landless to relocate the spaces of decision making in the global food system (Nyéléni, 2007). The discursive battleground lies in an ambitious redefinition of the political, the economic, the social, and the

FIGURE 5. Inventive gardening in an old above-ground pool. Photo by author.

ecological in the food system. The material struggle for land, food, and seed advances on multiple fronts, mostly on small farms and in local communities, and through small, but significant acts of defiance, as well as through acts of kindness and love—the "practice of freedom" (hooks, 2006), made in everyday ways by ordinary people.[7]

This articulation is significant, as it foregrounds the practices and priorities of power, agency, and decision making that food sovereignty enables for communities and individuals who have been marginalized in our contemporary food system. As I show, examining the emergence of food sovereignty in the gardens of farmworkers in Vermont allows us to consider the examples of agency, resilience, and power that are present in even the most marginal of spaces.

The concept of food sovereignty is inextricable from the food sovereignty movement and has developed principally through the mobilization of La Via Campesina. La Via Campesina is an international farmers movement that has devoted particular attention to the struggles and rights of third-world peasant farmers (especially women), the impacts of neoliberal trade and agricultural policies, and the importance of working in solidarity across international borders. In the Declaration of Nyéléni, Via Campesina defines food sovereignty as " the right of peoples to healthy and culturally appropriate food produced through ecologically sound and sustainable methods, and

FIGURE 6. Storing tomatillos for the winter. Photo by Jessie Mazar.

their right to define their own food and agriculture systems. It puts the aspi-rations and needs of those who produce, distribute and consume food at the heart of food systems and policies rather than the demands of markets and corporations."[8] Food sovereignty's emphasis on rights and issues of control shifts the focus beyond the equitable provisioning of food to address more fundamental inequalities related to land distribution, resource management, and social relations.

Eric Holt-Giménez argues: "Food sovereignty is a much deeper concept than food security because it proposes not just guaranteed access to food, but democratic control over the food system—from production to processing, to distribution, marketing, and consumption."[9] As I discussed in the previous chapter, the narrow means through which food security is defined and

FIGURE 7. Jalapeños ready for harvest. Photo by Jessie Mazar.

measured in the United States is inadequate for understanding the complicated and more nuanced relationships that immigrants develop with land and with food. Within a framework of food sovereignty, it is of central importance that food sources are consistent with cultural identities and embedded within community networks that promote self-reliance, mutual aid, and conviviality. Focusing on food sovereignty allows those who are working for more sustainable food systems to move beyond questions of access to a more comprehensive focus on entitlements to land, decision-making, and control over natural assets. Indeed, as Trauger notes, many food sovereignty advocates believe that food sovereignty is the prerequisite for achieving food security, rather than the other way around.[10] As described in the opening vignette, and as I will soon elaborate upon, Huertas allows the possibility for farmworkers to cultivate food with deep cultural meaning, and to exercise agency and choice over what foods they consume. This is particularly significant as it is the denial of food sovereignty, specifically the dispossession of rural lands and livelihoods in Latin America, that has motivated so many farmworkers to move north.

Although the food sovereignty movement has largely developed through the mobilization of rural peasant farmers, agri-food scholars and activists see great potential in furthering the movement in other contexts. Raj Patel argues that the vision of food sovereignty is "important not only because it has been authored by those most directly hurt by the way contemporary agriculture is set up, but also because it offers a profound agenda for change for everyone," as it "aims to redress the abuse of the powerless by the powerful, wherever in the food system that abuse may happen.[11]

As is the case across the industrial food system, within industrial dairy production abuses are rampant, and farmworkers bear the brunt of hierarchical power relations. Long hours, hazardous working conditions, and little time off conspire to make food sovereignty an unattainable goal for most farmworkers, especially if we approach food sovereignty as an all-or-nothing, encompassing movement. And yet, the farmworker gardens grown in the northern borderlands with the support of Huertas reveal compelling examples of these same exploited workers cultivating everyday practices of food sovereignty.

While some food sovereignty scholars and activists have expressed concerns about the Global North appropriating and ultimately rendering meaningless the food sovereignty discourses that have emerged from the Global South, scholars like Patel and Trauger are less concerned about this possibility. As Trauger emphasizes, "Food sovereignty works to break down North/South dualisms, which are a product of and constitutive of imperialism, the perpetuation of settler colonialism, and the existence of extractive corporate food regimes."[12] Like Trauger, I am hesitant to reify these kinds of binaries, particularly when examining spaces where the individuals from the Global South have migrated into and are remaking spaces in the Global North. Given that food sovereignty ultimately is required to, and has the power to, adapt to the political, cultural, and economic contexts where it is applied, it is in our best interest to examine these different contexts if we wish to support the growth and strength of the movement. In the next section, I turn to stories of emergent food sovereignty from farmworker gardens cultivated in Vermont's rural landscapes.

THEY TRIED TO BURY US—THEY DIDN'T KNOW WE WERE SEEDS

Within the group of Huertas participants, some farmworkers have extensive agricultural experience in their home countries and reflect upon their families' farms with a sense of fondness and nostalgia, while others were already disconnected from an agrarian tradition long before they arrived in Vermont to find work in the food system, often as a result of histories of dispossession that denied them food sovereignty. Emmanuel, whose story of generosity opened this chapter, is a prime example of the first group. Born and raised in 1950 in the Mexican state of Guerrero, Emmanuel is the father of eight children, six of whom live and work in various states north of the border. When he was just twenty-four years old, he started traveling north to work in U.S. agriculture, a livelihood he pursued for more than forty years. Until arriving on a Vermont dairy farm in 2002, he traveled back and forth from Mexico frequently, alternating between working on large farms that grew tobacco, lettuce, cabbage, cauliflower, and beets while in the United States and tending to his *maíz y frijoles* (corn and beans) while in Mexico. With increased border security following 9/11, Emmanuel and millions of other migrant workers have found themselves less able to visit their families in Mexico for fear that they would not be able to return to work in the United States. Because of this seismic shift, he found himself with a difficult choice: either remain in Vermont where he felt isolated and distanced from his family or return to Mexico with the understanding that crossing the border would likely be too risky and dangerous to attempt in his advanced age.

Over the years that I knew Emmanuel, a visit to his home always meant a walk through his gardens. During a visit in 2014, I asked Emmanuel why he had not grown a garden in Vermont previously given his extensive agricultural experience, enthusiasm for growing, and the number of years he had lived in the state. He replied that until he was approached by Huertas, he never even thought planting a garden was a possibility. Despite having a tremendous wealth of agricultural knowledge and experience and a deep love of growing food, he was unable to access the seeds and other necessary materials needed for his garden, a connection that was successfully established through participating in the project. After this brief discussion, he quickly returned to the tour of his garden, pointing out the sunflowers and *flor de viuda* (widow's flowers) he had planted around the perimeter of the space and the dry beans he had received in seed form from his family in Mexico. Over the course of our many visits, Emmanuel regularly requested that we take pictures of him in his garden so that he could share them with his children and so that he could bring them with him back to Mexico. In these instances, the sense of pride and sovereignty that is cultivated through these gardens becomes clear, as is the desire to share the bounty of the food produced in these spaces. What also becomes clear is his sense of impermanence in the United States, even as he became, quite literally, deeply rooted in U.S. soil.

As our visits with Emmanuel grew more regular throughout 2013 and 2014, and more focused on socializing than gardening, he also began to prepare elaborate meals in anticipation of having guests. These meals nearly always centered upon homemade tortillas that he prepared with Maseca purchased from the mobile vendors, accompanied by a rotating assortment of vegetables, chicken *mole, pozole, atole,* beans, salsas, rice, and candied squash that he prepared with the hundreds of butternut squash he grew. When asked if he cooked these kinds of dishes in Mexico, he gave a sly laugh and stated, "No, in Mexico, I was the king! I did not need to cook or clean, nothing!" Commenting on the *"machista"* ways of men in Mexico, he acknowledged his gender privilege during this conversation but also hypothesized that when he returned home for good, he most certainly would not continue to cook if he could find a woman who would do so. However, as his stay in the United States stretched longer than he had originally planned, he sought out the expertise of women, particularly when he was working in seasonal crop production where women were more commonly employed. These women shared with him their cooking knowledge and skills, which he began to employ in his own kitchen. While tortillas were an everyday staple in his Vermont home, as he repeatedly reminded us, cooking more elaborate meals was really only worth the time and effort if it brought visitors to his home. In this way, Emmanuel engages his culinary knowledge and foodways to rebuild a sense of community that was often absent when living in the United States.

Over the four seasons that I witnessed Emmanuel cultivating a garden that he always knew was impermanent, I gained a much deeper understanding of the complex and often competing relationships he held to work, to land, and to his foodways. While Emmanuel reminisced frequently about the land he cultivated in Mexico, until connecting to the Huertas project, he had never grown food for his own sustenance in the United States. He recalled his livelihood in Mexico with a deep sense of longing.

> We had everything- all the beans, everything! We bought only oil, this, more than anything is what we would buy in town, along with the salt, that's it. We knew everything. What else would we need to buy? Because where we were living we were always raising goats, cows, chickens, and when someone needed some money, you could sell a chicken, or a turkey, and there you go, now you have money! If you wanted to sell a pig, there you've got money. And if you sell your goats—five, or even six goats—there, you have got your money!

In contrast to this life of food sovereignty, the forty years that he spent in the industrial food system was instead a series of jobs ensuring the food security of others, not his own. Drawing upon the work of Lefebvre, Trauger asserts that "the struggle for autonomy entails a deep engagement with the spatiality and territoriality of that struggle."[13] In both Emmanuel's longing for his

FIGURE 8. Farmworker admiring his garden. Photo by author.

previous livelihood, as well as the claims he makes to space in his Vermont gardens, we see a clear struggle over space and territory.

After decades of working in U.S. agriculture, Emmanuel permanently returned to Mexico in January 2015 after his employer sold the remaining dairy herd and retired after several years of financial struggle. His return to Mexico occurred just months after he appeared in immigration court; he had been detained when ICE personnel entered his home after his housemate and his boss were stopped by a sheriff just outside their trailer due to a broken taillight. Though his housemate was not driving, the sheriff began asking for his information and then called ICE, who then entered the home and detained the three men living there. During Emmanuel's initial court date he was granted deferred deportation proceedings until late 2015, but seeing the limited opportunities for work he now faced in his advanced age, he made the difficult decision to return to his home village in Guerrero knowing that he would not likely return to the country he had known for forty years. Before he returned home to Mexico, he made sure to let us know that he planned to return to farming the land he had been accumulating in Guerrero, becoming once again autonomous over the food and land that sustains him.

While Emmanuel and his housemates lived and worked in a fairly rural area of northern Vermont, César had found work in an even more remote area of the state, the Northeast Kingdom. This border region, granted its moniker by Governor George Aiken in 1949, consists of Caledonia, Essex, and Orleans Counties. It is a beautiful but very rural space, popular with hikers, hunters, and those looking for relatively inexpensive agricultural land who are willing to traverse the roads that deteriorate further with every harsh winter. César was in his late thirties when Jessie interviewed him in the fall of 2015, and he lived and worked with his brother and another young man. Together, they labored on a dairy farm in the same region of the Northeast Kingdom where there has been a rural renaissance of producing specialty foods like artisanal cheese and craft beer.[14] These specialty value-added products have become more lucrative than milk from the industrial dairy farms that surround the farms where they are produced.

Coming from the Mexican state of Veracruz, César had grown up in a coastal region; Vermont's climate was a shock to his system. On the day of the interview, he prepared a seafood-based soup using some of the herbs from his garden that he insisted Jessie sample before the interview began. Despite the rural location of the farm where he lived and worked, César's household was categorized as having high food security. Unlike many farmworkers, he was able to accompany his boss to the grocery store every two weeks to do his grocery shopping, supplementing staple foods with the specialty Mexican goods delivered to his home. The garden that César and his housemates cultivated was not particularly successful the summer of Jessie's visit. They had lost most of their tomato plants to a late blight but were still enjoying a number of the herbs they had planted.

César explained that finding Mexican ingredients was challenging in the Northeast Kingdom: "It is difficult because there are things that are not here and we cannot find them, because we need a Mexican market and there are none here!" Despite feeling that he had enough money to purchase the food he wants and having the opportunity to do his own grocery shopping—an opportunity that few farmworkers experience—he found that the garden fulfilled an important connection to fresh produce. As he explained, it was not only the specific varieties that he grew but the freshness of the food that gave him greater agency over his meals. This freshness was something he had grown accustomed to in Veracruz, and he appreciated that even in the cold climate of northern Vermont he could approximate it through his garden. He shared, "When you want a vegetable, you go and get it fresh! You go get what you will eat that day and leave the others to grow." He provided Jessie with the example of preparing *pintos,* a corn-based dish similar to tamales, with beans that were growing in the garden. Unlike the frozen tamales that are delivered by mobile vendors, these fresh tamales, made with items that he had nurtured from seed, deeply fulfilled him and connected him to home. The ability to pick vegetables that he has grown with his own hands, when he wants them, is a perfect example of the everyday experience of food sovereignty.

César much preferred the fresh herbs that he grew to the dried ones he purchased in the winter when he had little choice. He explained:

> We have a lot of herbs and everything that we have is so good because it is fresh, and we just go and grab it, like the *epazote*. Just enough to put in the pot, and when we don't have it, we buy it dried but it does not have the same flavor or aroma. With *manzanilla* (chamomile), it is also not good when it's dry. Oregano is a good plant to grow, but here they usually sell it dry and it is not the same. I have a little plant that that I put in a pot and there it is! That is why the garden benefits us, because you eat fresh foods, those that still have their aroma.

It was this love of fresh foods that kept César attached to his garden, although he also expressed frustration that he was the only one using his spare time to maintain it. While his housemates spent what little free time they had on the internet or watching TV, César preferred to spend his time outside, growing items that provided him with the flavor of home, a greater degree of choice over the quality, and varieties that he enjoyed. Nevertheless, he shared the fruits of his labor with his housemates, reinforcing bonds of mutual aid and community in their kitchen.

As I have grown more involved with Huertas, what has been particularly striking to me are the daily lives of women, especially mothers with very young children, who are living at these dairies. Unlike Emmanuel, who would likely give up his cooking duties if he could find someone else to cook for him, for Alma, preparing meals that resemble those from home is what she loves most about her garden. Alma, whose story appeared in chapter 2, is a good example of the second group of gardeners, those who have little direct experience farming but come from agrarian regions. While her family in Chiapas owned a sizeable amount of land, it was devoted to growing coffee for export instead of providing food for her family to subsist upon. This pattern of production reveals that access to land does not necessarily translate into food sovereignty, particularly when growing products like coffee that are highly volatile in the global marketplace. Despite this disconnection from farming, Alma devoted significant effort to maintaining her family's connec-

FIGURE 9. Alma harvesting *camote* (sweet potato). Photo by Jessie Mazar.

tion to culturally meaningful foodways in Vermont even while facing significant challenges in accessing fresh foods on her own terms. As a novice gardener, Alma's success growing food for the first time in 2012 was impressive, especially given that the farm owner periodically cut off the water supply to her family's home during the hottest period of the summer to redirect it to the cows in the barn.

At this farm, Alma lived with her two small boys, her husband, and a few other men in a small manufactured home, though she later moved to a different farm with only her immediate family. For Alma, cultivating her own food has given her an opportunity to get outside and re-create some of the meals she misses from home, as well as to develop new agricultural skills that she had only witnessed from afar while living in Chiapas, Mexico. Although she has jokingly complained about the fact that her husband and children do not have enough appreciation for vegetables, she has continued to find new ways of sneaking them into the meals she prepares. Over the years that she was involved in the project, I had the fortune of regular visits and shared meals with Alma, and during that time her garden increased exponentially in size and productivity.

Unlike many of the gardeners we have worked with, Alma had little experience growing her own food before becoming involved in Huertas, despite having been raised in an agricultural community. However, she threw herself into the project with both feet, growing flowers and vegetables that she regularly shared with other volunteers who came to her home and with our project collaborators whenever she had a chance. Whether it is fresh salsa or a bouquet of recently picked flowers, Alma's produce brings her a firm sense of pride in her ability to create something from the ground where she resides. As this pride developed, Alma became increasingly active in local farmworker activism efforts and even taught cooking classes at a food cooperative in Burlington focusing on dishes from her home community. Despite the fact that these events required her to leave the home—which is a risky venture given where she lived—Alma's relationships to the local community deepened. And yet, even with this personal growth, her autonomy and sense of place were rooted to land that she does not own, a connection that remained tenuous and seemingly impermanent. Alma has since returned to her home village in Chiapas, following a number of personal family tragedies that forced her to return to seek the support of the family networks that remained there.

As with Alma, Sofía and her family grew deeply connected to their garden space, which seemed to exponentially grow each season. As described in chapter 1, Sofía lived with her young daughter and husband, along with several other workers, at a farm very close to the border. Before their return to Mexico, the Huertas project gave her and her daughter an outlet for creativity, experiencing the outdoors, and cultivating fresh food with deep cultural resonance. She reflected upon these experiences during a 2014 visit with my colleague Naomi:

> I used to only leave the apartment to go to the milking parlor to help my husband sometimes. I never went outside. I didn't see the sun. Three years ago I started to have a garden. I didn't know anything about having a garden here. Jessie and Teresa came to talk to me about it. They explained how to prepare the soil and asked about the plants I wanted. The boss gave us a place to plant in an area in between the barns and farm machinery. Immigration always passes by on the roads next to the farm so it was difficult to find a place that was not visible from the road.

Because of this continual fear of immigration enforcement, Sofía explained that prior to having a garden, there were periods where she would not leave her apartment for as long as two months at a time because there simply was not anywhere enjoyable to go. This apartment, described in detail in the previous chapter, is tucked behind a makeshift farm office and has a small kitchen and sleeping quarters for the workers, little else. It is the last place you might expect food sovereignty to develop.

As Sofía recalled in her conversation with Naomi, in deciding upon the location of the garden we had to take extra care that it was out of sight from the small state highway that loops around the barn and their housing unit. To get to the raised beds, Sofía and her daughter put on their rubber boots and mucked their way through the milking parlor and then the cow barn, wading through inches of animal waste to arrive at a sunny area tucked between two sections of a free-stall barn and bunker silos that store the majority of the cattle feed. Despite these obstacles, Sofía repeatedly expressed that the garden gave her and her daughter a reason to get outside, often as much as three or four times a day, and reconnect with dishes like *chiles rellenos* that she prepared with the produce that she grew with her own hands. As importantly, she expressed her appreciation of the project for the ways it allowed her to meet more people and form lasting friendships, breaking the monotony of isolation that she experienced.

During the summer months, the produce from her garden provided a significant percentage of the fresh vegetables her family consumed, and throughout the winter, she added dried herbs from the garden to flavor her dishes and saved seeds to replant the herbs the following year. For her, this was both a meaningful addition to her household's food supply and a practice of food sovereignty, though of course there are seasonal limitations. She explained:

> The rest of the year, the manager on the farm buys us the vegetables we ask for once a week. We make a list and request what we need. It's difficult to know how much I need each week, and there are times that we eat all the vegetables I ask for in a few days and then we don't have any for the rest of the week. Other times, we have too much, and they rot before we can use them. With the garden, I harvest what I need daily without the vegetables going bad or not having enough for the meal. Since I started harvesting this year I haven't purchased any vegetables. Every day I harvest what I want that day. I covered my garden a few weeks ago to protect it from the frost and am still able to harvest.

Sofía's garden continued to be one of the most productive we have seen, an abundant space where she grew corn, tomatoes, several varieties of *chiles*, tomatillo, lettuce, radishes, summer squash, carrots, watermelon, cucumbers, onions, and garlic, in addition to many different herbs (cilantro, oregano, mint, chamomile, *epazote*, dill, thyme, *papalo*, and *cepiche*). While the variety

FIGURE 10. Sofía's raised beds. Photo by author.

and quality of vegetables are of clear benefit, Sofía's ability to choose which vegetables she wants to pick and eat, and avoid waste, is perhaps even more significant in terms of food sovereignty. Unlike all of the other women involved with Huertas, Sofía has no interest in planting flowers, preferring to dedicate this precious space to food.

Over the last two years she lived in Vermont, she and her husband made special efforts to construct raised bed borders and extend the overall footprint of the garden, in addition to adding a large umbrella to provide shade for relaxation. This transformed the garden from a space of producing vegetables to one with multiple uses and meanings.

> One benefit of the garden is the distraction. If I didn't have the garden, I'd be inside all day in the kitchen watching TV. I don't get bored in the kitchen

FIGURE 11. Little gardener. Photo by Jessie Mazar.

but it's different being outside. Now I go outside and listen to the birds sing. I feel more free, like I'm in the fields in my village. The memories of what it was like there come back. Another benefit is to breathe fresh air and have fresh vegetables and herbs and no more rotten cilantro!

In these connections, we can observe the desire to create a sense of belonging and tranquility, even amid the challenging conditions and fear in which she lives. She often told us that when the time came for her to return to her home state of Guerrero, Mexico, she planned to take the skills she has learned through gardening in Vermont and grow vegetables for sale on land that is owned by her extended family.

Gloria, a mother of five, with four of her children living in the United States and one being cared for by her mother in Guerrero, has enjoyed a different level of freedom than most other women. Unlike Alma and Sofía, Gloria's husband has documentation to work in the United States, so she sees Vermont as her permanent home. She is one of the women I have grown closest to: I have seen her family grow and change, through a move, the birth of their youngest child, and a growing attachment to the state of Vermont. Gloria's love for her garden followed her from the small trailer on the rural farm where her husband has worked to the small home they now own in the nearest town. Through cultivating the garden, and more recently through raising chickens for eggs and meat, Gloria and her family have enjoyed the freshness of the foods they produce while maintaining a connection to particular recipes and dishes from home. At the same time, they also regularly experiment with new dishes inspired by her children's assimilation to the U.S. diet through attending public schools.

When I asked Gloria how her diet has changed since moving to the United States, she explained:

> Well, it has changed a lot. In Mexico there are different types of ingredients. And, here we have learned to eat new things and different things. And thanks to the program that you all have started, Huertas, because of this, we have more of the foods that we need to make our dishes. So, we don't have to miss our Mexico as much! For example, *epazote,* and the vegetables that we have, for example the *papalo quelite,* they are things that we have never been able to find in the supermarket here in the United States. We have never found them! Also the *tomatillo* and a few spices. The basil we can find, but only sometimes. We can also find the cilantro, but not always. But now, thanks to the program, now in the summer we are able to have all of these types of vegetables.

Gloria has experimented with different forms of preservation to extend the harvest into the much colder winter months, but she is constrained by the size of her kitchen and limited storage space. The foods she preserves are typically frozen, but she explained that her family quickly goes through what little amount they have room to freeze. This leaves her family mostly reliant on foods purchased at the grocery store in the winter, which is a dramatic change from the shopping habits she practiced in Mexico, where the growing season was much longer and fresh produce was available in small neighborhood markets year-round.

The diversity of foods that Gloria and her family cultivate in their garden is something that she deeply appreciates, even as it represents a slightly different form of agriculture than the farm her family maintained in Mexico. This farm, where they primarily grew "*solo maíz*" (only corn), was larger in scale and provided for the tortillas they consumed on a daily basis, but not all of the vegetables her family consumed. In her Vermont garden, Gloria is able to sustain the family tradition of planting peas, recalling with fondness what she learned from her father, "My family had a garden in our house and my father was always planting peas and now I always plant peas because of this.

I think this is a form of education that is very important for people." In addition to the peas that reminded her of her father, she also grew *quelites* (a catch-all term for different varieties of greens that often grow wild) and *epazote*, which she could not find anywhere else but in her garden. For these foods, she expressed a strong interest in learning how to save seeds, explaining, "Especially when the winter is approaching and we pull everything out of the garden I always think this is not trash, we should save the seeds! It would be good to know how to save and have it for the next year instead of throwing it away."

These five individuals are distanced from their home communities by thousands of miles, living and working on farms that they do not own, and in truth, could never hope to. Many forms of structural vulnerability conspire to deny them agency and sovereignty over their food, particularly as they grapple with the daily realities of living in a border region that demands that their bodies, and their basic needs, remain invisible. As the organizers of this project, we have had to balance the potential of the gardens with these structural constraints, carving out often hidden spaces where small instances of food sovereignty might be cultivated and connections to foodways restored. The joy that is found in planting a variety of *chile* or a type of herb and then preparing and sharing a meal with the foods that are grown by one's own hand is a unique form of agency. This form of agency is extremely rare in the lives of workers whose labor is devoted to feeding others rather than attending to their own physical, spiritual, and cultural hungers.

While the gardens are significant because of the food that is cultivated, their meanings extend even deeper than a basic sense of food security. For these individuals, these spaces have become a source of pride and joy, providing a break in the monotonous labor patterns that characterize the industrial dairy system. They provide a means to engage with the forms of traditional ecological knowledge that are always in danger of being lost. For some households, particularly those where women are present, gardens also provide a way to pass this knowledge down to the next generation, a generation who may never know Mexico and the true richness and complexity of their parents' foodways. For Gloria, the garden is a symbol of her permanent life in Vermont, whereas for the others, it represents an important, if impermanent connection. Finally, as I describe in the next section, these gardens also provide an opportunity for farmworkers and Huertas volunteers to bridge large gulfs of cultural difference and engage in mutual recognition.

Since Huertas became a formalized project in 2012, we have been supported by the work of a dozen student interns and many more short-term volunteers. As the academic supervisor for these interns, I have been pressed to negotiate my own long-term commitments and interest in the project with the more transitory and short-term routines of university students with their ever-changing class schedules, study abroad plans, and ability to commit to an unpaid position when their bills often demand that they devote what little free time they have to paid employment. Despite the many competing demands on our interns' time, I have been consistently impressed by the devotion and commitment that many of these individuals have demonstrated and the genuine love they have developed for the project. Four of our interns have committed to the project for more than a full academic year, sacrificing paid work in some cases, and in some others receiving competitive funding from the university in the form of student research grants and internship fellowships. Through their work, our interns have gained a deep level of understanding of the daily lives of farmworkers in the dairy industry, in particular the barriers they face in food access and nutrition. As I describe in this section, this understanding reflects the transformative potential of experiential learning for undergraduate students.

Emily is a volunteer who has developed a particularly close connection to Huertas participants and an understanding of their lives both before and after migration. Working as an intern, research assistant, and temporary paid staff member over two-and-a-half years, she saw her involvement with Huertas as a natural extension of her interests in social justice and sustainability. In an interview with my research assistant Jessie Mazar after her first full season of volunteering, Emily shared what she had learned through these initial experiences. Learning about the program from a class presentation organized by a previous intern, she explained:

> I have always had a passion for working with people and I didn't really know how that would manifest itself in Vermont, I didn't even realize that there was a Latino population in Vermont and I was studying Spanish and I had just gotten back from South America and I really wanted to find a way to be involved.... For me it was a way, it was the first thing I ever saw that just made sense, it was about the environment but not in the same way that a lot of the same things in Vermont are. I am from the South and

FIGURE 12. Huertas intern, Claire Macon, helping to build chicken coops. Photo by Naomi Wolcott-MacCausland.

> I feel like my relationship with the environment is very different than a lot of people who work here and I felt like Huertas, all of it just made sense to me.

In our later conversations, I learned that for Emily, Huertas addresses environmental concerns in a more grounded way, reflective of the environmental justice ethos of seeing the environment as those spaces where we live, work, and play, rather than a place of wildness and remoteness.

Over her years working with Huertas, Emily developed close relationships with several families, particularly with Gloria's, who asked her to be the godmother of their young child (an invitation she was honored to accept) and Alma's, whom she visited in Chiapas after they returned home. Living so far from her own family as she attended college, Emily found a sense of family and kinship that was often missing in her college life. At the same time, she sometimes felt overwhelmed by the magnitude of the struggles that these families faced. She reflected:

> I think that being a part of this project, there is a point where you realize that ... I feel like this a lot because I am relatively young ... not in comparison to a lot of farmworkers because a lot of them are my age, but in relationship

to being in the work community. But there is a point where you realize that the entire system has failed the people you are working with and that there is literally no one left for them to turn to except for these few people that they see, with Huertas, or Bridges to Health or Migrant Justice, or whatever tiny organization. Looking at these tiny organizations, of three or four people. If you are looking at Huertas, you realize that they are turning to you because they have no one else to talk to. Like Willa and Milena have told me that the only people that they see are me and the health worker that is in their county. And it is, like, of course they are asking you for groceries! And, of course they are asking you to help them buy shoes for their daughter because there is no one else they can ask. And I think it is a really scary moment, that is when I have felt very overwhelmed and this world is too big for me. Because I am 21 and this person who has so many people relying on her is asking me for this and I can't be there for everyone because I am one person.

As a project, we have had to balance the potential that our interns will be overwhelmed by their experiences with the deep value of this kind of experiential learning. While Emily describes these feelings of being scared and overwhelmed, these feelings were not paralyzing for her, but rather encouraged her to become more deeply involved and to learn more about the structural vulnerabilities that farmworkers face. As we worked together, she repeatedly told me that she learned more through her involvement with Huertas than in any of her traditional courses, and by the time she graduated, she had earned a full semester of credits for her field-based work and research assistance. To help our interns like Emily process their experiences in the field, we require that they keep field journals, attend a thorough orientation meeting, and go to regular check-ins, where we collectively debrief and reflect upon our work. The majority of the many hours I spent with Emily driving around rural Vermont were also devoted to verbally processing our experiences.

At the same time that Emily described feeling overwhelmed by the circumstances and conditions she witnessed in the field, she also reflected, "This has been such a transformation for me and it is just so much, it is so much more than just gardens." As she continued to volunteer and work with the project over the next year and a half following the interview, she regularly shared with me that her work gave her a sense of meaning and belonging in a region where she often felt not quite at home. The relationships that she developed with participants in the program taught her that she had a tremendous ability not only to empathize with farmworkers and their families but also to be a strong ally and advocate. Comparing where she was at the time of the interview to when she started, she shared:

I was so occupied with doing the project and not stepping on people's toes and not making it about me. And now that I am just like I feel waist deep in it, neck deep in it. I feel like I look back where I was, I never thought I would be getting texts from Alma when her grandma died, I didn't know I had the capacity to make that kind of connection.

This level of connection is a far cry from the "unbearable whiteness" that Julie Guthman assigns to students engaging in experiential learning about alternative food systems in her program at University of California–Santa Cruz.[15] Rather, it represents a meaningful attempt to bridge sometimes enormous differences of cultural and social privilege, resulting in a series of relationships that have transformed not only Emily's life, but also the lives of Huertas participants. The close professional relationships that develop between Naomi and me (as academic and field supervisors) with our interns are enabled by the relationships we have sustained with farmworkers over years. This careful building of trust and reciprocity is made possible by both the small size of our project and the care that we take to select and train the interns we send out to the field.

The understanding that Emily has gained about herself and the farmworkers with whom she has grown close also extends out to a deeper knowledge of the structural vulnerability and violence that farmworkers encounter. As an anthropology professor, my goal within the classroom and individual advising relationships is often just that: supporting students as they unpack the patterns in our society and the structures that both limit and enable individuals based on their position in society. Emily's ability to make this move has been particularly notable within our group of interns, and her field journals and the narratives that she shares about Huertas reveal a balance of theory and description that I have found uncommon in students her age. She shared:

> You talk and joke with Alma about opening a restaurant and then you hear about this hard life they live and you joke with people about being silly and then hear about them crossing the border and not having food or water for a few days and everything turns from black-and-white to color, and I think that is the point where Huertas becomes your whole life, you're living for it.

The contradiction that Emily had come to understand between Vermont's love of local food and appreciation of a back-to-the-land ethos with the violence experienced by farmworkers in this same state, represented for her a replication of "a lot of the big problems with neoliberal food economies on a small scale." This recognition, a complex example of applying theory to practice, represents a form of high-level learning that is sometimes rare in traditional college classrooms. By putting a face and a name to immense political economic processes and complex social theories, Emily has grown into an impressive young researcher and has contributed in significant ways to the study that forms the basis of this book.

In Emily's experiences, we also see another pillar of food sovereignty at work, the building of community and networks of mutual aid. As a professor who has supervised dozens of internships, I have become well aware of both the limits and potentials associated with experiential learning. To me, one of the largest barriers that must be overcome for this form of learning to be mutually beneficial, particularly when working in socially marginalized communities, is building relationships of trust. This trust can only be built if one continues to show up and be present. Emily's work has been remarkable in this regard. As she extended a semester internship into a commitment of two-and-a-half years by her own design, she proved to Huertas gardeners not only that she cared, but that she would continue to show up. Whether it was showing up in rural Chiapas to celebrate the quinceañera of Alma's oldest daughter or agreeing to be the godmother of Gloria's youngest daughter, Emily has formed the closest and most sustained relationships within our group of interns. This, in turn, has allowed the collaborative planting of gardens to grow into something even more meaningful, into spaces of conviviality and cross-cultural connection.

CONCLUSION

Since our first summer as a formalized project, we have planned annual fiestas as the gardens are bursting with produce, to bring many of these gardeners together and to celebrate and share the literal fruits of our labor. Over a large, gas-fired stove at the Wolcott-MacCausland family farm, the individuals and families described in these vignettes have come together to share homemade tortillas, prepare and can fresh salsas and black raspberry jam, and transform the baseball-bat-size *calabacitas* that were allowed to grow for too long into zucchini cakes. We have done this all with the goal of building a sense of commensality and community that is often missing from the daily lives of these workers. In a small way, these events have challenged the isolation that is produced by and reproduces Vermont's rural working landscape. In these fiestas and in the gardens themselves, we see the glimmers of sovereignty and

FIGURE 13. Salsa harvest. Photo by Jessie Mazar.

autonomy over the sources and diversity of foods these individuals are consuming. Yet in planning these events, we must remain constantly aware that for farmworkers, traveling even just a few miles from home—for a reason as simple as sharing extra tomatillos—puts them at risk for surveillance and potential detention by Border Patrol. These individuals take these risks, fully aware of the consequences, because of their deep desire for social connection.

In the snapshot of a man in his beloved gardens where he tends to "the gifts of the earth," the rejection of planting flowers in favor of vegetables, or the firm commitment to provide healthy foods for one's husband and children, we can observe how these individuals claim a sense of agency and a connection to meaningful meals in a borderland region that is far from welcoming. We also can observe how these individual efforts, and the broader objectives of the Huertas project, call into question the complicated dynamics of how food sovereignty efforts play out on the ground and the challenges of working toward greater autonomy over one's consumption in an environment that is beset by so few choices.

These narratives reveal that, even while these gardens are significant in rebuilding some sense of place and fostering practices of food sovereignty, our efforts are necessarily limited by constraints of a short growing season, demanding work schedules, and the deeper structural vulnerabilities these workers face. As we continue to develop the Huertas project, questions of food access are of central concern, but it is not a straightforward connection to mere calories or nutrients that we are aiming to enable. Rather, in working alongside individuals like Alma, Emmanuel, César, Gloria, and Sofía, we seek to expand the choices and decisions that socially marginalized individuals have over how to source their food and what kinds of foods are available close to home. While the *chiles* or *epazote* they cultivate are just one small contribution to the household's food supply, as these stories demonstrate, the meaning of these plants goes deeper than their nutritional value to more fundamental issues of self-sufficiency and sustaining ties to cultural identity.

Our project team is also aware that no matter how many gardens we plant, or how successful they may be, they are just one small part of addressing basic needs year-round. It is imperative to underscore that with Vermont's short growing season these gardens are only productive for a few months out of the year. While most of the gardeners make an effort to freeze, dry, and otherwise preserve foods for the winter months, all remain dependent on others to do the majority of their shopping for them—often the manager or owner of the farm who rarely speaks Spanish. In this way, their ability to choose and have regular access to food in these northern borderlands—particularly fresh foods with cultural significance—remains compromised, and their practices of food sovereignty remain constrained. While many of the Huertas participants have indicated that they have consistent access to food, as we have seen, they do not often have total control over what they are eating or when the food arrives. We have observed that gardens are one part of a broader patchwork of responses that have sprouted up because of unpredictable and inconsistent food access and that in this northern climate, year-round access to healthy, sustaining, and culturally relevant food is of utmost importance.

As a border state, many of the same fears, anxieties, and dangers that are connected to the southern border are reproduced in Vermont, with significant consequences for food sovereignty, health access, and the overall well-being of migrant workers sustaining the state's dairy industry. While the number of migrant workers in these northern borderlands is much smaller than at the U.S.-Mexico border or in more traditional destinations of migration, significant experiences of structural vulnerability have been expressed by the workers involved with Huertas. This vulnerability is both produced by and serves to reproduce the ongoing fear and anxieties of living and working in a landscape where one is so visibly out of place. These vulnerabilities have only intensified since the 2016 U.S. presidential election. In the summer of 2017, we were deeply saddened to hear that a number of the families who have been involved with Huertas were either fearful of being seen working in their gardens by Border Patrol or were making plans to return home because of the increasing anxieties that they felt. In this political climate, it seems that the gardens are even more necessary, even as they might seem more trivial amidst the massive threats to immigrant well-being and safety. A garden will not change the course of anti-immigrant sentiment and draconian immigration policies, but I am convinced that it is more than a Band-Aid. Rather, as Trauger suggests, these gardens represent spaces where love and kindness may flourish, even amidst the hatred and exclusion that is directed towards immigrant families. If our program provides just one family a source of comfort and sustenance in a time of increased uncertainty, to me it is worth the effort.

While the cultural and political contexts in these northern states are very different from those in California, Texas, and other areas with large numbers of migrant farmworkers, the political possibilities of Vermont's political progressiveness remain limited by a failed set of agricultural and immigration policies at the national level. More broadly speaking, we must recognize that our agricultural system is built upon a systematic and often violent denial of sovereignty to workers across the food chain, both in the United States and in their countries of origin. Until we as a nation are ready to come to terms with the needs of those who feed us, and do all that we can to ensure that they can feed themselves in a way that they deem appropriate and nourishing, the mealtimes of individuals like Emmanuel, César, Alma, Sofía, and Gloria will continue to be incomplete.

FOUR

They Are Out, They Are Looking

PROVIDING GOODS AND SERVICES UNDER SURVEILLANCE

There was a history of something happening, but I don't think it was with INS,[1] I think it was something related to the hospital. There was an incident that involved somebody getting deported. So, the community at that time—when I first started my job— something had happened in the last year or two, and fear was heightened enough that some of the farmers employing these families had stressed that they did not want families leaving the farm. So, not only were they afraid because of the INS building, but there was also pressure from their employers to please not leave the farm at all.

MEGAN, Health Department Employee

I have to go all the way to Burlington for the chicken feet. Sometimes Hannaford's has them, and I buy them out. I go to Burlington for that or for packages of gizzards at the Asian market. And I get the banana leaves and things that if I get to Burlington, I will just stock up and put it in my freezer and that way when they say "Oh, can you get me five packages of banana leaves?" Why yes, yes I can.

—ELIZABETH, Interpreter and Personal Shopper

LONG BEFORE I STEPPED INTO Elizabeth's living room and finally met her in person, I felt like I already knew her from the many stories that farm-workers, particularly women, had shared about the ways she had supported them. I knew her as a godmother and confidante, the woman who delivered banana leaves and chicken gizzards when she wasn't helping to deliver babies. The woman who accompanied expectant mothers to prenatal appointments and later celebrated the birthdays of their children. As Elizabeth opened her door and welcomed me inside, I hastily apologized for nearly running over the free-range chickens that strutted across the long driveway leading up to her home in northern Franklin County. She responded nonchalantly, "Oh, don't worry about that, they are pretty good about not getting themselves killed." Impressed by the speed and intelligence of these chickens, and excited to learn about Elizabeth's insights, I settled on the well-worn couch where she indicated I should sit as she prepared mugs of tea to drink during our interview. After the tea was ready and I explained the purpose of the research in more detail, I asked Elizabeth to describe, in her own words, the support she provided to farmworkers working in the dairy industry. Without skipping a beat, she answered, "Anything and everything, I mean, whatever needs there are—whether it is grocery shopping or filling out paperwork for school—it seems like there is always people that fall through the cracks otherwise."

Coming from a family with a Spanish-speaking father, Elizabeth had developed the linguistic and cultural skills that would make her an indispensable source of support long before she started working with Vermont's farmworker community. A skilled baker and former owner of a small business, Elizabeth has pieced together various jobs to make it in Vermont's tough rural economy. Much of this work has revolved around providing "anything and everything" to the farmworker community, not just out of the goodness of her heart but also as part of her formal and informal paid employment. With the goal of making sure that farmworkers do not "fall through the cracks," Elizabeth has navigated working for state institutions and for herself, with dozens of farmworkers having greater access to basic needs because of her efforts.

A key distinction between Vermont's relatively recent experience with migration from Latin America and states with longer histories is manifest in the patchwork of state and federal agencies, community-based organizations, and individual actors like Elizabeth who provide goods and services to the migrant community. Given the size of the state and the concentration of the relatively small farmworker population in the dairy industry, the network of individuals and institutions serving Vermont's farmworker community is a tightly knit group. Through their volunteer and paid labor, these service providers help to interrupt the marginalization of migrant farmworkers, often risking their own well-being, comfort, and personal boundaries in order to do so. As for the workers themselves, service providers confront stress and anxiety about ICE and Border Patrol surveillance as they navigate the rural border landscape to provide services and assistance. Their ability to maintain relationships with farmworkers and visit their homes and places of work depends upon bonds of trust and respect developed with farmworkers, but also with farm managers and owners.

This chapter draws upon key stakeholder interviews and ethnographic fieldwork to present the perspectives of those who, despite significant challenges, provide food, health care, and other basic needs to the migrant farmworker community. Extending the framework of Bordering Visible Bodies, I argue that these service providers must negotiate a contradictory politics of visibility wherein they must ensure that their own efforts are visible to funders, employers, and larger state and federal agencies, while they draw as little attention as possible to the presence of the undocumented farmworkers they serve. At the same time, farmworkers must gain the *institutional visibility* to meet their basic needs with the support of these service providers.[2] In this chapter, institutional visibility refers to the ways that immigrants are seen by, or become visible, to state and private institutions, and are viewed as part of the community that must be served. I ground this discussion of visibility in an analysis of the complex distribution web of food and food entitlements, focusing on the individuals and agencies that provide food and nutrition-related services. This chapter reinforces my broader argument that food access must be understood in a comprehensive and holistic manner that accounts for the structural conditions that facilitate and constrain the provisioning of food and other basic needs.

As illustrated in previous chapters, farmworkers in the northern borderlands experience a particular form of structural vulnerability that is amplified by the rural isolation they encounter in Vermont and the processes of bordering that constrain them to their homes or workplaces and from entering public spaces. In light of these constraints and the transportation challenges that farmworkers and their families face, many of the goods and services that they receive arrive directly to their front doors. Coming through both formal and informal channels, this includes the delivery of groceries and prepared foods, bible classes and other religious outreach, health care—including physical exams and immunizations—and until 2016, the delivery of Women, Infants and Children (WIC) food benefits. These goods and services constitute part of what migration scholars have referred to as the "resource environments" that migrants engage in to address their basic needs.[3] With the weakening of the state protections and entitlements available to immigrants and increasing anti-immigrant hostility, the informal resources that are part of these resource environments have become even more significant in recent years for Vermont's farmworkers.

To benefit from the goods and services made available through institutions, farmworkers must gain what Jamie Winders calls institutional visibility. Winders argues that institutional visibility is a precursor to the incorpo-ration, and, depending on the local social fabric, sometimes the exclusion of immigrants in their new communities.[4] When immigrants gain institutional visibility, they are seen as constituents, or part of the community whose needs must be considered and addressed. Although her analysis is rooted in Nashville, an urban locale, this concept is relevant for understanding the provisioning of goods and services to farmworkers in Vermont's rural areas. With a specific focus on urban governance and planning, Winders asserts that "drawing new immigrant destinations onto the maps of urban America reconfigures how we see and understand immigrants' impacts on and inter-actions with the social fabric of American cities."[5] I extend her analysis to examine how Latino immigrants are changing the social fabric of rural Vermont and gaining institutional visibility with a small group of agencies and organizations. However, because the group of formal institutions work-ing with farmworkers in the areas of food and nutrition is so small and farm-workers so geographically isolated, the efforts of individuals like Elizabeth are just as significant for filling in the gaps that remain in institutional pro-grams and services. This chapter first offers the perspectives of service provid-ers working within agencies and institutions and then transitions to the narratives of individual service providers who, while sometimes working within agencies in the past, now work within the farmworker community on their own accord.

WIC: FROM DOOR-TO-DOOR DELIVERY TO EBT

A federal program administered at the state and local level, The Special Supplemental Program for Women, Infants and Children (WIC) provides "grants to States for supplemental foods, health care referrals, and nutrition education for low-income pregnant, breastfeeding, and non-breastfeeding postpartum women, and to infants and children up to age five who are found to be at nutritional risk."[6] WIC benefits are one of the only federal nutrition programs that is not determined by immigration status but instead by income and nutrition guidelines. As of 2017 in the state of Vermont, "Pregnant women, new mothers, infants and children up to age 5 can enroll in WIC if their household income is less than $876 per week for a family of four, or if they are receiving Medicaid or Dr. Dynasaur, SNAP or Reach-Up."[7] In Vermont, WIC offices are located at the twelve state Department of Health offices, which also offer services in infectious disease control, tobacco and alcohol abuse prevention, emergency preparedness, lead poisoning prevention, and immunizations and school health. Given the importance of WIC for the food security and dietary health of infants and mothers, I made it a point to interview WIC staff members in both Franklin and Addison Counties. The caseload of the Franklin County office at the time of our interview was roughly fifteen hundred, with only nine of those cases being migrant women. For the Addison County office with seven hundred fifty cases, only five were migrant women. Despite making up less than 1 percent of the case load in these two counties, in my interviews with migrant women who receive WIC, I found that it made up an important part of their household food supply.

In the fall of 2015, I sat down for separate interviews with Megan and Deborah, two women working for WIC in Franklin County, and Patty and Kate from the Addison County office. Both interviews took place within the state Health Department offices, and these four women were busy with a large transition in the provisioning of WIC benefits. At the time of our interviews, WIC food benefits were still being delivered to mothers' homes, but the entire state was set to transition to an electronic benefits transfer (EBT) system. Following this shift in services, women eligible for WIC would receive a card to purchase their benefits, requiring them to visit a qualifying grocery store or share their card and PIN with a trusted person who could shop on their behalf. This transition would have a considerable impact in the small state of Vermont, given that more than half of the children born in the state are enrolled in the WIC program, and 40 percent of pregnant women in the state access WIC services.[8] This transition is a reflection of a broader neoliberal turn in the provisioning of state services, seen in the emphasis on efficiency and cost-effectiveness and the production of self-governing subjects.[9]

Deborah and Megan both anticipated that this transition would bring with it drastic changes to their work patterns, having grown used to the delivery system. However, at the time of our interview, Megan was still doing home visits, including visits to the homes of migrant women. She explained:

> Well, we are required to offer the same services to them that we would offer to anybody but one of the things that we do that is maybe different than the others is that we do home visits for them if they can't come to the office. Because especially at our old building we were right next to immigration, so that was an issue with them being . . . even if they did want it or have transportation, they just didn't feel comfortable coming to us, so we decided it was more important

for us to go to the families that needed us to. We, well … I have continued to do home visits for all of the families I have done in the past, but what we are doing, is when we have new families coming in, we are assessing: Do they have transportation? Are they able to come to appointments? If they are able to it is preferable that they come here just because the scheduling is a lot easier. If they can get here, it is good, they get to meet different people, they get out, and then it is less pressure on me to get those home visits and get the interpreter, I mean we still have to get one for here, but right now we have two families that come here for appointments and everybody else I still do home visits for.

While Deborah and Megan expressed concern about how this transition would impact rural women, including those born in and outside of the United States, they were also optimistic about some of the potential benefits of moving to the EBT system, particularly the likelihood that less food would be wasted because mothers could pick out specific foods they preferred from a range of options.

Over their combined eighteen years working with WIC, Deborah and Megan had observed that the household food security of their Mexican and Guatemalan clients had improved somewhat, particularly as the community had grown and as the network of formal and informal providers had become more well established and aware of community needs. This was in large part dependent upon the farm owners also gaining an understanding of what the employees and their families needed, as Deborah explained.

It seems to have gotten better, I know that a lot of work was done with the employers or his wife. I think in that case, the one who was having the most difficulty leaving, it was like, OK but here is the impact that is having and there are children here who at the time you [the farmer] are impacting, and WIC is great, but it is a supplemental food program and it is specific to the participants. So, if you are really thinking this family is going to live off of what is coming through WIC, you are sadly mistaken. So, the education process has to happen, employers are not always up to speed. And in some cases, education has to happen to say, "No, they still need access to grocery stores and someone still needs to be doing that shopping."

Deborah also noted that in her years working at WIC and living in Franklin County, she had also observed that the larger grocery stores had started carrying more Mexican products, a change that I have also witnessed in other Vermont counties with a significant number of dairy farms.

While maintaining a degree of optimism about the well-being of their Latina clients, both women expressed concern about the impact of Border

Patrol on their daily lives and food access. While we were discussing the proximity of some of the farms to the U.S-Canada border, I shared my observation that on the farms I had visited, it was very uncommon for farmworkers to leave their homes, and Deborah responded with a sense of anger, "No, because Border Patrol … they are out … they are looking. I had one park behind my car when I was at a home visit and take down my plate. And I am like 'Oh, so now I am on their hate list.' So, they are waiting for me to transport people and pull me over. Whatever! I don't transport people. But still, it is intimidating." Becoming visible to Border Patrol in this way put not only Deborah at risk but also the clients she was visiting, because it could potentially draw greater attention to which farms were employing foreign-born workers. At the same time, she took these risks not only because these visits were part of her regular workload but also because of her care and concern for the migrant women she served who were experiencing extreme isolation and marginalization.

When I asked whether she felt the surveillance of Border Patrol had an impact on the nutritional well-being of her clients, she replied:

> Yes, and I saw it with my own eyes, so it is not just as close as you get to the border kind of thing. I think they [Border Patrol] are also literally parking their vehicles there. And also, just in terms of the health for some of the families that are living that close to the borders is that they are scared when their kids go out and play. And as far as WIC is concerned about nutrition, and physical activity and stuff, you know it is great if they are eating well, but if they are running circles around the living room because they have so much energy and they can't get out and play, it is tough.

While Deborah had not been directly contacted by Border Patrol or law enforcement while she was doing home visits, she did carry the WIC attorney's business card with her at all times in case she was questioned, sharing that the office's "party line" was that all information about their clients was confidential and that field staff had no obligation to share it with either federal or local officials.

The concern for the health and well-being of these families was both a motivation and a source of distress for Megan and Deborah. During their home visits with migrant farmworker families, they gained an intimate insight into the structural vulnerability that they experienced in their daily lives and the substandard living conditions that many were forced to endure. These insights allowed farmworker clients and their needs to become more institutionally visible to them as health professionals. Megan and I came to understand through our conversations that we both knew several families very well, and when remembering her early visits with one family in particular she recalled:

> There was one that I was really concerned about and at the time there was a one-year-old and he was sitting in a high chair and there were so many flies that he literally wasn't flinching or trying to flick them away anymore it was just like he just sat there. I don't know if you saw the place before that, it was a small room and there were bunk beds and a hot plate and a fridge that didn't look like it was functioning all that well. And then there's a large door where the cows are and I remember thinking, "My goodness what if one breaks through the door?" They have this much space for a cow to try and turn around, it would take up all the space! So that was, not easy to work with at all. That was not a good situation from a human rights perspective.

These poor living conditions, coupled with the isolation and linguistic and cultural barriers that farmworkers encountered, raised Megan's concerns about the well-being of this family and reinforced the importance of visits with farmworkers in their homes. As WIC has transitioned to the EBT system, these home visits will likely grow more infrequent; they are seen as a costly and inefficient way of providing services and benefits, even if they allow professionals like Megan to have a deeper understanding of the challenges that their clients face.

Given that Megan and Deborah work with a program that is governed by income guidelines, most of the families they encounter are living in poverty and struggle with food insecurity. When comparing farmworker households with other poor households, Megan made an important distinction with respect to the causes of their food insecurity. She explained:

> Some of the other families that seem to struggle with food, it is more related to having money to buy food versus less on transportation and getting to food, whereas it seems that the farmworkers make okay money. Well, I don't know how much they are sending home, but I think more for them it is isolation. So, if you are looking at isolation as the issue—whether you are a migrant family working on a farm where they don't want you leaving or if you are a woman experiencing severe domestic violence, the reason for the isolation is different but the impact is the same.

Here, it becomes clear that Megan understands how a politics of visibility keeps farmworkers and their families fearful of being visible in public spaces, with significant impacts on their access to basic needs and overall well-being. While the Latina clients she served had different challenges than the other women she served, she also raises an important point about how, while rural isolation is shared across lines of ethnicity, race, and citizenship, it manifests in disparate ways based on these same factors.

Working in Addison County, which is further south of Franklin County and the U.S.-Canada border, Kate and Patty encountered fewer issues with Border Patrol on a daily basis. Nevertheless, Patty was fairly familiar with the nutritional barriers confronting farmworker households, having been involved with a county-wide coalition that had worked on issues relevant to farmworker rights and well-being. These experiences contributed to the institutional visibility of the farmworker community that informed Patty's work. Despite the fact that migrant women occupied such a small percentage of her office's caseload, she paid particular attention to whether the needs of the farmworker population were taken into account. She explained:

> I was really considering making sure we do outreach to farmworking [sic] families to ensure that they could come to the state office building, that it was a safe place to come, they could access WIC. And the other big piece I was really worried about was immunizations, so those have been really the focus in terms of the farmworker population, making sure that folks are immunized. There have been issues that have popped up over the years around TB, and usually it has been fine so far.

This focus on providing care and services to farmworkers was well received by the farmworker community, and it seemed through my interviews with staff at both WIC offices and farmworker clients that the Addison County office was perceived to be safer to visit than the one in Franklin County. Patty and Kate, for instance, noted that they rarely had to do home visits for the Spanish-speaking clients because they were able to arrange for rides for their checkups even while food benefits were still being delivered to their homes.

While Patty and Kate felt that Addison County farmworkers and their families were faring better than they had in previous years, there remained significant concerns about isolation and vulnerability. Patty did not see isolation as completely unique to farmworker families since it was experienced by other rural people in poverty, but she felt they experienced a different degree of feeling trapped in their homes due to cultural and linguistic barriers. She shared:

It has gotten better because they now can access drivers' licenses, but they were really a trapped, hidden population and I think that is true of a lot of people in Addison County who are suffering from generational poverty and struggle with transportation. It has been really interesting, because we were talking about the difference between us and Franklin County and concerns about Border Patrol and how that makes things different.

You know I remember early on meeting with the Middlebury police chief and he said, "look, we're never going to check immigration status because we don't want to have people afraid of the police, because when you have hidden populations, they are victims and they can engage in unsavory activities themselves," And sweet little Addison County just down the road from Middlebury College, there was a pretty significant prostitution ring not so long ago! So, if we don't address this really publicly and formally, this issue of , "Hey, who is putting the food in your mouth? Well it is undocumented workers who are living hidden lives!" And what does that mean for our broader community? We could really end up with things that have negative impact, community-wise.

Working in Addison County, which is not a border county, Patty feels that the community dynamics are very different from the areas that adjoin the border, like Franklin County. Like Megan, Patty demonstrates a keen understanding of the consequences of farmworkers leading "hidden lives" and advocates for the importance of farmworkers gaining institutional visibility, not only to agencies like WIC but also to the local police. Of course, the visibility to law enforcement is a complex matter, and while this particular police chief might be unwilling or uninterested in checking immigration status, this is very likely not the case for all local law enforcement. In fact, in an effort to limit cooperation between local law enforcement and federal immigration agents, in early 2017 Governor Phil Scott signed into law a bill making it illegal for any Vermont law enforcement agency to enter into a formal enforcement agreement with federal immigration authorities without the governor's permission.[10] In the chapter that follows, I will discuss the dynamics of bias-free policing in greater detail.

One concern that Patty and Kate shared was whether the food benefits as provided through the home delivery arrangements were culturally appropriate for the migrant households that received them. From the time that she had spent working with the Open Door Clinic, a free clinic for uninsured and underinsured adults based in Middlebury, Kate noted that the question of cultural appropriateness was not limited to the food benefits provided by WIC. There is a broader question of how traditional meals can be when farmworkers are laboring in the milking barn for upwards of seventy hours per week and have limited time to cook meals from scratch. She shared her observations:

> With WIC, we provide a very prescriptive food package, so whether it is meeting the needs of all folks, it's hard to tell. However, the food options . . . the traditional cultural dishes tend to go by the wayside because they are so busy with work. So that definitely is tough but I think, overall, they are incorporating a lot of traditional dishes in the household when they have women's help with the preparation. But the gentlemen, they are so busy.

As Patty noted, while the Mexican sections of the grocery stores in the area had significantly expanded, men were still primarily eating quick-to-prepare convenience foods and snacks, similar to "any single male shopping." With the transition to the EBT system, both service providers were hopeful that the migrant women they served would have more culturally familiar options at the grocery store, compared to what was delivered to their home. Further, during the summers WIC provides coupons to the local farmers market, and Patty noted that three of the five farmworker families on their caseload were making use of these coupons, which felt to her like a significant success given the limited hours of the market and the transportation barriers confronting many of these families.

One of the challenges that both the Addison County and Franklin County WIC offices faced is the lack of Spanish-speaking employees and the limited number of interpreters that are available for hire. This challenge was not unique to the WIC offices; other health-care professionals working with the farmworker community have expressed the same concern. The lack of professional interpreters is a reflection of the particular characteristics of the resource environment that is available to Vermont's farmworker community. In a state where just over 1 percent of the residents speak Spanish (compared to nearly half of New Mexico residents and 40 percent of residents in California and Texas), the demographic patterns that result from Vermont being a nontraditional destination of migration clearly carry over to influence what kinds of programs and services are provided to farmworkers.

DOING A LOT WITH VERY LITTLE IN
THE FIELD OF PUBLIC HEALTH

In Vermont, public health providers serving the migrant farmworker community are tightly networked and frequently collaborate to coordinate services, seek funding, and share information. With the limited funding available for the federal Migrant Health Program, and the ever-changing terrain of health-care debates in state and federal government, these public health providers do a lot with very little. One of the key players in providing health-care service to the migrant farmworker community is the Open Door Clinic, which holds regular clinic hours at their Middlebury location as well as an evening clinic in nearby Vergennes, serving both Latinx farmworkers and those who come to Vermont seasonally through the H-2A visa program, typically Jamaican workers in the orchard industry. The clinic heavily depends upon volunteers for their work, from the volunteer medical and dental directors to the college interns who help patients fill out paperwork. For the most part, this volunteer base is stable, even if it is somewhat transitory with some volunteers working for many years with others burning out more quickly.

The number of farmworkers seen at the Open Door Clinic fluctuates somewhat. In 2014 the total case number of farmworkers was 289 distinct patients, with a total of 1,369 visits (or what the clinic terms "interactions"), in 2017 the clinic saw 276 patients with 1,285 visits. Latinx farmworkers make up 41–52 percent of patients seen by the clinic on any given year. Given that the estimated population of all migrant farmworkers in Vermont is one thousand to twelve hundred, this is a significant number of patients, demonstrating the success that the clinic has had with providing outreach on the farms and through other channels. This outreach has improved the institutional visibility for farmworkers within an agency providing one of the most essential services: health care. With the permission of Alexandra, one of the clinic's bilingual outreach nurses, the waiting room of the clinic became a second home for me as I conducted food security surveys with farmworkers living and working in Addison County.

In the midst of completing these surveys, I had the opportunity to sit down and interview Alexandra and learn more about her experience and perspectives on working with this population. Over her years working at the Open Door Clinic, Alexandra had learned an immense amount about the challenges confronting farmworkers in the dairy industry, and also about the importance of balancing her role as a farmworker advocate with the need to maintain positive relationships and methods of communication with those who employ them. She had observed a spectrum with respect to employer-employee relationships, from those employers who express concern for the health of the employees in either a paternalistic or supportive way, to those employers who "don't even know the last name of their workers." In

some cases, conflict could arise even where relationships were relatively positive, as she explained.

> And I think it is really important as a health provider to maintain a good
> relationship regardless of what kind of people they [farm owners] are. We
> showed up to a farm once and the guys there, they had bed bugs, and they
> had already done one treatment and the bugs were back and they were pissed.
> They wanted to talk to the farm owner and we happened to be there and we
> speak English and Spanish and they wanted us to interpret. And they were
> just starting to say, "If this isn't taken care of, we are out of here!" and the
> farm owner was saying, "Did you guys do the washing, all of this stuff that
> you are supposed to do?" And he was upset about it, he was mad that he was
> going to have to spend another couple thousand dollars, and it got to a point
> where the workers were upset, the owner was upset.
>
> But we are there to provide health care and we can give them the resources
> to continue this conversation, but we can't be in the middle of it. And the
> workers are still there two years later and the owner gives us a giant donation
> every year, amazingly, and they worked it out. It's tricky, because we main-
> tain good relationships with the farm owners because that is one of the keys
> to providing access, and we can't be seen as taking one side over the other,
> because we are a health-care provider, we are neutral.

In remaining as neutral as possible during farm visits and while providing
care, Alexandra also sees the importance of connecting farmworkers to other
resources in the community that are better equipped to handle the drastic
violations of health and safety standards she has seen as a health-care provider. One of these resources is the Teleayuda line maintained by Migrant
Justice, mentioned in the previous chapter.

In our interview, I was particularly interested in Alexandra's knowledge
of the dietary health and food access of the clients she helped to serve. One
of the first observations she shared was the increasing numbers of Latinx
workers who were enrolled in their diabetes program. In the four years that
she had worked at the clinic at the time of our interview, the one or two
farmworkers who were enrolled in the program grew to a point where 80
percent of the patients in the diabetes program were migrant workers or their
partners. With an "inordinately high percentage of women" in the program,
many were enrolled and diagnosed after having suffered from gestational
diabetes. Attributing this growth to the dramatic changes that these individuals had experienced in their exercise and eating habits since arriving to
the United States, Alexandra wryly noted that she had not "been to a house
yet where there is not a Sunny Delight on the counter" and that decreased

consumption of fresh fruits and vegetables and increased consumption of heavily processed convenience foods and sugar-sweetened beverages were especially common. In addition to diabetes, other common health conditions linked to changes in consumption patterns brought people to the Open Door Clinic, including hypertension and liver dysfunction linked to increased alcohol consumption, particularly binge drinking. Alexandra found that these conditions were more common among older farmworkers and believed that they were due in part to older men not having been taught to cook for themselves in their home countries.

At the time of our interview, Alexandra felt that the Open Door Clinic's success had much to do with successful outreach campaigns and the positive experiences of the clients, who share information with others via word of mouth. The passage of the licensing bill also meant that fewer clients had to rely on others for a ride to appointments, given that a number of farmworkers in Addison County had secured licenses and were driving themselves or their friends and family members to the clinic. However, she had also noticed a trend in the increasing severity of the health problems that people were facing. She shared:

> The trend that I have seen is that we are seeing sicker and sicker patients, and I think the reason is because they are not going home to Mexico to seek treatment. Whether that is because they trust the clinic or because it is too hard to get back over the border I don't know what the reason is, but I do know it is because they are choosing not to go home. Whereas before, and still up north too, when somebody gets really sick they go home. So we are seeing cancer, we are seeing liver issues, we are seeing brain dysfunctions, seizures, and just all sorts of pretty serious stuff.

As a clinic providing mostly preventative and routine health services, the Open Door Clinic's role is to refer clients with these kinds of severe health issues to other providers, including local hospitals. This extends the resource environment that is available to individual farmworkers to include a larger network of agencies and organizations, even though many of these individuals have to pay out of pocket for these services because they lack insurance.

Despite working in a difficult field with few resources, Alexandra demonstrates an impressive commitment to her job and enthusiasm in providing the best care to farmworkers. During our interview, I made a particular effort to understand how she responded, personally, to the sociopolitical context of her work. The importance of maintaining professional boundaries is something that Alexandra and nearly all of the other service providers mentioned during our interviews. When we discussed our challenging experiences of working in the field, whether as a health-care provider or as a researcher, Alexandra reflected, "It is the unmet need . . . and the need is so great that you either have to have incredible boundaries, or a cold heart. And that happens a lot." Alongside this negotiating of boundaries was a genuine desire to better understand the cultural backgrounds of the clinic's patients and serve as a cultural mediator of sorts. She reflected:

> I find a big part is cultural and just constantly reminding myself or people in the office . . . constantly reminding themselves that it is a different population with a different experience and so talking very frankly about things [with farmworkers], "If you can't make your appointment, please call because the providers are coming to see you. If you can't make your appointment, you're wasting two hours of someone else's time," Because we have had a lot of no call, no shows, and then we have a wait list, and it is not their fault. I feel like the more you explain how the system works, the more willing they are to call, they know they are affecting other people, they are affecting their community. So I think it is a lot of just being clear on the process that I think we take for granted. Because if you grew up here, you know how that works.

As she worked to communicate with her clients about the medical system in the United States, Alexandra also strove to learn more about the histories and backgrounds of those she served. Feeling "humbled" by her work and feeling continually and productively challenged to think in new ways, she also realized early on that she could be a better provider if she traveled to Mexico and learned more about Mexican culture, since she felt that she "didn't know squat." A few years after our interview, Alexandra had the chance to do so, visiting southern Mexico with her family. This opportunity allowed her to gain greater insight into the cultural background of the clinic's clients, improving her capacity and motivation as a health-care provider.

Working closely with both Alexandra and the WIC office in Franklin County, Naomi helps to coordinate health-care access with farmworkers closer to the U.S.-Canada border through her role as program director for Bridges to Health (BTH). A program of UVM Extension, BTH works with farmworkers who need access to health care in addition to working with health-care providers to increase their ability to provide services. This assistance to health-care providers takes the form of technical assistance, cultural competency training, and assistance with interpretation. As needed, BTH also makes referrals to community resources and services that farmworker families are eligible for, including WIC and Head Start. Over the course of my research and my work with Huertas, I have grown to be close friends and colleagues with Naomi. She plays a crucial role in the network of organizations and individuals working with the farmworker community, and I knew it was essential that her perspective be included in my research. At the time when I interviewed Naomi, BTH was entering its fourth year, although for three years prior to that she was employed through funding available for health access programming in specific areas of the state. Although the program's staff is based in Franklin County, through UVM Extension and their work within a broader consortium, BTH helps to coordinate care in thirteen of the state's counties and provides technical assistance statewide. As discussed in detail in the previous chapter, the Huertas project is also an important means for BTH to deal with matters related to food and nutrition.

As for the Open Door Clinic, the success of Bridges to Health depends upon positive relationships with both farmworkers and farm owners. Naomi explained:

> The first challenge is really the power dynamic between farm employers and employees. We're really dependent on our relationships with the farm employer to have access to farmworker housing, so that is certainly is a challenge: to try and understand the relationship that exists for each farm and be respectful of it, yet at the same time be helpful to the farmworker that may be in less than ideal situations.

The fact that a majority of farmworkers are undocumented complicates this power dynamic, with some employers taking advantage of the vulnerability of their workers through paying low wages and providing substandard working and living conditions, and others paying fair wages and doing their best to provide adequate housing and fair working conditions. For the majority of farmworkers without legal status, there is often little they can do to improve their wages and conditions if they have an unsupportive employer other than seek work on a different farm.

Naomi also related these citizenship barriers to the financial challenges that her program faces, as well as the language and transportation barriers that are pervasive. She explained that because the majority of farmworkers in Vermont are undocumented, there is a limited pool of funding sources, since "it means that we have to be pretty open about the fact that we are serving a primarily undocumented population and it's kind of common knowledge, so it does limit the funding sources because we are not." If, for example, the state had a higher number of H-2A agricultural workers, or a different mix of workers' citizenship, the program might be able to access additional sources of funding. Nevertheless, the work that Naomi and her colleagues do with this invisible community must be rendered visible to compete for the limited sources of funding. This lack of available funding also impacts the kinds of language acquisition resources that UVM Extension can provide to farmworkers. The limited access to English language learning programs, as Naomi described, impacts both the degree to which farmworkers can advocate for themselves in the workplace and their ability to communicate more generally. These barriers mean that programs like the Open Door Clinic and BTH become even more crucial to the well-being of the farmworker community, even as their resources are stretched increasingly thin.

In her role at BTH, Naomi has also gained a deep knowledge of the food access barriers that farmworkers face, both through spending an immense amount of time in the field and through research that she has completed as part of her job. All of these experiences granted a high degree of institutional visibility to the farmworkers who are served by BTH. This knowledge, and the visibility of farmworker food insecurity, led her to start the Huertas project, which was described in detail in the previous chapter. From this work, Naomi feels strongly that there are geographic determinants of food access and that the barriers that farmworkers experience depend upon the proximity to the border of where they live and work. Naomi shared that access to culturally appropriate or preferred food is a barrier that persists for farmworkers in all areas of the state, whereas in border communities the more serious concern was access to any food, regardless of whether it was culturally appropriate or recognizable. She explained:

So, farther from the [U.S.-Canada] border, farmworkers and family members tend to have more consistent access to food, because they are going out into the communities to purchase it and they may or may not have their own transportation. In the case that they have their own transportation then they are only limited by their work schedule, versus if in those communities farther from the border they don't have their own transportation. They are still only going once or twice, once a week or every two weeks to access food, but they are going on their own, so they have an idea of what is available. Closer to the border, within 25 miles or so, the majority of individuals are not going out into the community so it is more about just being able to get any food when they want it.

Her observations echo those offered by the WIC staff members I interviewed and reinforce the fact that farmworkers in different areas of the state grapple with varying risks of being visible in public spaces like grocery stores.

Those farmworkers who are not shopping for themselves often lack understanding of what is actually available in Vermont's grocery stores. Many farmworkers end up with foods or varieties of foods that are not to their preference, while others might end up with a better selection, particularly if there is a better channel of communication or if the farm owner is hiring a bilingual person to do the shopping, a point I will return to in more detail. One concrete way that Bridges to Health has attempted to support the purchasing of more familiar foods is through creating a bilingual shopping guide booklet, with photos of different varieties, to facilitate communication between farmworkers and those who are shopping on their behalf. Naomi felt that over time, food purchasing had improved and become better suited to farmworker preferences and needs, in large part because of the growing network of service providers and other people familiar with the challenges confronting farmworkers. This network, or resource environment, also includes the individuals traveling door-to-door selling Mexican products and prepared foods, though some of these individuals would only deliver to households with a minimum order of fifty to one hundred dollars. She explained that even just six years prior to our interview, many farmworkers only knew their employer, whereas at the time of our interview, most households were getting food from a variety of sources as options expanded, limiting their dependency upon just one channel. As other providers mentioned, the availability of Mexican products in the grocery stores has also widened in the areas where Naomi worked, though these mostly consist of packaged goods rather than familiar cuts of meat or varieties of fresh produce.

Naomi echoed the findings from my own survey and household interviews by emphasizing that the challenges related to food access and security were not limited to monetary constraints, a point that distinguished the food security concerns of farmworkers from those of other rural residents. She explained:

> The ironic, or strange piece of this is that it is not always lack of access to income but rather lack of access to those resources. So if they can't get to a place where they can spend their money, then they are not accessing food. But it is not that they do not have money. That is not to say that the hourly rates on some farms aren't low, but the fact that they are working sixty- to eighty-hour weeks means that they are making in general at least $450, and right

now we're seeing the average of $550–650 dollars a week, which is a significant amount of money and tends to be much more than somebody who would be considered rural, low income in that situation.

Here again, we see the economic factors that distinguish farmworker experiences with food insecurity and a lack of food sovereignty from those of other rural Vermonters struggling with poverty.

In addition to the questions of availability and access, Naomi and I also spoke in depth about the health consequences related to farmworker eating habits that she had observed through her health outreach work and the time spent in farmworker households. For some of the children in these households, low weight gain and low iron levels had been recorded, as well as less exposure to a well-rounded diet, particularly access to fresh foods. For adults, constipation, gastritis, and acid reflux were also common, and she noted "health providers have attributed some of that to going long periods of time without eating and then eating a lot at once, drinking caffeine or caffeinated beverages on an empty stomach, [and] eating pre-prepared foods." The lack of a balanced diet and regular eating patterns, exacerbated by work schedules, therefore prevents the healthy digestion and absorption of nutrients. With respect to weight fluctuations, Naomi shared that weight gain was not common for men, who were working long and arduous hours. For women who were not working outside the home, however, a growing reliance on processed foods and more sedentary lifestyles often led to weight gain, a major source of dissatisfaction expressed by many of the women I interviewed.

Because Bridges to Health serves such a large number of farmworkers in Vermont, and given that the program's staff members spend so much time in the field working directly with this community, I made it a point to also interview a former health promoter to deepen my understanding of their observations and perspectives. Natalie, who had previously worked directly for Naomi in Franklin County, expanded upon the impact that border proximity had on the delivery of programs and services to farmworkers in this region. Stating early on in our interview, "In the northwest region we are definitely closer to the Canadian border, so there is more immigration and Border Patrol presence that can be intimidating," Natalie also noted that the food access channels that farmworkers could utilize were very dependent upon the power dynamics at each individual farm and that there was a wide spectrum in how well farmworkers were faring in their attempts to access food. She had seen well-developed systems and support networks at some farms where food shopping was predictable and there was a point person to do the shopping, but also another extreme where "there is no person and the employer doesn't offer them a way to get food and they have to fend for themselves and kind of figure it out by looking for someone they can pay to go and buy it for them or even risk having Border Patrol interactions and going out on their own to do that." The risk of encountering Border Patrol extended beyond accessing food to accessing health care, a barrier that BTH seeks to address through the programs and services they provide.

TRUNKS FULL OF BANANA LEAVES AND PHONE CARDS: THE INDIVIDUALS SERVING THE FARMWORKER COMMUNITY

In addition to the institutions serving the Latino farmworker community in Vermont, there is a small but committed group of individuals who work to provide access to transportation, legal services, health care, and basic needs like food and medicine. These individuals do so largely on a voluntary basis, out of a deep care and concern for the well-being of farmworkers, though some charge small fees for their time or gas expenses. To better understand why they devote so much of their time and energy to the farmworker community, my research assistant and I conducted three in-depth interviews with people referred to us either by the service providers mentioned above or farmworkers themselves. We focused on the northern border region of Vermont, given the particular challenges in access that farmworkers in this region experience.

Elizabeth

For Elizabeth, whose words opened this chapter, her informal work with the farmworker community followed many years of working in the formal sector, serving for many years as a Spanish-English interpreter for various state and local agencies. Following a change in the system that routed all interpretation services for government agencies through the Vermont Refugee Resettlement Program (VRRP), Elizabeth stopped working in this position, because the change left her earning far less per hour as a contractor through VRRP than through direct agency contracts. At the time of our interview, Elizabeth provided a range of services for farmworkers, including grocery shopping, assisting with paperwork and health care, delivering letters and packages to the post office, and for a limited number of families, providing some transportation. For some of these services, Elizabeth charges an hourly rate for her time but on a sliding scale, earning less than half of what she was making as an interpreter. For much of this work, she actually charges her time to the farm owners, as she is relieving them of time many had previously spent on shopping and running errands for the workers on their farms. On these farms, she receives cash from farmworkers for the goods, brings them the receipt, and then logs the hours spent on the errands, typically getting paid by the farm owners either weekly or biweekly.

Over her many years working with the Latino farmworker population, Elizabeth has observed a wide spectrum in employer-employee relationships; because of this, she is particular about whom she works with. She explained:

> I think it will always depend on the farm, and I think that will always be a factor. Some farmers are great, some really suck, as bosses, as human beings. I mean these are people that are working for you and making your business go, you should make them happy, that way everybody is happy. But they don't look at them as humans and I don't work with those kinds of people, and the workers are always resourceful and they always find a way to get things done because they have to.

Even with the care that Elizabeth takes to selectively work with farms with fair treatment of the workers, she still finds herself in a position of delicately navigating the on-farm relationships in addition to her own personal space and responsibilities. She continued:

> Although over time I have become much better about boundaries, because I wasn't at first, and I mean I got way involved in everything. And now, with my own kids and family, I started to resent it some because my phone would ring all the time, day and night: "Can I get a ride?", "Well. when do you need to go?" "Now." "No, sorry." I wouldn't do that to anybody! So emotionally it is often times draining. You know kids that aren't getting the attention that they need from their parents or farm owners that are treating their workers badly, I end up sort of walking a fine line because I try to keep everyone happy all the time, the farmer, the workers, because if I cross the farmers, then that is not going to do anybody any good. So I kind of have to keep it in the middle."

Still, Elizabeth had grown very close with some individuals, especially with women, through developing *comadre* relationships. She shared, "And there are certain people I am just closer to and I don't know why that has happened.

I mean I do know why, because I have known them for years and we go to the hospital and have a baby together and I cut the cord! So yes, I am a little closer to those people."

Through doing grocery shopping for farmworkers, Elizabeth has gained a deep insight into their diets and food preferences, as well as how these have changed over time. For some, particularly households of young men, grocery lists often center upon "frozen crap" that she sees as "insultingly expensive," like frozen burritos, pizzas, and other foods that are quick to microwave and consume in the small amount of time between milking shifts. For households where women are present, or if there is more actual cooking taking place in the home, Elizabeth is often purchasing fresh and frozen produce, including specialty items like spices, dried chilies, and frozen banana leaves to make tamales. She has also observed that the network of vendors delivering foods to the farms had expanded, delivering a greater diversity of items and with more regularity. While she knew that some of these vendors were charging a fair price for the goods they were delivering, she also knew that there were others who were exploiting the vulnerability of farmworkers, stating dryly, "People definitely know that there is a buck to be made one way or another, honestly or dishonestly." This dishonesty ranged from charging extremely high prices for Mexican products delivered on farms to isolated cases of armed robbery committed by criminals who were pretending to be couriers of cash remittances to Western Union. The later cases were extremely rare, but news of them circulated rapidly through farmworker communication networks.

I asked Elizabeth about her thoughts on the changes that had taken place in Vermont with the growing visibility of the farmworker community, even as individual farmworkers remain fearful of being seen in public. She responded, "I have seen a lot of the changes, and a lot of the lack of changes. I always say that progress is glacial; if it has anything to do with immigration really not much has changed." At the same time, she felt that the growing integration of families with children into the community, through school networks and even through everyday activities like shopping, was perhaps making the broader public more accepting. She explained that previously she would often warn people about going to the larger grocery stores because of the possibility of being "picked up" by Border Patrol, but told me in our interview that these warnings did not seem as necessary. However, she was not at all confident that this relative feeling of security would last, concluding with a sense of anger, "the Border Patrol activity seems to wax and wane. Like all of the sudden somebody sends a message from above and it says crack down, and they do, and then it passes, and it happens again." As has been made clear through my conversations with farmworkers after the 2016 presidential election, the renewed attention to cracking down on undocumented immigrants has brought with it a renewed fear of leaving their homes and places of work.

Nancy

While Elizabeth had built a strong set of relationships with a large number of farmworkers in Franklin County stemming first from her paid work as an interpreter, Nancy's connections were a bit more focused and completely voluntary. I had crossed paths with Nancy several times at the trailer shared by Emmanuel, Martín, and Gabriel, and on one or two occasions, we shared a meal that was prepared in anticipation of our visits. I had come to know Nancy as the person who made the blackberry wine and jam with the berries that Emmanuel had collected in the fields near the dairy farm, and as the kind older woman who often gave these three men rides, including to their immigration hearing in Boston. On one occasion, Nancy had even driven Emmanuel four hours to visit his son who lived in southern Maine, with a carload of produce that he had grown in his kitchen garden. The interview with Nancy was completed by my research assistant Jessie on a rainy summer day in the old farmhouse she shared with her husband, surrounded by beautiful gardens that Nancy carefully tended during the long days of her retirement. After several years of serving as a hospice volunteer, Nancy had first become involved with the farmworker community when she was asked to give rides to several men who were visiting Montpelier to help lobby for the passage of the licensing bill. Feeling that she could be more helpful as an informal volunteer, she soon became a close friend and grandmotherly figure to several individuals and families living in Franklin County.

Recovering from a surgery soon after meeting Emmanuel and his housemates, Nancy's relationship with these three men started in a place of reciprocity. In exchange for giving them rides, including to their court date in Boston after they were detained by Border Patrol, Nancy received help in her garden. She remembered:

> When I brought Emmanuel out here, I couldn't do much because of the hip replacement. And so I said, "look at my garden," and he would help me. And I couldn't pay him enough but he would not take any money anyway. And he

did it, he was like a miracle. Emmanuel was the one that knew what to do and Emmanuel made sure that they worked, and kept right on, so every time they would come, they got a lot done.

Over time, Nancy became close friends with these three men, and after she recovered, she became a regular visitor to their home, one of the few connections these men had made to the nonfarmworker community, other than their connections through the Huertas program.

In addition to the close relationship she built with Emmanuel, Martín, and Gabriel, Nancy had also become an important source of support for Sofía and Santiago, and their daughter, Mia. Estimating that she spent between three and five hours per week driving farmworkers around, Nancy regularly drove Sofía and Mia to appointments and often, to shopping excursions after these appointments. For this service, Nancy typically refuses any money that people offer her for her time, though she occasionally would accept half of what was offered to help pay for gas. At the time she spoke with Jessie, Nancy was tiring of some of these driving requests, even though she loved to spend time with people. She sighed, "But it's not, it's much more time than the mileage that costs me. They don't understand. Well they do understand and they also know it's a favor, like I don't want to see them have to beg."

At the same time that she was building strong relationships with people like Emmanuel and Sofía, during the interview she also expressed a certain bewilderment about their culture. When describing her impression of Sofía and Santiago's home, she stated, "They are living in one little bedroom, a small space and there's no room in the barnyard. It is no place for a family. And they know it! I also bought them two rocking chairs and a changing table, various things, and it's weird I think, Mexicans are weird." This statement shows that even as Nancy has developed close relationships with a number of families, she fails to fully grasp the structural vulnerabilities that leave individuals like Sofía and Santiago without greater agency over their living conditions. It also represents a certain degree of paternalism and ethnocentrism that is pervasive even for those who are attempting to do good.

The dangers and risks associated with border proximity were also a common theme in the interview with Nancy, in addition to how these risks left farmworkers in a severe position of structural vulnerability. Despite revealing a certain degree of ethnocentrism, Nancy understood from her experiences that being a person of color in Vermont (or as she termed it a "colored person"), made someone hypervisible, sharing, "I'd see them on the streets—

they [dairy farmers] didn't hire Mexicans for a while. And so, you know, you see a colored person, a really different nationality than white, you kind of notice it." While Nancy's observations about the visibility of farmworkers in space are apt, this dangerous conflation of nationality and race is revealing of the not-so-subtle ways that racial hierarchies become implicit in the minds of even the most kindly of people. Continuing with this observation, Nancy shared how this played out in food access concerns:

> Well, they are basically at the mercy of their employer in order to get the food they can eat, because they can't get it themselves. There's all kinds of obstacles, even before it was like they were afraid to go into the grocery stores, afraid they would get arrested. Because they are out and they are vulnerable. Usually they have the farmer shopping for them. . . . But Emmanuel loved to go peruse the vegetables and pick out his own stuff. Others don't really care about that.

In comparing this level of fear with the experiences of two women from Mexico who had secured citizenship, she concluded, "The world is the oyster if you are legal."

Robert

Like Elizabeth's, Robert's involvement with the farmworker community had also begun through paid employment. Working as an English instructor through the Migrant Education Program, Robert was assigned to eighteen dairy farms in the rural Northeast Kingdom of Vermont until the funding for his position ended. During an interview with Jessie at the library of a small college near his home, Robert shared how this position transitioned into the informal volunteer role that he now holds, helping to shop and send remittances for farmworkers in one of the most rural regions of the state. Early on in his instructor position, Robert realized that the interest in and energy for learning English was highly variable for the seventy-five individuals who qualified for the program on his assigned farms. To qualify, individuals had to be under twenty-two years of age and working in agriculture. Robert described why his students were often less than enthusiastic about the English lessons:

> Because of work schedules, because of interest, because of being too tired, because of everybody else in the room all the time, because "I have to make a phone call to my family" or "my family called me" or because "I really need to sleep now" or "my schedule changed," or whatever, all the various things.

With the frustration that he often felt and the desire to be of real service, Robert started to open his visits with a more open-ended question of "Hi, how is it going, what do you want? What do you need?" When he started asking questions, Robert started to realize that more pressing needs included health care, phone cards, clothing for the long cold winters, and assistance with sending money to families back home.

On his own time, Robert soon found himself making regular trips to Walmart to purchase long underwear, gloves, hats, heavy socks, and all the "appropriate winter gear" that would make long hours working in a cold milking barn more bearable. With greater access to smartphones, the need for phone cards had declined over time, but at one point, he was ordering 600 five-dollar phone cards every four to six weeks from a "Guatemalan lady in New York State." With a trunk full of clothing and phone cards, Robert soon found that these tangible products were in much more demand than the English lessons he was being paid to deliver. More than phone cards and long underwear, what was most needed in this rural area was someone who farm-workers could trust to take money to Western Union with explicit instructions for sending these remittances to families waiting in rural communities and small cities in Tabasco, Chiapas, and northern Guatemala.

Often delivering as much as $2,000 through a complex and highly profitable international financial services company, Robert soon found himself "cut off" by this company, at which point he roped in his wife to help with these services. When she was cut off, he started sending funds with a short-ened version of his name, and at the time of the interview, was no longer asked to show identification because he was well known to everyone in the local office. As he started providing these extra services, Robert was still being paid to teach English. As he explained, his boss was not at all happy about these additional efforts. He shared, "In fact, they didn't want me doing anything besides teaching English classes. Because that is what they were funded for. My first boss was mad. And he was mad in the worst way. He was extremely paranoid about any other activity other than teaching English." While part of the fear was related to funding, it is quite possible that Robert's boss was also concerned that these activities might catch the attention of Border Patrol. However, when Jessie asked whether he had experienced any problems, Robert replied, "Never, they must have known who I was, I used to drive a giant orange van with some distinct features on it. I mean a big orange van, come on! It was good for food and for driving people. And they never ever stopped me. I was never stopped. They must have known."

When the funding for his position ended, Robert felt more able to continue relationships with his former students and volunteer in a flexible way that suited his retirement schedule. During his many visits, Robert had gained an intimate view into the working and living conditions of some of the most isolated farmworkers in the state. When asked about his impressions of food access for these workers, Robert explained that he had not seen anyone "starving" or without access to any food, but emphasized that the food situation could not be separated from the working conditions. He stated, with a sense of anger:

> The real issue for food, and this may not be part of your study, but as you know, the work situation is horrific, and in some cases is without totally any consideration of physical health. And under those circumstances your eating schedule is thrown completely off. So, you have that twelve-hour shift with no break in-between for any period of time, to eat anything. So, twelve hours without eating, well what do you do? The shift is from four in the morning to four in the afternoon, so you come home, you are so tired, you can barely stand and you're crying of hunger. If there is a bag of chips on the table, I am wolfing down half a bag of chips while I am getting my slab of meat cooked in a quart of oil, and that is it and I am going to gobble that down and sit there like this and watch TV and then I am off to bed. . . . So what does that do to your stomach?

Robert knew what this does to the stomach: it leads to ongoing suffering from acid indigestion, a common problem noted by both Alexandra and Naomi in their public health work. Because so many of the men he knew were suffering from this physical malady, he also started carrying Prilosec around with him, making special trips to a community health pharmacy to purchase a ninety-day supply for the same amount a two-week supply would cost in a Walgreens or CVS. As Robert wrapped up his thoughts on food access, he concluded, "It is unfortunate that they are displaced in terms of their food as with everything else."

In these discussions, we see a clear example of Robert's ability to generalize the individual suffering of farmworkers to the exploitative labor patterns that are endemic to the industrial dairy system and his frustration with the narrow scope of some of the agencies that provide services to the farmworker community. While English-language literacy is certainly conducive to improving the well-being of farmworkers, as he notes, it is not always the top priority of farmworkers who have limited time to address their basic needs while financially supporting family members back home. This reveals that even as farmworkers might gain a high degree of institutional visibility with formal agencies and organizations, this visibility is not necessarily adequate in meeting a comprehensive set of needs and desires. The efforts of individuals like Robert, as well as Elizabeth and Nancy, are therefore essential in contributing to a resource environment through which farmworkers can access what they need, when they need it.

CONCLUSION

In a border environment where farmworkers are geographically and socially isolated and have few transportation options, the agencies and individuals discussed in this chapter provide a crucial bridge to accessing both basic needs and social life off the farm. We must recognize that whether or not they are formally employed by an institution or agency, these individuals who aim to provide goods and services come to their work with their own motivations, biases, and commitments. As seen in these narratives, these men and women often go above and beyond their official work duties out of a deep concern for the well-being of the farmworkers they serve and because of the close relationships they have developed. Sacrificing their own material resources, time, and personal boundaries, they contribute to a resource environment that, even in its patchwork form, helps to ensure that farmworkers have better access to food, health care, and a means of supporting their family members both in Vermont and in their countries of origin.

In a small state like Vermont, the network of individuals and organizations working with the farmworker community is tightly knit. Indeed, most of these individuals discussed in this chapter knew each other well and had provided referrals or shared information with the goal of addressing farmworker needs. This kind of network is certainly different from states where the farmworker population is larger and the food system more expansive in size and productivity. And yet, despite its patchwork nature, in some important ways the small size of the network makes it more flexible and able to respond to changing social and economic conditions. Communication travels rapidly within this network, and if there is a new concern in the farmworker community, these service providers are quick to learn about it. At the same time, each of the individuals described in this chapter must navigate a complicated set of power dynamics as they go about their paid or voluntary work. In striving for a balance when dealing with the requests from and relationships with farm owners, farmworkers, and their own families, they devote much more than just their time to this unique form of care work.

In the areas where agencies do not or cannot provide services, individuals like Elizabeth, Nancy, and Robert have come to fill in the gaps. While this arrangement has a number of benefits to it, it is also precarious. If one or all three of these individuals decides to move on to other volunteer or paid work, it is certain that it will create a vacuum that will leave farmworkers with a weaker resource environment and more dependence on other parties looking to profit off of their vulnerability. The precariousness of this situation also points to the importance of maintaining institutional visibility for the farmworker community and continuing support and funding of the agencies and organizations described in this chapter. However, at a time where funding is even harder to come by, this also calls for farmworkers to have greater rights and more agency to access what they want and need, on their own terms. In the next chapter, I will describe the groundbreaking efforts of farmworker organizers in Vermont who have been working with this goal in mind as they challenge the most fundamental hierarchies of power that persist in the industrial food system.

FIVE

Resilience and Resistance in the Movement for Just Food and Work

It is something that opens your eyes, the huge violation of human rights. Before that it is like, "That is just how it is here." You get accustomed to it, tell yourself you can get used to it and that you have to do it out of necessity. But it is not the reality, after you start to see that there are solutions, that you can resolve it together. We see that people are suffering and people need to talk and really see what the solution is.

ERNESTO, Farmworker Organizer

This is a program that gives the workers a seat at the table and provides dignity and a real voice, but it's also a program that gives the farmers a community.

JOSTEIN SOLHEIM, CEO of Ben & Jerry's, speaking
about the Milk with Dignity program

IT WAS AN UNPRECEDENTED DAY OF CELEBRATION IN EARLY October 2017. On the brick walkway of Burlington's Church Street, directly in front of Ben & Jerry's flagship store, the CEO of one of Vermont's best loved companies—together with farmworkers from Mexico—signed the groundbreaking Milk with Dignity (MD) agreement. Young men and women from Chiapas, Tabasco, and other southern Mexican states shared the microphone with CEO Jostein Solheim, expressing their excitement about the future of the MD program and reflecting on the long years of campaigning that had brought them to that day. This sharing of the microphone represented a sharing of power that is uncommon in most corporate food production, and the agreement that was finally signed on this warm autumn morning would not have been possible without the leadership of farmworkers and the support of their allies. Based on a model of worker-driven social responsibility, the MD program is designed to guarantee equitable working and living conditions on the dairy farms that provide companies like Ben & Jerry's with dairy products. Drawing inspiration from the Coalition of Immokalee Workers (CIW) and their successful Fair Food Program, the MD program aims to highlight the needs and priorities of those who typically remain voiceless in the complex supply chains of our industrial food system: the immigrant laborers working on the ground.

Over the last twenty years, the food movement has increasingly picked up steam and brought with it significant changes in how food is grown, distributed, and consumed around the world. While some food activists emphasize reform-oriented actions, other approaches call for a complete and revolutionary change to our food system, or the dismantling of the "corporate food regime."[1] The latter tends to more fully acknowledge and challenge the labor exploitation that persists in our food system. This chapter situates the lives of farmworkers and recent farmworker organizing in the state of Vermont within these demands for change, responding to calls for food movement scholars to foreground issues of labor inequality and worker justice. In tracing the victories and potential future of farmworker organizing in Vermont, I assert that The Other Border is not only a place of great inequalities in the food system but also a space where new possibilities for food justice are emerging. Part of what has made farmworker organizing successful in Vermont is the greater visibility it has granted to the daily lives of farmworkers and the struggles they face, which is crucial, yet also exceedingly difficult for a community that is typically relegated to the shadows of the industrial food system. At the same time, this greater visibility has also led to the increased surveillance and scrutiny of farmworker leaders, who have become visible and vocal within recent policy debates and public campaigns like the one leading up to the signing of the MD agreement. This surveillance has at times led to the detention and even deportation of farmworker activists.

This chapter primarily focuses on the history, major accomplishments, and stated goals of Migrant Justice, an organization formed in 2009 and based in the Burlington area (though working in most of the Vermont counties where dairy production takes place). Migrant Justice defines itself as a farmworker-led organization and states, "Our mission is to build the voice, capacity, and power of the farmworker community and engage community partners to organize for economic justice and human rights."[2] The organization is primarily guided by the leadership of the Farmworker Coordinating Committee, (known more informally as the "CoCo") a group of eight to ten farmworker leaders who play a key role in defining the organization's priorities and campaign directions. In addition to their accomplishments with the

MD program, Migrant Justice has campaigned against racial profiling at the local and state level and has secured access to driver's privilege cards for any state resident, regardless of citizenship status. For an organization that was founded less than ten years ago, the successful campaigns carried out during the organization's relatively short history are impressive, given how much they have influenced governmental policy, public discourse, and corporate practices.

I begin this chapter by discussing my own involvement with farmworker activism in the state, in order to highlight the ways that research and activism can coalesce and become in some ways symbiotic. Just as important, this discussion allows me to be up front about the methodological difficulties that arise when one's positionality and objectives relative to the field are ever-shifting and at times competing. I then provide a timeline of farmworker activism in Vermont since 2009, outlining the major accomplishments, and the setbacks, that farmworker leaders and their allies have experienced. From there, I bring in data from interviews, participant observation, and analysis of original documents to situate Vermont farmworker activism and its accomplishments within the broader food movement. I conclude by outlining various trends and critiques in the food movement, showing how the farmworker campaigns led by Migrant Justice push against the neat categories outlined by food movement scholars.

NAVIGATING THE ROLES OF RESEARCHER AND ACTIVIST

Before turning to my analysis of farmworker activism in Vermont, I feel it necessary to situate my own work relative to this activism. Soon after moving to Vermont in the late summer of 2011, I reached out to staff members at Migrant Justice, then called the Vermont Migrant Farmworker Solidarity Project, to share my research background and interests, and to inquire about how I could support their work. Given my previous research on food access within Latinx immigrant communities, I envisioned that I would extend these interests through investigating similar issues within Vermont's farmworker community. Although my previous research concentrated on the intersections of migration from Latin America and urban food systems, I understood that if I wished to do the kind of ethnography that I was trained to do—the kind of anthropology that is grounded in the place where I live—I would either need to focus on rural food systems or change the scope of the community I work with. In Vermont, the small Latinx immigrant community that does exist is decidedly not urban and is much more geographically spread out than the community in Seattle that was the focus of my dissertation. After being active in food justice organizing for several years in Seattle, I was also looking for an opportunity to pursue my activist work in Vermont.

The staff members at Migrant Justice were receptive to my introduction, and soon after my initial email we sat down in their office and brainstormed potential ways we could work together. Over the next months, I found myself engaging in a number of volunteer roles with their organization: driving farmworkers to meetings, helping with fundraising and phone banking events, helping to edit and provide feedback on grant applications, and eventually assisting and advising with the research they were beginning on the industrial dairy supply chain. In exchange, my growing understanding of the conditions of dairy production gained through this involvement was foundational in shaping the directions of my research. When conducting pilot interviews for this study beginning in 2012, I found the staff members at Migrant Justice helpful in identifying and connecting me with potential interviewees to help hone my focus on food access issues, and I completed two preliminary interviews with farmworkers working and living closer to the Burlington area through their connections.

After a few years of semi-regular volunteering, I was asked to join the board of directors, or what Migrant Justice refers to as the *Junta de Apoyo*. Feeling the pressures of pretenure academic life and wary of how I would balance my research commitments with my activist commitments, I declined this offer but said that it was something that I would definitely consider again in the near future. As the codirector of Huertas, I also wanted to ensure that my efforts to support the farmworker community did not become spread too thin. The staff of Migrant Justice were more than understanding, and I continued to volunteer when and where I was able. With the results of the 2016 U.S. presidential election, however, my frustrations and concerns for immigrant rights issues were further galvanized, and I felt in a better position to extend my involvement, particularly after my tenure file was complete and headed up the ladder of administrative approvals. When I was approached again about serving on the Junta in late 2016, I knew that this was a better and perhaps an even more politically necessary time, and I began to serve in January of 2017.

While I have gained a degree of insider knowledge about the organization's structure and campaigns while serving on the Junta, I restrict my analysis to publicly available information. Both out of respect for Migrant Justice and in keeping with the scope of my institutional review board approval, I have chosen to focus my analysis in this chapter on information that has been made publicly available through the media, public documents, and my formal interviews with organizational staff. Through drawing on this information, I offer a timeline of the organization's campaigns using media pieces and public commentary, as well as my own perspectives from attending public rallies and marches organized by Migrant Justice. As will become evident, this organization has achieved a number of groundbreaking milestones over the past several years, and their work has the potential to significantly shift the unjust power dynamics that are pervasive in industrial milk production.

Of course, it should be said that separating my positionality as a researcher and as an ally to farmworker activists is not easy, and as should be clear by this point in the book, I am not neutral on the injustice that plagues our food system and its workers. While I aim to exclude the insider knowledge I have gained through my involvement with Migrant Justice, it nevertheless informs my analysis in this chapter and my understanding of the farmworker community. I do not disclose the details of campaigns or private organizational details that I am privy to as a board member. I am indebted to the organization and its staff and farmworker leaders, both for their time in providing feedback on this chapter, but more importantly, for providing an opportunity for me to gain a more grounded knowledge of farmworker experiences. These insights are inseparable from the knowledge that I have gained in an official research capacity and as the codirector for the Huertas project. It is incredibly fortunate that my involvement with the organization overlaps with a period of groundbreaking accomplishments and campaign successes, and it has been both instructive and personally rewarding to be a supporter of the organization's efforts and see the possibilities for food justice that are emerging.

A TIMELINE OF ACCOMPLISHMENTS— AND SETBACKS

The Birth of a Movement

As is often the case in the birth of activism, the organizing campaigns for and by Vermont's farmworkers were prompted by tragedy. On December 22, 2009, a young farmworker named José Obeth Santiz Cruz died when he was caught in a gutter cleaner on the Howrigan dairy farm, located in Fairfield, a small town in Franklin County. As the author of a news article published shortly after his death explains, "Neither migrant-worker advocates nor the Vermont State Police know much about José Obeth Santiz Cruz, and that, in its own way, is as telling as what little is known about this young man who died in Fairfield last Tuesday."[3] As word about his death rippled through the farmworker community with the aid of farmworker advocates, it was learned that he was from the rural Tojolabal Mayan village of San Isidro, near Las Margaritas, Chiapas, and that a number of his relatives were also working on Vermont's dairy farms. However, it took over a week for officials to determine his name, age, and where he was from.

Repatriating his body to his home community would cost upwards of $10,000, an extraordinary sum for his family. Realizing this, Brendan O'Neill, then a teacher for the Vermont Migrant Education Program, organized a candlelight vigil held at the Vermont Workers' Center and a fundraising drive for his repatriation and funeral costs. This community mobilization quickly multiplied, and by early January 2010, the Vermont Migrant Farmworker Solidarity Project was born, with O'Neill coordinating its efforts. The first goals of this newly formed group centered upon establishing ties with Santiz Cruz's family in Chiapas and sending a delegation of three Vermonters to accompany his body back to his home community.[4] This series of events would be recorded in the first film released about Vermont's farmworker community, appropriately titled *Silenced Voices*.

Silenced Voices opens with a scene of Santiz Cruz's coffin being carried by several men in his home village, with the sounds of wailing women interspersed with Mexican folk music. After a few minutes of following the coffin through the village streets in the back of a white pickup adorned with flowers, the film returns to Vermont to show scenes of the countryside and of migrant workers in milking barns. Switching quickly back to San Isidro, the film then begins to capture the words of Santiz Cruz's mother, Zoyla, who shares how she learned of her son's untimely death before turning to reflect upon the argument that they had about his decision to leave Mexico. Having lost three other sons, Zoyla was fearful for José Obeth's safety as he planned to cross the border and find work in the United States. After an extended conversation with Zoyla, the filmmakers then turn to an interview with a woman from the village who had previously crossed into the United States to find work in Vermont, while showing scenes of village life. Crossing back into Vermont, the film then features interviews with dairy workers still living in Vermont, showing the conditions of their work before returning to interview the parents of two sons who moved to find work in Vermont, one of whom was being detained at that time by immigration officials. Over a total of twenty-five minutes, the film presents a powerful series of narratives and images from rural Vermont and rural Mexico, emphasizing the transnational connections between these two places. This film was my first exposure to the realities confronting farmworkers in the state, and it has become an essential teaching tool in my classroom and the classrooms of many other teachers and professors.

Targeting Wage Theft

While the death of Santiz Cruz was a primary motivation for organizers to establish the Vermont Migrant Farmworker Solidarity Project (VMFSP), the group quickly realized that their work did not end with the return of his body to Mexico. Following this tragedy, organizers turned to a grassroots orientation for their work, building and drawing upon farmworker leadership (particularly through the emerging Farmworker Coordinating Committee) to develop the numerous public campaigns that have unfolded since. In late 2010, the VMFSP launched one of their first public campaigns, which targeted issues of wage theft. This campaign focused on supporting a young female farmworker and her two coworkers (her father and boyfriend) to file a formal complaint with the Vermont Department of Labor for unpaid wages of $4,494 against Robert Jr. and David Mack, owners of the Mack dairy farm in Charlotte, Vermont. The filing of the claim followed a three-day strike, which yielded nothing from the farm owners. After a year of pressure, some of the back wages were paid, but by that point, the three farmworkers had found work on a different farm. Nevertheless, given ongoing issues with unpaid wages that were reported to the new Teleayuda hotline that the VMFSP had established to channel worker complaints, the Mack farm became the focal point of a march and public demonstration in August 2012.

Now calling themselves Migrant Justice, this public demonstration included organizing a bike tour by nearly fifty "Human Rights Riders" from Burlington to Charlotte, a distance of roughly thirteen miles. Following the ride, farmworkers and their allies organized a roadside rally and delivered the "Cabot 'Sour Cream' Award" in recognition of what the organization deemed human rights abuses, calling on the farm owners to pay the wages that were, at this point, still being withheld. This public event was the first one I became involved with, and I was appointed to drive a number of signs and other materials to the farm, where they would then be used in the public demonstration that occupied a small state road that passes by the Mack farm. Via this role, I had the opportunity to witness both the public demonstration and the response from the farm owners, who called on state police to intervene. The demonstration was peaceful but highly visible, and certainly not routine for the small and sleepy town of Charlotte. After the public demonstration, Migrant Justice leaders left a large poster of the "Cabot 'Sour Cream' Award" at the farm. Natalia Fajardo, then a staff member of Migrant Justice, made this public statement about the demonstration: "We are not here to just denounce this immoral and inhumane farmer. We are also here because we are working to make sure that all of these so called 'green' or 'fair' dairy products live up to their image, whether it's Cabot Cheese or Ben & Jerry's. There is no Fair Milk without Human Rights."[5] This discourse on human rights has since come to shape Migrant Justice's campaigns and organizing efforts.

Fighting for Fair and Impartial Policing

In 2011, Migrant Justice kicked off a broader campaign around bias-free policing supported by a number of organizations in the state, including the now-inactive Addison County Farm Worker Coalition and the Vermont Workers' Center. The campaign against racial profiling and the collusion of local and state police with ICE and Border Patrol, referred to by Migrant Justice as "*No Más Polimigra,*" continues to this day. In the summer of 2011, this organizing focused on pressuring then Governor Peter Shumlin to take a stand against the Secure Communities Program, which allows local law enforcement to share information, including fingerprints, with Immigration and Customs Enforcement. Made mandatory under the Obama administration beginning in 2008, a number of states, including Massachusetts, Illinois, and New York, were at that time limiting their participation in the program, and Vermont was among a number of states that were yet to sign on to the program. Migrant Justice leaders delivered a petition signed by seventy farmworkers to the governor's office in August 2012, asking him to reject the Secure Communities Program, as well as releasing an open letter to Vermont farmers to take a stand against the program, emphasizing its negative consequences for employers who depend on migrant labor.

Although farmworker leaders were not able to meet personally with the governor to discuss their concerns, they sat down with Diane Bothfield, then deputy secretary of the Vermont Agency of Agriculture, Food, and Markets. Over the following weeks, Shumlin made public remarks questioning the federal program.

> We want to make sure that Vermont is a state where, when we host migrant workers, we treat them with respect and dignity. We have a raging immigration debate going on in America. There's no question, in my view, that our immigration policies in this country are broken, and that the federal government is . . . frankly, some of their policies are out of step with how we treat our farm workers in Vermont.

Despite this stance and the ongoing pressure of farmworker leaders, Vermont began to participate in the Secure Communities Program in May 2012, seeing no way to reject the federal mandate. However, in the months leading up to this decision, and in many months to follow, a number of high-profile farmworker arrests led Migrant Justice to challenge biased policing through other avenues. Important to note is that Secure Communities was suspended by President Obama in November 2014 because of challenges coming not only from pro-immigrant activists but also from local and state governments, inspiring Obama's transition to the "Priority Enforcement Program" that would ostensibly target only those suspected of serious crimes or seen as a threat to national security. The suspension of the Secure Communities Program was temporary, however, as it was reactivated just after the inauguration of Donald Trump in January 2017.

Even as Vermont became part of the Secure Communities Program, a number of efforts at the state and local level were designed to challenge racial bias in policing and to stop state and local police officers from acting as immigration enforcement agents. This organizing work of Migrant Justice took a particularly visible turn when two farmworkers—one of whom, Danilo Lopez, had become outspoken about the Secure Communities Program—were taken into custody following a routine traffic stop on September 13, 2011. As passengers in a car pulled over for speeding, Lopez and Antonio-Meza Sandoval were transferred from the state troopers who performed the stop to Border Patrol agents who issued an "Immigration Detainer" after the state troopers asked to see their identification or visas, despite the fact that they were not driving. The driver of the car, a U.S. citizen, was allowed to go without so much as a speeding ticket, while Lopez and Sandoval were held at the Middlesex State Police Barracks. Later that day, several activists, including members of Migrant Justice, arrived at the barracks and attempted to block Border Patrol from taking the two men away, with three activists detained and cited for disorderly conduct. Although Lopez and Sandoval were released later that day, with citations to appear in court at a later date, the events raised a considerable degree of public controversy and prompted Governor Shumlin to order an investigation into the police handling of the traffic stop. While publicly applauding the quality of the state police, Shumlin stated his position clearly:

> Look, Vermont State Police are the best in the world, they do a great job . . . but my question is, do we have adequate policies that give them the protection they need to ensure they're doing the policy we think is right when it comes to this rather complicated question of how we deal with guest workers in Vermont? Farmers can't survive without them. We know the federal government wants to send them home. And we don't.[6]

In November 2011, Shumlin put his words into action as he unveiled his policy on Bias-Free Policing, after meeting in person with farmworkers and Migrant Justice organizers the previous month. This policy mandates that state police shall not ask about immigration status when investigating a civil offense but may do so in the case of criminal offenses. However, if suspected unauthorized crossings occur along the border, state police are instructed to call federal authorities for help.

Although the policy developed by Shumlin and his staff was well received by both law enforcement and farmworkers and their allies, it fell short in fully protecting farmworkers from biased treatment by local law enforcement. After concerns that Franklin County sheriffs were targeting farmworkers on the basis of race, Migrant Justice organized to strengthen the previous policy through lobbying for Vermont S.184 (Act 193), which requires (1) every state, local, county, and municipal law enforcement agency to adopt a fair and impartial policing policy and (2) law enforcement to collect and make public roadside stop data related to race, among other requirements concerning the electronic recording of investigations having to do with homicide or sexual assault. S.184 was signed into law by Shumlin on June 17, 2014.

Following the 2014 law, Migrant Justice continued their work to ensure bias-free policing, helping to guide the work of the Vermont Criminal Justice Training Council as it developed a model Fair and Impartial Policing Policy (FIPP) that was adopted in June of 2016. Local police agencies and constables had the opportunity to adopt the policy in its entirety or ensure that their own policies covered the "essential elements" of the FIPP. The policy was fully reviewed by the state attorney general's office in 2017 and deemed to comply with federal immigration law. A subsequent bill, the Racial Justice Reform Bill, Act 54 (H.308) helped to establish greater oversight by establishing a panel to address racial disparities in statewide criminal and juvenile justice systems, as well as a provision to revisit the FIPP, with the intent of maintaining the rigor of the policy. However, the Vermont Criminal Justice Council advanced a new version of the policy in late 2017 that weakened a number of protections for immigrants, and, according to the group Justice for All, limited the accountability and transparency that the policy called for. The weakened policy was approved in December 2017 by Vermont police, despite strong opposition from Migrant Justice leaders. Migrant Justice continues to work to strengthen bias-free policies at the local and state level.

Demanding Freedom of Movement

One of Migrant Justice's most visible and successful campaigns focused on securing the ability for farmworkers, regardless of citizenship status, to obtain driver's privilege cards. Beginning in early 2012, Migrant Justice applied pressure on local and state representatives to support bill S.238, kicking off the public component of the campaign with a series of testimonies delivered at the Vermont State House on February 29. Over the next several months, the bill traveled through various committees and received a number of public hearings. It was opposed by a few organized groups, such as the Vermont Bankers Association. This association in particular expressed concern about the need to request additional identification that would demonstrate U.S. citizenship from their customers if undocumented immigrants were to receive driver's licenses. Despite this opposition, the Vermont Senate gave preliminary approval to the bill (27 supporting, 2 opposing) on April 5, 2013, moving the bill to the Vermont House which approved the bill the next month (105 in support, 39 opposing). Governor Peter Shumlin gave final approval to the bill on June 5, with the bill going into effect on January 1, 2014. The driver's privilege cards have a different appearance and format than the standard state driver's license, and they do not comply with the REAL ID laws, meaning that they do not count as federal identification. There is nothing barring U.S. citizens from applying for the driver's privilege cards, which Migrant Justice encouraged their supporters to do as an act of solidarity with farmworkers.

Amidst the organizing for driver's licenses, Migrant Justice also launched a public campaign to block the deportation of Danilo Lopez, whose arrest had prompted the conversations on bias-free policing and who had played a central role in the licensing campaign. After a number of appeals, Lopez was ordered to leave the United States by early July 2013. Through a widespread letter-writing campaign and leveraging the national attention raised in connection with the immigrant rights network Not1More, Migrant Justice asked ICE to use "prosecutorial discretion" to overturn Lopez's deportation order, while urging the state's congressional delegation (including Senators Bernie Sanders and Patrick Leahy, and U.S. Representative Peter Welch) to support this request. Sanders, Leahy, and Welch all wrote letters of support, with additional letters coming from Governor Shumlin and Burlington Mayor Miro Weinberger. Highlighting the leadership role that Lopez had played in the state, Migrant Justice called for a "stay of removal," which was eventually granted on July 16, 2013.

From Fair Housing to Milk with Dignity

In the summer of 2014, Migrant Justice turned their focus to the poor housing conditions that farmworkers often experience while working on dairy farms. The public face of this campaign centered on protests against a Ferrisburgh farm where workers experienced sewage backing up in the water pipes of the trailer that was provided by the farm owner, Ray Brands, as well as calling for back pay for the workers who had left the farm because of the sewage issue. Farmworkers, including Victor Diaz who had worked at the farm for more than two years, also raised complaints about the camper that they were provided to live in. According to Diaz, the camper had a leaky roof and was not large enough for the four farmworkers expected to sleep there. Brands quickly paid the back pay of more than $1,800 but expressed frustration about what he saw as "mob justice" when he was targeted by the protestors.[7]

Building on the attention raised about farmworker housing conditions, the public mobilization of the Milk with Dignity campaign, arguably the largest and most ambitious campaign organized by Migrant Justice, began in 2015. The public face of the campaign followed a number of meetings between Migrant Justice and staff at Ben & Jerry's, including representatives from their "Caring Dairy" program, Social Mission team, and public relations department. Through these meetings, Migrant Justice aimed to educate the company on the labor abuses and unfair working and living conditions that plague many of the dairy farms in their supply chain. This education, as well as the direction for the campaign, were informed by the farmworker survey carried out by Migrant Justice (discussed in chapter 2 in more detail), which documented the poor working and living conditions that many dairy farmworkers encounter. Based on this data, farmworker leaders and Migrant Justice staff formulated a Code of Conduct, which was guided by a framework of worker-driven social responsibility (WSR). The development and results of this Code, while specific to the dairy industry, is inspired heavily by the work of the CIW and the methods they used to set the standards for their Fair Food Program. Adapting the CIW model to Vermont has required Migrant Justice to carefully consider the different contexts that are present in the dairy industry with year-round, rather than seasonal, employment. It has also required the organization to carefully study the dairy supply chain to fully understand the most promising leverage points for their campaign and which companies are likely to sign on to the program. Ben & Jerry's, with its stated commitment to issues of social justice and history of purchasing fair-trade ingredients, was the most promising company to pressure first. Purchased by global behemoth Unilever in 2000 for $326 million, Ben & Jerry's has maintained its social mission despite what many feared would be a total corporate takeover, not only of the brand but of their emphasis on supporting progressive causes.

Migrant Justice has outlined the development of the Milk with Dignity program in detail throughout their press materials and social media, and has regularly been featured in local and national press for the campaign. The five main elements of the Milk with Dignity program include: a farmworker-authored Code of Conduct, farmworker education (focusing on educating about their rights under the Code of Conduct), the establishment of a third-party monitoring body for enforcement and auditing, economic relief (in the form of price premiums going to farmers following the Code), and the guarantee of a legally binding agreement that defined the contract as legally enforceable.[8] A key turning point in the campaign was a December 2014 meeting with Ben & Jerry's Social Mission team, when Migrant Justice officially asked Ben & Jerry's to sign on to the program and accept the Code of Conduct. Although Ben & Jerry's did not immediately agree to the conditions of the Milk with Dignity program at this meeting, the conversations that began in earnest then would continue over nearly three years of continued public mobilization and negotiations.

Throughout the first half of 2015, Migrant Justice worked tirelessly to promote the Milk with Dignity campaign, organizing a number of events, including partnering with CIW staff on a public screening of the film *Food*

Chains, which documents the work of the CIW, and a subsequent panel discussion about the links between the Fair Food and Milk with Dignity programs. Organizers from Migrant Justice had the opportunity to visit Immokalee, Florida, to see the results of the Fair Food Program and to learn more about the WSR model, and CIW members made the trip north to visit with farmworker organizers in Vermont. This cross-fertilization of farmworker campaigns attracted national attention, with local and national press outlets offering detailed coverage of the possibilities of extending the model developed by the CIW to Vermont's dairy industry. The increased attention by the press also helped to raise a growing public dialogue about how a socially minded company like Ben & Jerry's, with a stated commitment to a diverse array of environmental and political issues and fair sourcing of their ingredients, could ignore the demands of farmworkers producing the key ingredient in their ice cream.

Migrant Justice sought to leverage this conversation into a series of national actions at Ben & Jerry's scoop shops in sixteen different cities on June 20, 2015. The action in Burlington, Vermont, centered upon a march to the flagship store on Church Street, followed by a rally featuring a number of speeches from farmworkers active with the organization. Just one day before the day of actions was set to start, Migrant Justice learned that Ben & Jerry's was ready to agree to a written agreement of cooperation and to negotiate the terms of the Code of Conduct in earnest. The protest march subsequently turned into a celebratory march of more than 120 people, with farmworker leader Victor Diaz delivering a letter to Rob Michalak, the Global Director of Social Missions at Ben & Jerry's, signed by forty-five organizations in support of the Milk with Dignity program. Soon after the agreement was made, the *New York Times* ran a feature article about the Milk with Dignity campaign and other farmworker organizing projects around the country.[9] At this point, it appeared that the Milk with Dignity program would soon be implemented, and many Vermonters standing in solidarity with the campaign, including the author, were all too happy to start purchasing Ben & Jerry's ice cream again in good conscience.

However, despite ongoing negotiations between Migrant Justice and Ben & Jerry's, and the formal establishment and staffing of the Milk with Dignity Standards Council, more than two years would pass before this initial commitment was formalized into a written commitment. In April 2017, Migrant Justice decided to renew the public mobilization of the campaign, feeling that Ben & Jerry's was dragging their heels in negotiations. Centering public

FIGURE 14. May first action at Ben & Jerry's. Photo by author.

actions around the annual "Free Cone Day" that the company has offered since 1979 to thank their customers, Migrant Justice organized a public demonstration on April 4, 2017, at the flagship Burlington location to remind the company and its customers that the Milk with Dignity agreement remained unsigned and unimplemented. Rather than responding with frustration, Michalak made public statements about the company's willingness to continue negotiations and stated, "We're very much supportive of people's right to make the statements they need to make."[10] However, because both parties had signed a nondisclosure agreement, the details of the negotiations, including what specifically could not be agreed upon, were not made public. The protests continued the following week outside of a Ben & Jerry's board of directors meeting at the company's corporate headquarters in South Burlington, and a march in downtown Burlington on May first, in recognition of International Workers Day. The May first march concluded with a rally in front of the federal building in Burlington, in part to call attention to the anti-immigrant rhetoric and actions of the Trump administration.

On June 17, 2017, as Migrant Justice was still waiting on a written commitment from Ben & Jerry's nearly two years after their verbal commitment, the organization led a highly publicized thirteen-mile march from the Vermont state capitol building in Montpelier to the Ben & Jerry's factory in Waterbury. CIW leaders joined the march, adding to the crowd of over two

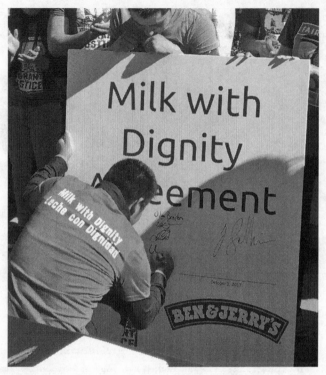

FIGURE 15. Public signing of the Milk with Dignity Agreement. Photo by author.

hundred people who made the long trek along Vermont's state highways on a hot and humid summer day. While the march was successful in garnering greater visibility for the campaign, two farmworker leaders, Esau Peche and Yesenia Hernandez, were detained by Border Patrol agents afterwards as they returned home. I will discuss these arrests, as well as the arrests of other Migrant Justice leaders, in more detail in the section that follows.

To leverage and extend the energy that was built through the march, Migrant Justice organized a series of talks for a "Human Rights Can't Wait" speaking tour in September 2017 in ten cities along the east coast, including Philadelphia, New York, New Haven, and Boston. The speaking tour, which visited a number of colleges and universities, would culminate in another national day of action planned for October 5. Just two days before the day of action, Migrant Justice announced that Ben & Jerry's was now willing to offer their written commitment to the program, a victory that inspired the press event on October 3 in which CEO Solheim and Migrant Justice leaders publicly signed the written agreement. The news of the campaign was shared in local, national, and international media, thrusting Migrant Justice onto the international stage of food justice movements.

The Milk with Dignity program will be monitored by a third party, the Milk with Dignity Standards Council, which will coordinate regular audits on participating farms where farmworkers and their employers will be regularly interviewed. As James, a Migrant Justice staff member, explained to me in a 2015 interview, this third party is not intended to be distant from the program, as is often the case in fair trade models, but rather a "permanent institution in Vermont that will create a relationship with the farmers" that will act more like a guide rather than a punitive force. If, during an audit, it is seen that a farmer is not following the Code of Conduct, he/she will be issued a Corrective Action Plan to bring that farm into greater alignment with the program. James emphasized that the auditing model is not designed as a "gotcha!" program, but rather is designed with a more comprehensive goal of identifying problems so that the employers understand the standards and codes, with the ultimate goal of ensuring that they follow through and provide fair working conditions. However, the program has zero tolerance for grave abuses such as sexual abuse. Migrant Justice is hopeful that the economic benefits that are funneled to the farmers through the Milk with Dignity agreement, specifically receiving a premium for their product from Ben & Jerry's, will offset the costs of compliance.

With Visibility Comes Surveillance

Despite the numerous successes that Migrant Justice has experienced in their relatively short history, the organization has been plagued by the arrests of a number of their members and leaders. The second high-profile arrest of a Migrant Justice member, following the 2011 arrest and release of Danilo Lopez, took place on April 21, 2016. Victor Diaz, then twenty-four years old, was taken into custody outside a restaurant in Stowe, Vermont, by federal immigration officers and placed into a Dover, New Hampshire, prison. Diaz, who had become well known through protests of living conditions at the Brands dairy farm, but also through his involvement with the Milk with Dignity campaign, was arrested upon becoming an "enforcement priority" after a DUI conviction the previous November. After mobilizing a petition and letter campaign, Migrant Justice delivered more than thirty letters and more than two thousand signatures to Diaz's attorney, who then presented them to the judge presiding at his hearing at the Boston Immigration court. Despite providing previous support following the arrest of Danilo Lopez, Senator Leahy declined to ask for prosecutorial discretion for Diaz. Senator Sanders did submit a letter to the Department of Homeland Security on Diaz's behalf, however.[11] The judge released Diaz on May 3, less than two weeks after his arrest, on $1,500 bail, the lowest allowable amount, and he soon returned to Vermont to continue his organizing work. At the time of writing, Diaz was still living in the state and active with the organization.

The next arrest, of twenty-three-year old farmworker leader Miguel Alcudia, took place on September 22, 2016, in Vergennes, Vermont, on charges that he had overstayed his visa. After being followed by an unmarked car from the farm where he worked while he was on his way to the bank, Alcudia was detained by federal officials, despite having no criminal history. Migrant Justice quickly organized a protest at the ICE Center in Saint Albans, demanding Alcudia's release, as well as a rally in Burlington where more than one hundred fifty people demonstrated in front of the federal building. Utilizing the same tactic as before, Migrant Justice gathered dozens of support letters and fifteen hundred signatures on an online petition organized in conjunction with Not1More. Alcudia was released on October 13, after spending three weeks in prison, with the judge dropping the entirety of the $21,000 bail, a move that is typically reserved for individuals who are not considered priority for deportation. As with Diaz, Miguel is currently in Vermont as of early 2018, still active with Migrant Justice.

The next series of arrests took place over a span of two years within the Burlington area, an urban setting that had previously been viewed as relatively safe by a majority of farmworkers. Alex Carrillo, age twenty-three, was detained on March 15, 2017, in a "targeted traffic stop" as he arrived at the Chittenden County courthouse for a hearing on DUI charges from 2016. Although he did not make it into the courtroom, the charges against him were dropped by the state in his absence. Arrested in front of his wife and four-year-old daughter, both U.S. citizens, Carrillo was transferred to a federal immigration court in Boston. Just two days later, Enrique "Kike" Balcazar and Zully Palacios were detained by four undercover ICE agents after being pulled over in South Burlington as they drove down Shelburne Road. Both Migrant Justice leaders, Palacios was arrested for overstaying her J-1 exchange visitor visa, and when it was determined that Balcazar was in violation of U.S. immigration laws, he too was detained. Migrant Justice organized a mass mobilization about the arrests of these three individuals, including a public march and demonstration of more than five hundred people in Burlington, launching a campaign in conjunction with Not1More that collected over ten thousand signatures demanding their release and hundreds of letters, including one from Senator Sanders. In addition, a public demonstration at the Boston courthouse took place during their hearings with the support of organizations including Cosecha, the ACLU of Massachusetts, and a number of labor unions.

The arrests of Carrillo, Palacios, and Balcazar, all occurring shortly after the inauguration of Donald Trump, raised questions about whether ICE was retaliating against Migrant Justice leaders for their public activism. The attorney representing all three individuals, Matt Cameron, called the arrests a "clear, simple case of retaliation," and contended that his clients were unfairly targeted.[12] These arrests promoted a flurry of national media attention, with coverage coming from local and regional papers but also from the BBC, *Democracy Now!*, and the *Boston Globe*. Following the hearing, Palacios and Balcazar were released on a reduced bail of $2,500 each (Balcazar's had been previously set at $14,000, and Palacios was being held on no bond) but Carrillo was held after being denied bail, with the judge citing his now-dropped DUI charge. While Palacios and Balcazar are still active in Migrant Justice's work as of early 2018, Carrillo decided to return to Mexico after accepting a "voluntary departure order" with the hope that he can return on a marriage visa, contingent upon receiving a U.S. immigration visa while he is in Mexico and a "hardship waiver," given his separation from his family.

Two later arrests, those of Esau Peche and Yesenia Hernandez, occurred on the evening after the Milk with Dignity march on June 17, 2017, and seemed to further demonstrate that ICE was targeting leaders and members of Migrant Justice. As they returned to the farm where they worked in Franklin County, Peche and Hernandez were detained by Border Patrol agents after the way they were driving appeared "suspicious"; they were pulled over in what was called a "routine traffic stop." While Border Patrol denied knowledge of their participation in the march, the agency refused to offer further details on what made their driving behavior suspicious enough to warrant stopping them, or what the agency termed "reasonable suspicion of illegal alienage." Amidst a series of protests organized by Migrant Justice, Peche and Hernandez were held until after their hearing in Boston on June 30, 2017, when they were eventually released on $6,000 bail each.

In November of 2015, as Migrant Justice was deeply engaged in the Milk with Dignity campaign, I had the opportunity to interview James and Ernesto, two Migrant Justice organizers, with my research assistant Jessie Mazar also in attendance. As we sat in the organization's small conference room, with volunteers and other staff members hard at work in the adjoining space, I learned even more about an organization that I had, at that point, supported for more than three years. I gained a more personal perspective on the campaigns and how the organization has fostered leadership development for its core farmworker organizers, many of whom I had grown to know well through my volunteer work with the organization.

Following in the footsteps of his parents, Ernesto worked on Vermont's dairy farms for about two-and-a-half years, experiencing a profound shift in consciousness after realizing that the working and living conditions that he and his family were experiencing were both widespread and oppressive. The normalization of unjust labor conditions in the industrial food system, a phenomenon that Seth Holmes describes in his analysis of Washington's berry farms, had become intimately familiar for Ernesto, who arrived in Vermont in 2011.[13] He explained the turning point when he realized that his story was not unique but rather shared by other exploited farmworkers:

> To see how hard it was for me working here with my father, who was here almost eight years, and to see how my mother . . . to see the hard work, the exhaustion on their faces, and it is hard to realize, that you don't have a voice within the industry. The dairy industry in Vermont is so important, and I have learned a lot, personally. I never imagined I would be an organizer, I came here to work with my family, that was my goal, to help my family in Mexico. . . . The first time I went to an assembly with Migrant Justice, I really wanted to meet a group of workers, and I get there and I am hearing the same stories of my friends that are like mine, like they also can't leave their homes, so that taught me a lot.

In the time that he has been active with Migrant Justice, Ernesto has also had the opportunity to learn about the broader struggles shared by farmworkers across the different sectors of the food system, most notably through his visit to Immokalee and ongoing conversations with CIW organizers about the Fair Food model and how it could be adapted to Vermont.

Through their organizing work, Migrant Justice places a heavy emphasis on this method of sharing narratives and experiences, seeing it as key to the development of solidarity between their core members as well as developing shared priorities for action. Often referring to this as a process of *concientización,* or consciousness-raising, the organization is guided by the ideas of philosopher and educator Paolo Freire on the importance of popular education in developing a critical consciousness about the systems of inequality and the political contradictions that persist in one's society.[14] James followed up Ernesto's recollection of his own *concientización* to reflect:

> I think that when the organization has done our best job is when we have had a good method of popular education, and that is exactly what Ernesto is explaining. To see that things are the same. To create a space where people can share their experiences and then after people analyze the causes, and then search for solutions, and then get plans of action, and then we act, and then we reflect again. That has been the model since the start that we wanted to come to, we see that we just need to bring people together and that is what will happen. We just need to create the space, to organize the space for it to be a safe space and a space of reflection.

He continued, "So it was a theory from our fights, it comes out in all of our campaigns, trying to share experiences. To share and analyze the problems, and see what we can do. . . . So it has worked the best when we have done that. And we have done it with a lot of intention. And I think that is the secret in moving forward." This method of developing plans of action around collectively defined solutions was key to the design of the Milk with Dignity campaign and its model of worker-driven social responsibility.

As Migrant Justice has worked tirelessly to create spaces and channels for farmworkers to share experiences and raise their collective consciousness, the organization has also been central to changing the public conversation about farmworkers in Vermont. In doing so, they have helped to challenge the processes of bordering that attempt to render farmworkers invisible. When I asked James to share his thoughts on the changes he had seen in Vermont, he responded by sharing a story about a class visit he had made on behalf of the organization earlier that same day.

> We asked how many people knew that there were Mexican workers behind the dairy workforce here? And almost all of them did, and that would not have happened five years ago! I think there is more consciousness and the community has advanced a lot in having more power and a voice in all that is Vermont, but I think there is still the perspective depending on the region. Like I think there are still employees in Walmart who talk to *la migra.* And things like this that show that there still is a lot of racism to be faced, there

is discrimination, but I think we have won space to make the conversation about food systems more critical.

As Migrant Justice has become increasingly active and recognized since 2009, they have helped to shape the public's understanding of the inequalities that persist in Vermont's industrial dairy industry, an industry that is a source of significant pride for the state and is rich in symbolic meaning. As discussed repeatedly in the preceding chapters, the image of Vermont's dairy industry that circulates through advertising campaigns and celebratory reports by agencies like the Vermont Dairy Promotion Council fails to capture the realities facing migrant farmworkers, and sometimes even erases their presence and contributions entirely. As James later notes in this same interview, in a state where the narrative surrounding food is often celebratory rather than realistic, the narratives offered by Migrant Justice help to paint a more complex picture of Vermont's food system.

In helping to raise the public's consciousness about the contributions of farmworkers and their living and working conditions, Migrant Justice has significantly challenged the politics of visibility that keeps undocumented workers invisible in their workplace and has also made strategic decisions about when, where, and how to make individual farmworkers and their struggles visible. Farmworker leaders active with Migrant Justice have unapologetically appeared in the news to share their stories and have helped to produce publicly accessible media such as the *Nadando Contra La Corriente* [Swimming against the Current] television program that is produced in collaboration with a local television channel maintained by the local organization Center for Media and Democracy. In making farmworkers and their struggles visible, Migrant Justice has challenged the status quo of the "social and spatial relations of agricultural labor reproduction" that Don Mitchell has argued is central to the continued marginalization and exploitation of farmworkers.[15] Their successes in elevating discussions of farmworker rights in public discourse also reflect Nelson's observations about the claims to cultural citizenship that are made in immigrant struggles over basic rights, in the case of her research, farmworker housing in Woodburn, Oregon. As Nelson notes, these claims reflect a demand for belonging and spatial claims to citizenship that are typically denied to undocumented workers in our food system.[16]

As the priorities of the organization have become increasingly guided by what Migrant Justice refers to as the *base*, or the base of the farmworker community, the organization has turned to the discourse of human rights as the primary framework for their campaigns as they draw upon their results of their popular education efforts. For Migrant Justice, the four main elements of this framework include the right of mobility (guiding the licensing campaign), freedom from discrimination (guiding the anti-*polimigra* campaign), the right to health (which has taken shape through participating in a broader campaign for universal health care led by the Vermont Workers' Center), and the right to just work and a dignified life (guiding the Milk with Dignity campaign). Although the right to food or food access has not figured heavily into the priorities of Migrant Justice (as it often does in human rights discourse), food has served a central role as a means to bring the farmworker community together. The organization has supported the entrepreneurial activities of women in the community through hiring them as caterers for the organization's celebratory events and has also explored the development of a mobile cooperative market that would deliver food to farmworkers at a fair price. The idea for the mobile market, while generating interest from Migrant Justice staff, has not gone beyond the planning stage, since it stemmed mostly from the work of student allies rather than the farmworker base.

During our interview, Ernesto spoke most passionately about the meaning of just and dignified work and the development of the Milk with Dignity campaign, noting how the community defined the main problems it was facing in order to inform the priorities of the campaign and the Code of Conduct:

> It was in 2012 where we started this campaign Milk with Dignity, and it was good to go from farm to farm to do surveys, ask people, and that was important so that between all of the workers, we defined what is a just workplace, what is a dignified life. And we did about one hundred eighty interviews and from there the community defined what the problems are, like right now, 40 percent of the workers do not have a day of rest, 40 percent do not receive minimum wage of Vermont, and with these results, in the assemblies we talk about these problems—now we know what they are, what do we do?

As Ernesto explained, after the farmworker community had identified their shared problems and priorities, the next step was to look at different models of farmworker campaigns, including the Fair Food program of the CIW.

As is the case for all Migrant Justice organizers, Ernesto deeply respects the accomplishments of the CIW. As he acknowledged the importance of the contract that the CIW has signed with companies like Taco Bell, McDonald's, and Walmart, he emphasized that for the workers, the workplace dignity and respect that they gained through their organizing was even more significant in their lives. For Ernesto, it was this dignity and respect, seen in basic rights like the right to shade and water in the fields, that reflected a human rights orientation. Although the working conditions and labor demands of Vermont's dairy industry and Florida's tomato fields are certainly different, the campaigns share this attention to human rights. Indeed, the discourse of human rights features prominently in all of Migrant Justice's public campaigns and materials, including the tagline that graces the organization's recent line of T-shirts released during the 2016 U.S. presidential campaign, "Can't Trump Human Rights!"

(SOMETHING OTHER THAN) REFORM OR REVOLUTION?

In their 2011 article, Eric Holt-Giménez and Annie Shattuck examine the possibilities of food movements to bring about substantive change in the global food system. They offer a comparative framework for categorizing the varying political and social trends in what they and fellow food scholar Philip McMichael term the "corporate food regime" and the global food movements that intersect with and challenge this regime.[17] Categorizing these trends into four areas: Neoliberal, Reformist, Progressive, and Radical, Holt-Giménez and Shattuck situate these movements in response to the global food crises that arose after the political-economic shocks of the 2008 global financial crisis, a time in which corporate power became more solidified even as the weaknesses in global financial institutions were painfully revealed. They argue:

> Today's food movements, responding to the social, economic and environmental crises unleashed by the corporate food regime, are important forces for social change. But it is the balance of forces within the food movements that will likely determine the nature and the extent of reform or transformation possible within the double movement of the corporate food regime.[18]

Holt-Giménez and Shattuck locate farmworker movements in the radical trend, which "seeks deep, structural changes to food and agriculture" and is typically framed by the discourse of food sovereignty.[19] They emphasize that because of the dramatic increase in migration between the Global South and the Global North, this radical space within the broader food movement often overlaps with immigrant rights movements.

Alison Alkon and Julie Guthman extend the project of classifying the trends within the food movement in the introduction to their edited volume focusing on food activism in the United States and Canada. Together, they outline the two areas of critique that have been offered in attempts to strengthen alternative food systems, the first focusing on food justice and the other focusing on neoliberalism.[20] The food justice critique centers on an analysis of how structural racism intersects with, and is often amplified by, power dynamics within the food system (including alternative food systems), whereas the neoliberal critique focuses on the tendency to employ market-based solutions in place of demanding or facilitating state interventions or regulations. In her contribution to this edited volume, Laura-Anne Minkoff-Zern grounds these critiques in her analysis of the successful farmworker campaigns led by the United Farm Workers and the CIW. Rather than expressing a wholly cynical view about market-based solutions, Minkoff-Zern argues that as the CIW has facilitated a shift from a focus on individual consumers to large-scale buyers, they have developed a worker-centered food movement that "creates an opening for consumers and workers alike to break down the divides between consumer and producer, urban and rural, and individual and community-based approaches to changing the food system."[21] This moves beyond the call for consumers to vote with their dollars, so to speak, to asking them instead to engage their power as citizens through participating in CIW campaigns and, when necessary, participating in boycotts. Similar to what I have described about the orientation of Migrant Justice, Minkoff-Zern notes that the CIW has long engaged with tactics such as popular education, public protest, and concentrated efforts to develop leadership within the farmworker base.

Migrant Justice has a clear place within the food justice movement; the organization offers a critique of the structural racism that not only is built into state policy and action (particularly those related to policing) but also pervades the working and living conditions on dairy farms. Migrant Justice activists make an explicit connection between the rights of farmworkers with broader immigrant rights issues, echoing the point raised by Holt-Giménez and Shattuck. The organization certainly reflects a radical ethos in their organizing work as they align their goals with class struggle and the rights of workers across the food system, seen in their active membership in the Food Chain Workers Alliance and their frequent collaborations with the CIW and the Vermont Workers' Center.

When examining the development and goals of the Milk with Dignity program, it becomes less clear where this campaign fits within the categories outlined by Holt-Giménez, Shattuck, Guthman, and Alkon. It could be argued that the Milk with Dignity campaign is reflective of the neoliberal trend, as it emphasizes a market-based solution through the pressures it places on dairy corporations rather than upon the state. While Migrant Justice did not call for a boycott of Ben & Jerry's at any point during the campaign (unlike the UFW, which called for the grape boycott, and the CIW, which has called for boycotts of companies like Wendy's), they repeatedly sought the solidarity of consumers and emphasized the importance of consuming goods that ensure the well-being of workers. However, like the CIW they focus their efforts on pressuring large-scale buyers rather than individual consumers. While Alkon and Guthman's critique of the neoliberal approach in food movements is certainly appropriate in a number of cases, the emphasis on making demands of the state perhaps reveals an implicit assumption that those who would make such demands are able to do so because of the benefits of citizenship. For undocumented workers in Vermont's dairy industry, it has proven more promising to look for solutions in the WSR model rather than calling for reforms to federal policies that largely exempt agricultural workers, particularly immigrant workers, from state protections.[22]

In examining the campaigns and campaign successes of Migrant Justice, it becomes clear that, while the organization is engaging with many of the dominant discourses of the broader food movement, it draws deeper and more specific inspiration from the farmworker movement. The mobilization of Migrant Justice is perhaps the newest chapter in the long history of U.S. farmworker organizing, which first gained national attention through the struggle of the United Farm Workers (UFW), and has since continued through groups like *Pineros y Campesinos Unidos del Noroeste* [Northwest Treeplanters and Farmworkers United], Community to Community Development, *Familias Unidas por la Justicia* [Families United for Justice], and the CIW.[23] Pictures of Cesar Chavez and the UFW eagle flag adorn the walls of the Migrant Justice office, and the National Education Association awarded Migrant Justice their César Chávez Acción y Compromiso Award in 2017. The *grito* that Migrant Justice organizers shout in Vermont's streets— *"Si se puede"*- is borrowed from the mouths of Dolores Huerta and Cesar Chavez, who marched from Delano to Sacramento, California, amongst thousands of farmworkers and their allies. The UFW's emphasis on meeting farmworkers in the fields where they worked has a parallel in the long days of field visits that Migrant Justice organizers pay to dairy workers in Vermont. The marches organized throughout the Milk with Dignity campaign echo the 1966 UFW march during the height of the Delano grape strike.

And yet, despite their inspiration in the work of the UFW, Migrant Justice's tactics are clearly guided more deeply by the newer model of the CIW, in large part because of the ongoing collaboration between the two groups. As a longtime staff member of Migrant Justice explained to me, *"Usamos el grito de UFW, pero el modelo del CIW"* [We use the shout/call of the UFW, but the model of the CIW]. Rather than focusing primarily on organizing through a union structure to demand grower contracts and insist upon a union-certified label, both the CIW and Migrant Justice have demanded change through shifting corporate purchasing practices and putting a structure into place to ensure that those changes are continually monitored and evaluated. In my interview with James from Migrant Justice, he distinguished the work of Migrant Justice and the CIW from that of UFW by stating that while the UFW placed primary emphasis on unionization (perhaps at the expense of ongoing monitoring of workers' rights and working conditions), Migrant Justice and the CIW have focused more energy on the implementation and monitoring of the Codes of Conduct developed by farmworkers, which are guided by the principles of WSR.

The future development and scaling up of the Milk with Dignity program and its human rights framework, even beyond the corporate food system, looks very encouraging given the recent development of the Worker-Driven Social Responsibility (WSR) Network. Founded in 2015, this network aims to "afford protection for the most vulnerable and lowest-wage workers in global supply chains" and is critical of the failures of corporate social responsibility schemes and multistakeholder initiatives that seek to bring in NGOs and other institutions into the processes of setting and monitoring workplace standards.[24] As of late 2017, the WSR Network is comprised of a coordinating committee including the Business and Human Rights Resource Center, the Centro de Trabajadores Unidos en Lucha [The Center for Workers United in Struggle], the Coalition of Immokalee Workers, Migrant Justice, the National Economic and Social Rights Initiative, T'ruah: The Rabbinic Call for Human Rights, and United Students Against Sweatshops.

The WSR statement of principles outlines six main points of the WSR model that must be agreed upon by those who endorse the model.

1. Labor rights initiatives must be worker-driven.
2. Obligations for global corporations must be binding and enforceable.
3. Buyers must afford suppliers the financial incentive and capacity to comply.
4. Consequences for non-compliant suppliers must be mandatory.
5. Gains for workers must be measurable and timely.
6. Verification of workplace compliance must be rigorous and independent.[25]

According to WSR Network, this model offers a completely different solution to human rights abuses within global supply chains than corporate social responsibility programs, which, according to their analysis, are more often than not public relations strategies that fail to focus on the needs and priorities of workers. Included in the rights that the WSRN prioritizes are "the right to freedom of association, the right to a safe and healthy work environment (including the right to work free from sexual harassment and sexual violence), and the right to work free of forced labor or violence."[26]

While it is certainly the case that Bangladeshi sweatshop workers and Vermont's farmworkers are worlds apart in how they live and labor, the forces of exploitation are similar. The WSR model is powerful in that it recognizes the common forces that endanger and exploit workers in these disparate supply chains. Showing a healthy distrust for both corporate behavior and state-based enforcement agencies, and concentrating on the knowledge of workers who are in the best position to speak about workplace conditions, WSR represents a compelling possibility for rendering visible and eliminating the egregious abuses of human rights that persist in the supply chains that deliver the consumable goods that we all have come to expect. Whether it is Ben & Jerry's ice cream, tomatoes on our hamburgers, or the clothing that we wear, WSR demands that we, as informed consumers, have a critical role in supporting workers and the organizations they are forming and leading. As importantly, the WSR model seeks to complicate a too-neat binary of reform versus radical approaches to social activism, revealing that even approaches that engage with the market can be quite radical if they are guided and led by those with the least social, political, and economic power.

CONCLUSION

On a crisp May first morning, I joined more than three hundred people for the March for Dignity that started with a rally across from the Migrant

Justice office in the Old North End of Burlington and ended with a rally in front of the federal building just north of Burlington's Church Street Marketplace. Along the way, Migrant Justice organizers staged a demonstration and rally in front of Ben & Jerry's flagship store, complete with a skit featuring people in black-and-white dairy cow costumes and an attempt to pack the scoop shop with as many activist bodies as possible. Commemorating International Worker's Day, the crowd was a mixture of Migrant Justice activists, members of the Vermont Workers' Center, students, allies, and members of Brass Balagan, a radical street marching band known for their red jumpsuits and commitment to supporting "anti-imperialist causes." Carrying puppets, banners reading "No Borders, No Wall," and dozens of hand-painted monarch butterflies perched atop long wooden poles, the crowd brought downtown traffic to a crawl and caused onlookers to pause with interest. The crowd was larger than in years past and especially vocal about their disdain of the anti-immigrant rhetoric that was spewing from the newly installed administration in Washington, DC. As a volunteer legal observer decked in a neon green baseball cap bearing the logo of the National Lawyers Guild, I was instructed to keep a neutral stance and keep an eye on the crowd to ensure that any interactions with law enforcement or counter-protestors were recorded in detail. As I have learned more about the injustices facing immigrant workers in our food system, maintaining a neutral stance on this day, or any day, has become supremely challenging.

The small state of Vermont might seem like the least likely place for farm-worker activism to take hold. In the fields of California or Florida, where there is a larger concentration of farmworkers on each individual farm and a larger population of farmworkers overall, it makes sense that unjust conditions would inspire the campaigns of the United Farm Workers or the Coalition of Immokalee Workers. Farmworkers in Vermont face a different reality. Spread around the rural landscape in remote corners of the state, there are a number of geographic, social, and cultural barriers that keep farm-workers separate. What Migrant Justice has accomplished in this context, to bring farmworkers together and make their voices heard, is nothing short of astounding. Building upon the successes and struggles of food and farm-worker activists that have paved the way before them, Migrant Justice is creating change in an industry that for too long has remained dependent upon the exploitation of immigrant labor. Through their campaigns that focus on state and local policy and the innovative Milk with Dignity campaign, their work is making farmworkers and their contributions more visible

FIGURE 16. Difference of opinion. Photo by author.

and recognized, not only in Vermont but internationally. In doing so, they are creating new possibilities for food justice that are defined by those who are most familiar with the injustice in our food system.

During events like the March for Dignity or the public signing of the Milk with Dignity campaign, Migrant Justice brings farmworkers from the invisible margins to the visible center. The bodies whose labor sustains the dairy industry join with other bodies, those of workers, allies, religious leaders, and students. This joining together reminds us of the power of collective action and working across cultural and economic borders. The symbol of the monarch butterfly, which has become central to the struggle for immigrant rights, reminds us that just as borders are built to keep others out, they can be remade to welcome them in. And not just as workers, but as people with agency, dreams, families, and purpose.

Conclusion

> Here it's nice because we have some work and in Guatemala, no.
> But we miss things, like all of our family, because they're all still
> in Guatemala. It's really difficult to be separated from our family,
> but we are obligated to come here.
>
> IRMA, 2016

> There has been a change, since the new president entered. With
> the law that they are going to deport all of the migrants. And
> because of this, a new terror began for us. . . . We don't trust that
> we can go out. And if we go out, we are always looking over our
> shoulder for *la migra* or the police.
>
> MARTÍN, 2017

FOR VERMONT'S FARMWORKERS, FOOD IS EVER PRESENT, even in
its occasional absence. Whether it is a question of the cultural significance of
the foods that farmworkers can access, or the seventy-hour workweeks they
endure to sustain the production of the state's most prized commodity, food
and all that it represents figures heavily into their motivations for migrating
to and the realities of living and working within the northern borderlands.
As I set out on this project to examine food security within Vermont's
migrant farmworker community, I knew that my focus on food would inevitably push me to consider deeper and broader questions. This is the exhilarat-
ing and confounding nature of ethnography—it never fails to lead you to
ideas and theories you weren't expecting, and it is always a story without a
natural end. Concluding this story, one that seems far from over, is exceedingly difficult. Over the coming months and years, I know that many things
will change, in the lives of individual farmworkers, in Vermont's food system,

and in our national conversations about food justice, workers' rights, and immigration. And yet, a book has to end somewhere. Rather than force a complicated story into a falsely neat ending, in this conclusion I have chosen to outline the main areas where this research has pushed me to consider those deeper and broader questions: the promise and complications of doing ethnography at home, the politics of visibility in the borderlands, the everyday meanings of food sovereignty, and the transformative potential of worker-led food movements.

THE PROMISE AND COMPLICATIONS OF DOING ETHNOGRAPHY AT HOME

It seems the anthropologist always finds herself in the throes of theoretical and methodological crises. Whether we are wringing our hands about the process and politics of representation, the postcolonial situation, or questions of ontology, anthropologists seem to be a pretty nervy bunch. Having (justifiably) come under fire for so many years because of our ugly imperialist and racist histories and present days, we vacillate between turning inwards to our navels and outwards towards village X with a rather schizophrenic pace. We mumble about finding the self in the Other, the Other in the self, all while drafting our next research proposals and studying the latest developments in voice recorder technology.

From the time of Bronislaw Malinowski observing the Trobriand Islanders from the door of his tent, field methods have been contaminated by what Paul Rabinow calls intersubjective symbolic violence.[1] Ethnographic research has been rightly critiqued for its imperialist and colonizing tendencies. Much of this critique centers upon the power inequalities that are inherent in all field research, with the researcher historically being the one in the position of power. Nevertheless, field research still remains the hallmark of cultural anthropology, and it is rare for the cultural anthropologist to earn her wings without going into the "field" somewhere. Since I was a graduate student, I have made the conscious decision to develop my field research projects close to home. This orientation has put me into a certain category of anthropologist, and I sometimes still have the feeling that my fieldwork isn't quite *real* enough, that the old standards of taking antimalarial pills and cruising around in NSF-funded Land Rovers are still somehow the expectation. Perhaps needless to say, antimalarial pills are not necessary when researching on Vermont's dairy farms, though a Land Rover would sometimes come in handy during mud season.

· My decision to do local ethnography was guided by my first field experiences on the Pine Ridge Reservation in South Dakota nearly twenty years ago, a place that continues to experience the deep and painful legacies of colonization. Through this project, I witnessed the long-term relationships that my undergraduate advisor had developed with her research participants and the obligations that came along with these relationships. As a former public defender, she was often called to interpret legal documents, assist with land claims, and more often than not, serve as a taxi service around the remote rural reservation. These obligations were not bounded by the official summer field season; they remained in place even while she was at home teaching and advancing up the tenure track. While these obligations were time consuming and often demanded great patience on her part, they revealed to me the immense amount of trust and respect that she had earned over the decades she has worked there. This was a formative exposure to fieldwork for me, and I was no longer able to think of my own research outside of this model.

As I write this conclusion I am sitting at my kitchen table looking out at a frigid Vermont winter day, less than two miles away from the Mack Farm and within a seventy-five-minute drive from the homes of all the farmworkers whose stories have appeared in the preceding chapters. More than five years ago, I joined with Migrant Justice organizers to rally against the substandard working conditions at this farm, and as I drive by it multiple times each week, this memory is always close at hand. No matter where I go in Vermont, whether it's the dairy aisle at my local grocery store or the state's only taco truck unexpectedly located in the middle of a corn field, I am constantly reminded of the proximity of my research. I sometimes envy my colleagues who pack up at the end of the field season, putting hundreds or even thousands of miles between their academic offices and their field sites, allowing them a critical distance to pore over their field notes and interview transcripts as they coax their findings into academic prose. At the same time, I have found that I thrive on the continual blurring of home and field. For me, the constant reminders of the significance of my research are motivating and productive, even as they sometimes test personal and professional boundaries. On some days, this proximity has meant that I can squeeze in an interview before teaching my afternoon classes; on others, I can run down the hill from campus to engage in participant observation at an immigrant rights march, where some of my interviewees are leading the charge. At the same time, this proximity sometimes leads me, and my husband, to wonder when I am off the clock and when I am on.

In the ever-changing fields of food systems, migration, and border studies, ethnography offers an especially promising approach to analyze systems of power, inequality, and meaning. As a set of intentional—yet unpredictable—practices grounded in everyday life, ethnography allows researchers to hold everyday experience and broader social and cultural processes in constant tension and gain insight into their interconnections. When doing ethnography close to home, the researcher learns more about her own community and her place within it. However, like all fieldwork, this kind of ethnography is not immune from considerations of power. Throughout this project, I have struggled to come to terms with the wide gulfs of power and privilege that exist between farmworkers and myself. As I drive to and from interviews or garden visits, I must contemplate my own freedom of movement and the unearned privileges that come from my citizenship, ethnicity, profession, and social class. As I do my own grocery shopping, I must recognize the security of my own food access and the nearly unlimited choices I make over what I consume. These differences of power and privilege frequently push me to reflect upon the true motivations for this research. Why not "study up," as Laura Nader would encourage me to do, turning my gaze instead to the behemoth dairy corporations and conglomerates who profit off migrant labor?

While I agree with the importance of studying those in power, I also believe in the potentials of developing solidarity and forming alliances through critical ethnography with those not in power, those who demonstrate remarkable resiliency and autonomy in less visible ways. The role of the ethnographer, in this case, is to bring greater attention to this resiliency and autonomy so that we might interrogate power relationships more deeply, with the ultimate goal of challenging them. In this vein, I have drawn inspiration from ethnographers who call for "an anthropology of liberation," inhabiting a "space of betweenness," and a critical ethnography that moves from politics to a "politics of positionality."[2] As an ethnographer whose positionality and research objectives are inseparable from my politics, the insights of these critical thinkers have been instrumental in carrying out this project.

Nearly thirty years ago, critical ethnographer Faye Harrison called for an anthropology of liberation that must "subvert the established discipline and lay the foundation for a new field of inquiry . . . based on conscious political choices about standing on the side of struggle and transformation."[3] Cindi

Katz echoes Harrison and argues for a re-envisioned ethnography, because it "offers the possibility of traveling intellectually and strategically between the macrological structures of power—that is, the global processes of capitalism, imperialism, and patriarchy—and the micrological textures of power played out in the material social practices of everyday life."[4] As we consider how research is both transected by and located within relationships of power, critical ethnographers must reflexively question how our writing and research either enables or prohibits marginalized voices from being heard. In transforming our objective as critical ethnographers from "mere politics" to a "politics of positionality," Soyini Madison argues that self-reflexively turning the ethnographic gaze back upon ourselves forces us to become accountable for our analyses and representations.[5] For Madison, this does not mean that in our analysis, we can avoid speaking for others, but rather we must foreground and amplify their words and narratives to the best of our abilities. This book is the result of my attempts to follow the guidance of these groundbreaking ethnographers.

Conducting a study grounded in the local community has presented me with an opportunity to craft my skills as a researcher and as an ally in the movement for food justice and immigrant rights. Crafting these sides of my self has required me to (sometimes unsuccessfully) balance time commitments, professional and personal relationships, and critique with compassion. It has pushed me to consider whose side I am on, and how a question as mundane as what ends up on a farmworker's dinner plate is linked to the histories and materialities of transnational politics and movements. Through this project I have also learned a tremendous amount about the potentials of engaged research to facilitate dialogue and open up possibilities for social change within the food system. While I do not view this project as participatory research in the truest sense of the word, I have worked hard to make it not only relevant but also useful to my community. By sharing my findings with Migrant Justice, at local Hunger Council meetings, at events coordinated by UVM Extension, and through a number of other local venues, I hope that in some small way, I have helped to challenge the politics of visibility that continues to silence the voices and erase the experiences of farmworkers in the state. Most significantly, my ongoing work with Huertas and with Migrant Justice has provided me with the opportunity to take what I have learned about the particular forms of vulnerability and resilience that are evident in the farmworker community and become part of the movement that is creating change in our local food system.

Throughout the preceding chapters, I have argued that a politics of visibility keeps farmworkers who live and labor in the northern borderlands invisible in their workplaces and hypervisible in public. The perpetual erasure of farmworkers from representations of Vermont's working landscape borders farmworkers into marginality and fails to acknowledge their significant contributions to the state's agricultural economy. Due to the dominant whiteness of the state's rural areas, farmworkers are viewed as outsiders when they do venture into public spaces—as different, as speakers of a foreign tongue. In this respect, Vermont presents a much different reality from other agricultural regions with longer histories of migration from Latin America and more socially and culturally integrated Latinx communities. As farmworker organizing efforts have gained traction over the last several years, the veil of invisibility has been lifted by and for some farmworkers at key points in the campaigns for bias-free policing, driver's licenses, and Milk with Dignity. The visibility and recognition of farmworker struggle has been key to the successes of these campaigns yet has resulted in the increased surveillance of vocal farmworker activists. As I write this, we are in a period of increased hostility against immigrants that is endorsed by and circulating within the highest levels of our government; there is growing concern that immigrant activists are being targeted for deportation. Just this past week, ICE arrested fourteen construction workers in a raid at the Vermont hotel where they were staying. This mounting hostility and fear is both pushing Vermont's farmworkers deeper into the shadows and simultaneously making farmworker organizing and the building of alliances even more momentous and necessary.

When I embarked upon this project, I knew from my previous research that building trust and rapport would be crucial when working on matters of immigration and food security. What I was not prepared for was the degree to which immigrant households were feeling the impact of living and working so close to the border. As so many do, I had a vision of Vermont as some sort of green utopia, a place where the Bernie Sanders ethos spread far and wide and the model of local democracy allowed progressiveness and acceptance to flourish. In some aspects, there is truth to this vision, and there is a sense of political possibility in Vermont that might be out of reach in a redder state. And yet this vision is tempered by the reality that Vermont is still a border state. Whatever progressiveness might exist at the local and state level only stretches up to the very real physical border that divides this nation from our northern neighbors. For those who have crossed at least one national border to find work in the state's dairy industry, this Other Border figures heavily into every choice they make about meeting their basic needs.

Though my research has focused primarily upon food access, discussions of the border arose in nearly all of the food security surveys and household interviews I completed. Farmworkers often shared their experiences of crossing the border into the United States, emphasizing the economic realities that pushed them out of their home communities in Mexico and Guatemala. However, these interviews also revealed that the U.S.-Canada border shapes their daily experiences in immediate ways if not in equal ones. When the decision to go to the grocery store or out for a quick meal is always and necessarily bound up with the risks of encountering Border Patrol or ICE personnel, access to food or any other basic need is severely compromised. This fear and anxiety is painfully but precisely described by farmworkers who experience life in Vermont as *encerrado,* as prisoners to the iconic dairy farms that are celebrated in images of the state's working landscape. This feeling of being *encerrado* underscores that borders are ever present in the lives of farmworkers and manifest at multiple levels—around the dairy farm, within the U.S-Canada borderlands, and at the national divisions between the United States and their country of origin.

As farmworkers experience the proximity and reality of the border on a daily basis, service providers too feel its presence. As they work tirelessly to provide access to health care, food, and transportation options, both providers in the fields of public health and nutrition programming and volunteers understand that the work they do is made both necessary and more difficult by the particular geography of the borderlands. Throughout the duration of this project, service providers working in different counties of the state have expressed that working with farmworkers is much more difficult and risky in the border counties compared to places like Addison County, which is just over an hour south. Farmworkers who had lived in both areas echoed this, with those living and working further south often expressing sympathy for those in the northern part of the state. These particularities of geography remind us that all landscapes must be examined with an attention to the lived realities of space and place, realities which are inherently shaped by differences of race citizenship, and other markers of identity.

Amidst the growing fears and anxieties following the 2016 U.S. presidential election, these geographic dynamics have shifted. It often seems like no place in the country, let alone Vermont, is a safe place for immigrants. As of early 2018 the federal government is embroiled in a debate over the Deferred Action for Childhood Arrivals (DACA) program, and our commander in chief is instructing the Department of Justice to explore the possibility of charging state and local officials with criminal charges if they implement or enforce sanctuary policies in their jurisdictions. While the legality—and morality—of these proposals is contested, the message they send is deeply symbolic: undocumented immigrants are not welcome, and those who stand in solidarity with them will be likewise subjected to the power of the state. This kind of fear-mongering perpetuates the processes of bordering that increasingly extend from the lines dividing nation-states to the "borders within" that immigrants experience even on a psychological level. As is so often the case, those who are arguing for stronger borders and stricter immigration policies fail to consider the ramifications of these policies on our food system.

While farmworkers in Vermont experience a unique confluence of historical, economic, and cultural factors, what unites their struggles with those of farmworkers around the United States is their invisibility in most mainstream discussions of food and immigration. Although academics and activists have long called for attention to the contributions of farmworkers and their daily struggles, popular food authors such as Michael Pollan and Mark Bittman have only recently used their platforms to remind us that considerations of our food system are inseparable from considerations of labor. While greater visibility is crucial, there is no easy answer to the predicament that is now confronting immigrant workers in our food system. According to the Bread for the World Institute, more than 70 percent of U.S. farmworkers are foreign-born, about one-third of meatpackers are immigrants, and an estimated 10 percent of restaurant workers are immigrants.[6] All of these figures are likely underestimates, given the off-the-books arrangements that many immigrant workers have with their employers.

In Vermont, as in all states across the nation, there is serious concern about who will fill these positions in our food system should there be the promised ramping up of border enforcement and an increase in deportations of the "bad hombres" that are said to be invading our country. In a time of increased hysteria about our borders, what this anti-immigrant rhetoric fails to account for is how dependent our food security is on immigrant workers and the complex political-economic histories that have left millions of Latin Americans with limited livelihood options back home. We are fed due to the labor of individuals who have been dispossessed in their home countries, only to be further exploited as workers in the U.S. food system. In a cruel twist, the continued invisibility of farmworkers and food workers is crucial to maintaining the violent status quo of how food makes it from farm to plate. The borderlands of Vermont represent a microcosm of what is taking place at the national level with respect to immigration and food, with the industrial dairy economy jostling for center stage with the exciting developments in more localized and sustainable models. As we move forward with supporting the more sustainable models, we must not forget the needs of those who sustain the industrial ones.

THE EVERYDAY MEANINGS OF FOOD SOVEREIGNTY

It is likely that living and working conditions will improve for some of Vermont's farmworkers because of the Milk With Dignity program, but there is also little doubt that farmworkers in the dairy industry will continue to be marginalized as the pressures for industrial consolidation and further industrialization inevitably increase. Even as marginality is isolating and exploitative, it also creates the spaces for resilience, for struggle, and for autonomy. Extending the discussion that began in Robert Park's 1928 work on the "inventive force" of marginality, Devon Peña challenges the sociological representations of the marginal as living in a state of isolation or anomie.[7] He views "marginals as liminal beings full of creative and transformative potential. They are fully capable of expressing their own voices and in doing so can challenge and undermine dominant views and ideologies."[8] In the gardens that farmworkers cultivate with the support of Huertas, we see the transformative potential of developing and sustaining deeper relationships with food, even within a community whose labor is dedicated to the production of a mass commodity. For individuals coming from agrarian backgrounds, these gardens provide a bridge to a livelihood and an identity that is in danger of being lost or forgotten as each generation moves further from its past, both geographically and temporally.

It is true that the gardens that Huertas helps to cultivate are small in scale and are limited by a short growing season and the busy schedules associated with working in a milking barn. Nevertheless, the program continues to see considerable success more than eight years since its informal beginning. Many of the farmworkers whom I first met in 2012 continue to grow gardens with support of the program. Each year, we see new households becoming involved. This enduring involvement and the constant interest that the program generates within the farmworker community point to the deep meaning that these gardens hold for the gardeners, who cannot wait for the ground to thaw after a long winter so they can start planting. From my interviews with Huertas participants, audio recordings and written transcriptions cannot capture the smiles that are shared when people explain the dishes from home they create with the produce grown in their garden or the eyes that light up when they describe sharing these dishes with their U.S.-born children. The pride of growing black beans from seed and then preparing tamales from these same beans is better expressed through nonverbal cues of communication and the communal consumption of those tamales, rather than the words shared in an in-depth interview. The benefit of ongoing field research is that I have had the good fortune to bear witness to these stories and experiences of food sovereignty and the contexts in which they unfold. Through sharing in many of the meals that result from these gardens, I have quite literally ingested their richness and meaning. It is my hope that the stories that I have shared in the preceding chapters have helped to make the connections between gardeners and what they produce more three-dimensional and illustrative of this meaning.

Amy Trauger argues that food sovereignty is embodied in "small, but significant acts of defiance, as well as through acts of kindness and love."[9] Set against an industrial food system that is determined to homogenize our sustenance and flatten the cultural richness of food, the acts of defiance, kindness, and love that emanate from farmworker gardens represent a form of food sovereignty that is everyday—not spectacular—and embedded in small pieces of land that are not owned by those who cultivate them. For clear and obvious reasons, the food sovereignty movement, as articulated in the Declaration of Nyéléni, has emphasized that the rights to use and manage land and the other resources needed to produce food should be in the control of food producers. Vermont's farmworkers are in no way in charge of the means of production, and the dairies where they work are certainly not under their control, even if their labor is necessary for their continued production. However, the gardens that Huertas supports are under their control, even if in a tenuous and often impermanent way, and even if the land is owned by their employer. This bifurcated relationship to land and to food signals that even in the most marginal of circumstances, the possibility for agency and autonomy exists.

In my work codirecting Huertas and engaging in ethnographic research with many of the participating farmworkers, I have had the opportunity to witness not only the connections that are made through and in the gardens themselves but also the personal relationships that are built between gardeners and the volunteers for the project. While our internship program is certainly far from perfect, the friendships and alliances that have developed over time point to the transformative potential of experiential learning that is carefully designed to benefit all parties involved. At its heart, food sovereignty is about connection. Connection to place, connection to food, and connection to community. In our work with Huertas, we often share that the food grown in the gardens we help to build is the by-product of the social connections we are attempting to forge. For farmworkers grappling with deep and painful experiences of isolation and social disconnection, these connections are what inspire us to continue with our project, even as we face a number of obstacles related to ongoing funding and other forms of support.

When we started the Huertas project, we were guided by the discourse of food security. And even now, as we apply for small sources of funding, this is the term that we typically use because of its coherence in the world of food systems and nutrition. However, as Eric Holt-Giménez emphasizes, food sovereignty goes deeper than food security, reaching into more fundamental questions of choice, democracy, and power. As we have planned and planted gardens over the last several years, we have increasingly been guided by these deeper meanings that food sovereignty calls for. This has altered the way we run Huertas, moving from a rather top-down system of delivering extra plants to putting most of our energies into collecting information from farmworkers about the exact number and types of plants they would like to grow. This has moved us from getting participants involved at the time of planting to instead having some participants work alongside Huertas staff and volunteers in the greenhouse, as we collectively sweat under a hot June sun to divide seeds and seedlings into groups destined to be delivered to each farmworker household. However, I still ask myself: What would it take for Huertas to become fully and completely guided by the principles and priorities of food sovereignty? The best answer that I can come up with is that we, as Huertas staff, would need to become obsolete, because farmworkers gained the ability to take over the reins of the project. But this would necessitate a different kind of borderlands environment and a level of freedom that currently seems out of reach in our political climate.

In chapter 2, I shared the story of Andrés, a single father from Chiapas who has lived and worked in Vermont since 2011. I described how Andrés and his son form a tightly knit bond that benefits from the son's fluency in

English and the father's dedication to ensuring his son is loved and well cared for. What did not appear in that chapter was a description of Andrés's garden, which in hindsight is a bit surprising to me, given that I have known him as long as I have been involved with Huertas and that his participation in the program has endured over the years. In this garden, Andrés has put into practice years of experience growing food, both in Mexico and the United States, and a wealth of traditional ecological knowledge. When reflecting on this omission as I conclude this book, I realize that I have yet to come to terms with Andrés's painful decision to not plant his garden in 2017, just a few months after the inauguration of Donald Trump.

Located just next to the small state highway that wraps by his home, Andrés's garden was a lovingly tended space that produced a wealth of food for his family. This space now remains empty, a tangle of expired plants from the previous years. In early 2017, Andrés decided to stop gardening because of the heightened fears and anxieties that he has experienced since the presidential election. He is concerned, rightly so, that working in this proximate but visible space will put him at risk of being seen by Border Patrol. He is unwilling to take this risk because of his concern for his son. In learning about his decision, my Huertas colleagues and I were heartbroken and enraged. We were heartbroken that a man who demonstrates such a clear love of growing food feels afraid to do so. We were enraged that this fear is enabled by a growing hostility towards immigrants and an ever-more violent criminalization of their existence. While Andrés's fears are shared by most other farmworkers, he is—for now—the only person who has decided not to garden because of these fears. In this story we see another side of food sovereignty: the violent denial of it.

THE TRANSFORMATIVE POTENTIAL
OF WORKER-LED FOOD MOVEMENTS

Despite the very real inequalities that continue to dominate the lives of migrant workers across the U.S. industrial food system, we find ourselves in a moment where food is at the center of calls for social change and greater equity. Farmworker-led movements have a long and compelling history in the United States, and the struggles of Filipino and Latinx farmworkers who joined together to transform California's grape industry with the United Farm Workers planted a seed that is now carefully tended by groups like the

Coalition of Immokalee Workers and Migrant Justice. The emerging Worker-Driven Social Responsibility Network, to which both CIW and Migrant Justice belong, promises to unite workers across different sectors to ensure that their voices and priorities are front and center in any attempt to improve workplace conditions. This approach recognizes the agency and knowledge that even the most marginalized of workers possesses, from Vermont's dairy farms to garment factories in Bangladesh.

The Milk with Dignity program represents the first attempt to apply the worker-driven social responsibility model within the dairy industry and is the first successful attempt to replicate the approach taken by CIW within a new sector of agriculture. As dairy farmworkers in the Northwest, New York, and Wisconsin start to organize and demand improved working conditions, extending the WSR model across the dairy industry could help to improve the working conditions of those who produce a key commodity. In Washington, Oregon, and Idaho, farmworkers in the Darigold supply chain have organized with the United Farm Workers since 2014 to challenge the poor conditions that both workers and cows face on Darigold farms. In New York State, the Workers' Center of Central New York and the Worker Justice Center of New York have produced a comprehensive report entitled *Milked* that documents the dangerous working conditions on New York's farms and provides a set of well-informed recommendations to eliminate the exploitation of migrant farmworkers in the state. In Wisconsin, the plight of dairy farmworkers has received renewed attention since the election of Donald Trump; grave concerns exist about the survival of the industry in the event that immigrant workers are increasingly targeted by immigration enforcement. In these key dairy-producing states, adopting and adapting the Milk with Dignity model would have real potential for workers in one of the most dangerous sectors of agricultural labor to unite in demands for more comprehensive and sustained change.

As is evident through Migrant Justice's long campaign for Ben & Jerry's to implement the Milk with Dignity program, it is clear that sustained public pressure will always be needed to bring large corporations into alignment with the demands of workers. For a company like Ben & Jerry's, with a stated commitment to social and environmental causes, accepting the Milk with Dignity agreement and ensuring the fair treatment of workers in the dairy supply chain seemed only natural, if only to protect their image and brand. Indeed, this is why Migrant Justice chose Ben & Jerry's as the first target for a program they hope to expand to other companies and brands in the coming years. As seen in the comments by Ben & Jerry's CEO Jostein Solheim that appeared in the introduction to chapter 5, the company was quick to include their participation in the Milk with Dignity program into their brand messaging following the signing of the contract. For companies with a less evident social mission, finding the best leverage points to bring them into agreement with the principles of WSR requires in-depth investigation and attention to the values of their consumer base.

Across the hyperconsolidated and industrialized dairy industry, the branding that is sold to the consumer continues to focus on the image of the small-scale family farm. Indeed, an anthropomorphized Holstein is much more likely to appear on the label of a milk carton than a farmworker from Chiapas, Mexico. For WSR approaches like Milk with Dignity to fundamentally alter the conditions of production, the first hurdle to overcome is the invisibility of the workforce who sustain the dairy industry. According to a 2015 study conducted for the National Milk Producers Federation, 79 percent of the U.S. milk supply was produced on farms using immigrant labor.[10] Despite this dependence on immigrant workers, it can be safely assumed that the average consumer knows little about the challenges these workers face in the food system, and even less about the conditions that pushed them to migrate in the first place. Where the CIW has been so incredibly successful is in rendering more visible and transparent the supply chains that provide large corporations with key ingredients for their products. Consumers have an important role to play in demanding more transparency in the routes that food takes from the farm to their plates.

Critiques have been raised about consumer-led food movements, and the unfairness of the calls to "vote with your fork" is evident when wealthy consumers have more of a say about what they ingest than those with less purchasing power. However, increased consumer involvement and worker-led food movements are not mutually exclusive. What I have learned through my years of studying and participating in food movements is that the problems are too great to be approached through one tactic alone. To dismantle the unsustainable practices that plague our food system—from the chemicals that are used on fields to the sick days that food chain workers have access to—we must launch our attack from all sides. We must balance our demands for structural policy reform with our demands for change in the private sector and be strategic about the best timing for each. At the same time, if just labor conditions are to be central to a just food system, consumers must take the lead from food system workers who have the best vantage point about the changes that are most necessary. A key challenge is developing platforms for workers to share their experiences, both with each other and with the broader public. The Milk with Dignity program has seen success so far precisely because farmworker leaders have developed these platforms and have made their voices heard.

While there is still a long way to go for farmworkers in Vermont to gain dignity in the workplace and full social integration, Migrant Justice and their allies have not just talked about conditions in the dairy industry but have taken concrete steps to improve them. Many Migrant Justice leaders are called upon to speak at public events, receive awards that recognize their successes, and participate in conversations within Vermont's local and state government about the development and reform of policies that impact farmworkers. When any issue relevant to immigration or labor rights becomes newsworthy, their perspective is sought and their expertise is recognized. Their impact is not limited to the state of Vermont, however, as the organization is recognized not just locally but across the country for leadership in the food justice movement. For a small grassroots organization that began less than ten years ago, their successes in transforming the food system are remarkable and, with the hopeful success of the Milk with Dignity program, will only continue to grow.

SOME FINAL THOUGHTS

Throughout this book, I have aimed to foreground the voices and experiences of Vermont's farmworkers and their families. I have done so with the goal of portraying these individuals in complex ways that acknowledge that they are much more than just workers, even as their lives are often governed by the work they do. They are members of loving families with enduring ties to their home communities in Latin America and to those who remain there. They are fierce and resilient activists who demand dignity and fairness in the workplace. They are mothers and fathers who, through their labor on dairy farms and in the home, pursue the vision of greater opportunities for their children. They are not criminals, even as they are criminalized. They are not bringing problems but rather sustaining our food system. They are not coming from "shithole" countries but rather have made the difficult decision to leave places that have experienced long histories of dispossession, colonization, and violence.

Engaging with the framework of Bordering Visible Bodies has allowed me to situate the narratives and experiences of individual farmworkers within a structural analysis that examines the politics of visibility that farmworkers encounter while living and working in the borderlands. In viewing the border as both a place and as a process, I have shown the impact that the physical site of the border—and the processes of border making—have on the daily realities of farmworkers and their access to basic needs. Examining these realities through the lens of food has provided both the material and symbolic grounds for understanding the complex relationships between people and what sustains them. Activists and scholars in the food system are leading the charge to understand and transform how food makes its way from farm to plate. In the context of a food system riddled with both deep contradictions and exciting possibilities, this book has examined the lives of workers who are working to put food on the table in a distinctive but not entirely unique place. While there are particularities, this story is not exclusive to Vermont. It is a story that can be heard wherever food is harvested, cooked, or served by immigrant hands.

It is important to me that the last words in this book are not my own, but rather those of a farmworker. In an interview with Jesús, a man from Chiapas who had worked on a Vermont dairy farm for four years, the topics of conversation ranged from the foods he missed from home to his analysis of structural racism. Towards the end of the interview, Jesús reflected:

> The line between Mexico and the states, it's something very hard, very difficult. They are more vigilant now because of so many people. You have no idea how many people try to cross daily to look for a better future for our family. For our sons, for our parents, searching for a better situation economically. And we are thousands and thousands of Latinos, not just Mexicans but also South Americans who come. That's why they protect the border so much. And every day it becomes more dangerous and harder to cross and come into the states. I don't know if you have seen in the news, but a lot of the police are racist and they don't like the Hispanics. Also, it is not just the police, there are a lot of citizens who are racist. They see a Hispanic or a Black man and they are always looking at them like they are making trouble and will call immigration or the police. That's why daily the lives of Hispanics are becoming more difficult.
>
> I have always said that no one is indispensable in this world. We all need each other, in one way or another, we need each other's help. There are racist people but they need people, they need help from the Hispanics. Often times they would rather hire Americans, but then they will regret it, because not many Americans will work as many hours. They will only work eight hours, and if they work more . . . they will ask for more money. But for us what we want is to work, we have family in Mexico, we want something better. That is the difference.

Semi-Structured Interview Guide for Farmworkers

EATING/PREFERENCES

1. Tell me about what you ate today and yesterday or describe a typical day of eating for you.
   a. How has this changed since living in your country of origin?
2. Tell me about your cultural food preferences.
   a. Do you have special foods for your religion?
3. Tell me about obtaining and preparing the ingredients for
   a. your favorite meal,
   b. a typical meal,
   c. a holiday meal.
4. What guides your decisions in picking out food?

HOUSEHOLD STRUCTURE

5. Who does the majority of shopping and cooking in your household?
   a. Why do you organize the work in this way?
6. Do you share foods or resources for getting food (such as federal vouchers) with other people outside of the household? If so, how do you go about sharing?
7. Do members of your household have different food preferences and/or needs?

FOOD ACCESS

8. Where do you obtain the majority of your food?

9. Does your food consumption change based on the season, and if so, how?
    a. What about over the course of a month?
10. Do you get any of your food through hunting/fishing/gathering?
11. Where else do you go for food?
12. Are there any foods that you have trouble accessing, and why?
13. Do you feel like you have enough money to purchase the food that you need?
14. Do you have any challenges in eating a diet that is varied and nutritious?
    a. If yes, what are they?
15. Does your household utilize any food-related programs? For example, WIC or food stamps.
    a. If so, which ones? What are your thoughts on these programs?
16. Do you or your house have a garden?

If they do have a garden, continue on to this section.

17. How has the garden impacted your access to food?
18. Are you growing anything in the garden that you cannot find at the store?
    a. Are you growing anything special to your culture?
19. What other roles does the garden play in your life?
    a. Do you feel that participating in Huertas has contributed to your sense of community?

MIGRATION

20. Please tell me about your motivations for migrating to the United States.
21. Could you talk a bit about your experience migrating?
22. Was food security a motivation for your decision to migrate to the USA?
    a. Was it hard to provide food for you and/or your family in the country from where you migrated?

APPENDIX 2

Semi-Structured Interview Guide for Service Providers

1. What are the programs/services/products that this organization/agency/farm /retail outlet provides?
2. What do you perceive to be the food needs of Latino/a immigrants in Vermont?
3. How does this organization/agency/farm / retail outlet respond to these needs?
4. What resources do you provide to Latino/a immigrants or Spanish-speaking individuals?
5. Do you believe that the needs of Latino/a immigrants have changed over time?
6. Do you believe that the food needs of Latino/a immigrants are unique in relation to other communities in Vermont?
7. What are the challenges that this organization/agency/farm / retail outlet faces with respect to working with the Latino/a community?
8. What are the opportunities that are presented to this organization/agency/farm /retail outlet working with the Latino/a community?

NOTES

INTRODUCTION

1. In this book I use *Latinx* as a gender-neutral term to refer to individuals and communities of Latin American descent. Other terms, including Latino/a, Hispano/a, Mexicano/a, also appear throughout the book, particularly when quoting interviewees and discussing how they describe their own ethnic and racial identities. I have chosen to use Latinx in order to be inclusive of multiple and pluralistic gendered identities and sexual orientations, while also recognizing the complicated and contested nature of all terms.

2. For useful critiques of the local/global binary, see Born and Purcell, "Avoiding the Local Trap"; Gray, *Labor and the Locavore;* and Guthman, *Agrarian Dreams.*

3. Garcia, DuPuis, and Mitchell, *Food across Borders,* 1.

4. Anzaldúa, *Borderlands,* preface.

5. For definitions and critiques of the terms *deterritorialization* and *reterritorialization,* see Deleuze and Guattari, "Anti-Œdipus"; Elden, "Missing the Point."

6. Paasi, "Shifting Landscape of Border Studies."

7. Paasi, "Bounded Spaces in a 'Borderless World,'" 215.

8. Johnson et al., "Interventions on Rethinking 'the Border,'" 62.

9. Baker and Chappelle, "Health Status and Needs"; McCandless, "Conserving the Landscapes of Vermont"; Wolcott-MacCausland, "Health Access Negotiations."

10. The five places named in this sentence are discussed respectively in Latham, "Governance of Visibility"; Winders, "Seeing Immigrants"; Nelson, "Farmworker Housing"; Licona and Maldonado, "Social Production"; and Esbenshade, "The 'Crisis' over Day Labor."

11. For extended discussions of the ways that nativist discourses construct immigrant bodies as contaminating the body politic, see Chavez, *The Latino Threat;* Cisneros, "Contaminated Communities"; Molina, *Fit to Be Citizens?.*

12. Licona and Maldonado, "Social Production," 520.

13. Casper and Moore, *Missing Bodies,* 3.

14. Giroux, "Reading Hurricane Katrina."

15. Mintz, *Sweetness and Power.*

16. ACLU of Vermont, "Surveillance on the Northern Border."

17. McCandless, "Conserving the Landscapes of Vermont."

18. Secure Communities is federal program implemented under the second Bush administration but expanded under Obama that facilitates the sharing of fingerprints and other data collected by local police agencies with ICE aiding in deportations.

19. Bromage, "Shumlin Says VT Should 'Look the Other Way.'"

20. Harvey, *Brief History,* 2.

21. Campbell and Hendricks, "NAFTA and Dumping"; Patel, *Stuffed and Starved*; Relinger, "NAFTA and US Corn Subsidies."

22. Baumann, "Mexican Farmers"; Freidberg, *Fresh.*

23. McDonald, "NAFTA and the Milking of Dairy Farmers"; Shields, *Consolidation and Concentration .*

24. In the state of Vermont, a class action antitrust complaint was filed in 2009 against Dairy Farmers of America, Inc., Dairy Marketing Services, Dean Foods, and HP Hood. The lawsuit charged these four parties of conspiring to lower the milk prices received by farmers.

25. Parsons, "Vermont's Dairy Sector."

26. Vermont Dairy Promotion Council, *Milk Matters.*

27. Radel, Schmook, and McCandless, "Environment, Transnational Labor Migration, and Gender"; Wolcott-MacCausland and Shea, conversation with author, May 2016.

28. Sifuentez, *Of Fields and Forests.*

29. Hinrichs, "Consuming Images."

30. Heintz, "Selling the Herd"; Sneyd, "Total Number"; Vermont Dairy Promotion Council, *Milk Matters.*

31. Heintz, "Selling the Herd."

32. Parsons, "Vermont's Dairy Sector."

33. Decena and Gray, "The Border Next Door"; Nicholson, "Without Their Children"; Parra and Pfeffer, "New Immigrants in Rural Communities"; Sexsmith, "'But We Can't Call 911.'"

34. Andreas, "Mexicanization of the US-Canada Border."

35. Keller, Gray, and Harrison, "Milking Workers, Breaking Bodies"; Radel, Schmook, and McCandless, "Environment, Transnational Labor Migration, and Gender."

36. Wolcott-MacCausland, *Vermont Dairy Farms.*

37. Wolcott-MacCausland.

38. Food Chain Workers Alliance, "Hands That Feed Us."

39. At the time that this chapter was written, dairy workers are not eligible for the H-2A visa given that they work year round and this program is designed for seasonal work permits. Elected representatives in Vermont, most notably U.S. Senator Patrick Leahy, have proposed to expand the program to include dairy workers.

40. Hertz, "USDA ERS—Farm Labor."

41. Hertz.

42. Hertz; Kandel, "Profile of Hired Farmworkers"; Southern Poverty Law Center, "Injustice on Our Plates."

43. Southern Poverty Law Center.

44. National Center for Farmworker Health, "Agricultural Worker Factsheet."

45. Hertz, "USDA ERS—Farm Labor"; Kandel, "Profile of Hired Farmworkers"; National Center for Farmworker Health.

46. Kandel.

47. Kandel; Southern Poverty Law Center, "Injustice on Our Plates."

48. Food Chain Workers Alliance defines a livable wage as 150 percent of the Lower Living Standard Income Level (LLSIL) for a family of three. This level varies depending on region. See Food Chain Workers Alliance, "Hands That Feed Us."

49. National Agriculture Workers Survey, "Income and Poverty."

50. Food Chain Workers Alliance, "Hands That Feed Us."

51. Migrant Justice, "Milk With Dignity Campaign."

52. Kandel, "Profile of Hired Farmworkers."

53. Southern Poverty Law Center, "Injustice on Our Plates."

54. Southern Poverty Law Center.

55. This is likely to be an underestimate, because the Bureau of Labor Statistics keeps certain fatality information confidential and the eventual cause of death is not always linked back to chemical exposure.

56. Southern Poverty Law Center, "Injustice on Our Plates."

57. Kandel, "Profile of Hired Farmworkers"; Southern Poverty Law Center.

58. Southern Poverty Law Center.

59. Bon Appétit and United Farm Workers, *Inventory of Farmworker Issues.*

60. Frymer, *Black and Blue;* Goluboff, *The Lost Promise of Civil Rights;* Katznelson, *When Affirmative Action Was White.*

61. The state of California is an exception to this rule, with the 1975 California Agricultural Labor Relations Act (CALRA) establishing collective bargaining for farmworkers in the state. This law was passed in large part due to the successful organizing efforts of the United Farm Workers Organizing Committee.

62. Douphrate et al., "Work-Related Injuries and Fatalities"; Harrison, Lloyd, and O'Kane, "Overview of Immigrant Workers on Wisconsin Dairy Farms"; Harrison and Lloyd, "New Jobs, New Workers"; Keller, Gray, and Harrison, "Milking Workers, Breaking Bodies"; Sexsmith, "'But We Can't Call 911.'"

63. Sexsmith.

64. Baker and Chappelle, "Health Status and Needs."

65. Wolcott-MacCausland, "Health Access Negotiations," 1.

66. McCandless, "Conserving the Landscapes of Vermont."

67. Harrison et al., "Development of a Spanish-Language Version."

68. Harrison, "Ethnography as Politics."

69. Sanchez, "Californian Strawberries"; Holmes, "Structural Vulnerability and Hierarchies"; Holmes, *Fresh Fruit, Broken Bodies;* Kearney and Nagengast,

Anthropological Perspectives; Palerm, "Immigrant and Migrant Farm Workers"; Quesada, Hart, and Bourgois, "Structural Vulnerability and Health."

70. Quesada, Hart, and Bourgois, "Structural Vulnerability and Health," 340–41.

CHAPTER ONE

1. Andreas, "The Mexicanization of the US-Canada Border.
2. Paasi, "Bounded Spaces in a 'Borderless World.'"
3. Paasi, "Border Studies Reanimated," 2304.
4. Farmer, *Pathologies of Power*, 8.
5. Holmes, *Fresh Fruit, Broken Bodies*, 157.
6. De León, *The Land of Open Graves*, 40.
7. De León, 284.
8. De León, 17.
9. Quesada, Hart, and Bourgois, "Structural Vulnerability and Health," 340–41.
10. DuPuis, *Nature's Perfect Food*, 118.
11. Hinrichs, "Consuming Images."
12. Bromage, "Why Wagner Hired Migrant Workers."
13. De Genova, "Migrant 'Illegality'"; De Genova, "Introduction"; De Genova, "Production of Culprits"; De Genova and Peutz, *The Deportation Regime*.
14. Baker and Chappelle, "Health Status and Needs"; Wolcott-MacCausland, "Health Access Negotiations."
15. Wolcott-MacCausland, "BTH Data."
16. In chapters 4 and 5 I will go into further detail about Migrant Justice's history, objectives, and accomplishments, as well as my involvement with the organization, drawing upon participant observation as well as interviews with Migrant Justice staff.
17. Migrant Justice, "Milk With Dignity Campaign."
18. Gray, *Labor and the Locavore*, 56.
19. Licona and Maldonado define the social production of Latino/a visibilities and invisibilities as the "spatialized practices by individuals, families, communities, institutions, and the state that render Latin@s (or through which Latin@s render themselves) visible or invisible across contexts, with repercussions for survival, community integration, and political praxis." See Licona and Maldonado, "Social Production," 518.
20. Licona and Maldonado, 521.
21. Nelson, "Racialized Landscapes."
22. Mitchell, *Lie of the Land*.
23. De León, *The Land of Open Graves*, 156.
24. Washington Post Staff, "Full Text."
25. Heintz, "Fear on the Farm."

CHAPTER TWO

1. The following offer excellent critiques of both the concept and the measurement of food insecurity: Cafiero et al., "Validity and Reliability"; Coates, Webb, and Houser, *Measuring Food Insecurity;* Coates et al., "Commonalities in the Experience"; Deitchler et al., "Validation of a Measure of Household Hunger"; Hadley, Patil, and Nahayo, "Difficulty in the Food Environment"; Jones et al., "What Are We Assessing"; Messer, "Anthropological Perspectives on Diet"; National Research Council, *Food Insecurity and Hunger;* Webb et al., "Measuring Household Food Insecurity."
2. Patel, *Stuffed and Starved.*
3. Coleman-Jensen et al., "Household Food Security."
4. Carney, "Compounding Crises of Economic Recession"; Carney, *Unending Hunger;* Dhokarh et al., "Food Insecurity Is Associated with Acculturation"; Himmelgreen et al., "'I Don't Make the Soups Anymore.'"
5. Sanchez, "Californian Strawberries"; Holmes, "Structural Vulnerability"; Holmes, *Fresh Fruit, Broken Bodies;* Kearney and Nagengast, *Anthropological Perspectives on Transnational Communities;* Palerm, "Immigrant and Migrant Farm Workers"; Quesada, Hart, and Bourgois, "Structural Vulnerability and Health."
6. Borre, Ertle, and Graff, "Working to Eat"; Brown and Getz, "Farmworker Food Insecurity"; Cason, Nieto-Montenegro, and Chavez-Martinez, "Food Choices"; Essa, "Nutrition, Health, and Food Security Practices"; Harrison et al., "Development of a Spanish-Language Version"; Kilanowski and Moore, "Food Security and Dietary Intake"; Kresge and Eastman, *Increasing Food Security";* Minkoff-Zern, "Knowing 'Good Food'"; Moos, "Documenting Vulnerability"; Quandt et al., "Household Food Security"; Sano et al., "Understanding Food Insecurity"; Villarejo et al., "Suffering in Silence"; Weigel et al., "Household Food Insecurity"; Wirth, Strochlic, and Getz, "Hunger in the Fields."
7. Brown and Getz, "Farmworker Food Insecurity."
8. Kresge and Eastman, *Increasing Food Security.*
9. Minkoff-Zern, "Knowing 'Good Food.'"
10. Sano et al., "Understanding Food Insecurity."
11. Harrison et al., "Development of a Spanish-Language Version."
12. Coleman-Jensen et al., "Household Food Security."
13. The Economic Research Service of the USDA makes the Spanish version of the HFSSM available free of charge. The full survey and the scoring rubric is located under "Survey Tools" on the USDA website.
14. Ready, "Challenges in the Assessment of Inuit Food Security," 277.
15. Coates et al., "Commonalities in the Experience."
16. Baker and Chappelle, "Health Status and Needs"; Wolcott-MacCausland, "Health Access Negotiations."
17. Coleman-Jensen et al., "Household Food Security."
18. Sano et al., "Understanding Food Insecurity."

19. Sen, *Poverty and Famines.*

20. Gray, *Labor and the Locavore.*

21. Bove and Sobal, "Foodwork in Newly Married Couples"; Sobal, "Men's Foodwork in Food Systems."

CHAPTER THREE

1. Trauger, *We Want Land to Live,* 2.

2. Mazar, "Resistance and Resilience."

3. Mares and Peña, "Environmental and Food Justice"; Mares, Wolcott-Mac-Causland, and Mazar, "Eating Far From Home."

4. Klindienst, *The Earth Knows My Name,* xxi.

5. Mares and Peña, "Environmental and Food Justice."

6. Klindienst, *The Earth Knows My Name,* xxii–xxiii.

7. Trauger, *We Want Land to Live,* 2.

8. Via Campesina, "Declaration of Nyéléni."

9. Holt-Giménez, "From Food Crisis to Food Sovereignty," 246.

10. Trauger, *We Want Land to Live,* 23.

11. Patel, *Stuffed and Starved,* 302.

12. Trauger, *We Want Land to Live,* 6.

13. Trauger, 3.

14. Hewitt, *The Town that Food Saved.*

15. Guthman, "'If They Only Knew.'"

CHAPTER FOUR

1. INS is the acronym for Immigration and Naturalization Services. The functions of INS were transferred to Citizenship and Immigration Services (USCIS), Immigration and Customs Enforcement (ICE), and Customs and Border Protection (CBP) following the events of 9/11.

2. Winders, "Seeing Immigrants."

3. Levitt and Schiller, "Conceptualizing Simultaneity"; Sexsmith, "'But We Can't Call 911.'"

4. Winders, "Seeing Immigrants."

5. Winders, 59–60.

6. USDA Food and Nutrition Service, "Women, Infants, and Children."

7. Vermont Department of Health, "Apply to WIC."

8. Vermont Department of Health.

9. For an extended discussion of the neoliberal aspects of the WIC program, see Mason, "Responsible Bodies."

10. Dobbs, "It's Law."

CHAPTER FIVE

1. Holt-Giménez and Shattuck, "Food Crises, Food Regimes and Food Movements."
2. Migrant Justice, "About Migrant Justice."
3. Galloway, "Young Man's Accidental Death."
4. Migrant Justice, "Tragic Death of Migrant Farmworker."
5. Migrant Justice, "Human Rights Riders and Farmworkers."
6. Ledbetter, "Vt. Gov. Wants Police Directive."
7. Associated Press, "Vermont Migrant Farm Workers."
8. Migrant Justice, "Farmworkers Call on Ben & Jerry's."
9. Greenhouse, "Farm Labor Groups Make Progress."
10. Thomson, "Farmworker Rights Leaders Plan to Protest."
11. True, "Migrant Justice."
12. Jickling, "After Arrests."
13. Holmes, *Fresh Fruit, Broken Bodies.*
14. Freire, *Education for Critical Consciousness.*
15. Mitchell, *The Lie of the Land.*
16. Nelson, "Racialized Landscapes."
17. Holt-Giménez and Shattuck, "Food Crises, Food Regimes and Food Movements"; McMichael, "Food Regime Genealogy."
18. Holt-Giménez and Shattuck, 113.
19. Holt-Giménez and Shattuck, 128.
20. Alkon and Guthman, *New Food Activism.*
21. Minkoff-Zern, "Farmworker-Led Food Movements Then and Now," 158.
22. For an excellent genealogy of the failure of the state to protect farmworkers, see the discussion of agricultural exceptionalism in Gray, *Labor and the Locavore.*
23. For an excellent history of the role of farmworkers and farmworker revolt in California agriculture, see Mitchell, *The Lie of the Land.* For a deep history of the United Farm Workers and their tactics, see Garcia, *From the Jaws of Victory.* For an excellent analysis of PCUN and farmworkers in Oregon, see Sifuentez, *Of Fields and Forests.*
24. Worker-Driven Social Responsibility Network, "Mission."
25. Worker-Driven Social Responsibility Network, "Endorsers."
26. Worker-Driven Social Responsibility Network, "What Is WSR?"

CONCLUSION

1. Rabinow, *Reflections on Fieldwork in Morocco.*
2. These three concepts come, respectively, from Harrison, "Ethnography as Politics"; Katz, "All the World Is Staged"; and Madison, *Critical Ethnography.*

3. Harrison, 88.
4. Katz, "All the World Is Staged," 500.
5. Madison, *Critical Ethnography*.
6. Wainer, "Immigrants in the U.S. Food System."
7. Park, "Human Migration"; Peña, *The Terror of the Machine*.
8. Peña, 217.
9. Trauger, *We Want Land to Live*, 2.
10. Adcock, Anderson, and Rosson, "Economic Impacts of Immigrant Labor."

BIBLIOGRAPHY

ACLU of Vermont. "Surveillance on the Northern Border." 2013. https://www
.scribd.com/embeds/168829662/content?start_page=1&view_mode=scroll&show_
recommendations=true.

Adcock, Flynn, David Anderson, and Parr Rosson. "The Economic Impacts of
Immigrant Labor on U.S. Dairy Farms." College Station, TX: Center for North
American Studies, Texas A&M Agrilife Research, 2015. http://www.nmpf.org
/files/immigration-survey-090915.pdf.

Alkon, Alison Hope, and Julie Guthman, eds. *The New Food Activism: Opposition,
Cooperation, and Collective Action.* Oakland: University of California Press,
2017.

Andreas, Peter. "The Mexicanization of the US-Canada Border: Asymmetric Interdependence in a Changing Security Context." *International Journal* 60, no. 2
(2005): 449–62.

Anzaldúa, Gloria. *Borderlands/La Frontera: The New Mestiza.* San Francisco: Aunt
Lute Books, 1987.

Associated Press. "Vermont Migrant Farm Workers to Focus on Housing." *The
Brattleboro Reformer,* May 17, 2014. http://www.reformer.com/stories
/vermont-migrant-farm-workers-to-focus-on-housing,347209.

Baker, Daniel, and David Chappelle. "Health Status and Needs of Latino Dairy
Farmworkers in Vermont." *Journal of Agromedicine* 17, no. 3 (2012): 277–87.

Baumann, Susana G. "Mexican Farmers Affected By Agricultural Subsidies From
NAFTA, Other International Agreements." *The Huffington Post.* January 11,
2013. Updated July 28, 2014. https://www.huffingtonpost.com/2013/01/11/mexican-
farmers-agricultural-subsidies_n_2457845.html.

Behar, Ruth. *Translated Woman: Crossing the Border with Esperanza's Story.* Boston:
Beacon Press, 1993.

Bon Appétit Management Company Foundation, and United Farm Workers.
Inventory of Farmworker Issues and Protections in the United States. 2012. http://
www.ufw.org/pdf/farmworkerinventory_0401_2011.pdf.

Born, Branden, and Mark Purcell. "Avoiding the Local Trap: Scale and Food Systems in Planning Research." *Journal of Planning Education and Research* 26, no. 2 (2006): 195–207.

Borre, Kristen, Luke Ertle, and Mariaelisa Graff. "Working to Eat: Vulnerability, Food Insecurity, and Obesity among Migrant and Seasonal Farmworker Families." *American Journal of Industrial Medicine* 53, no. 4 (2010): 443–62.

Bove, Caron F., and Jeffery Sobal. "Foodwork in Newly Married Couples: Making Family Meals." *Food, Culture & Society* 9, no. 1 (2006): 69–89.

Bromage, Andy. "Migrant Farmworkers to Shumlin: Denounce Immigration Enforcement Program." *Seven Days,* August 18, 2011. https://www.sevendaysvt .com/vermont/migrant-farmworkers-to-shumlin-denounce-immigration-enforcement-program/Content?oid=2179897.

———. "Why Farmer Chris Wagner Hired Migrant Workers to Milk His Cows." *Seven Days,* November 1, 2011. https://www.sevendaysvt.com/vermont/why-farmer-chris-wagner-hired-migrant-workers-to-milk-his-cows/Content?oid= 2180415

———. "Shumlin Says VT Should 'Look the Other Way' on Illegal Immigration, Republicans Pounce." *Seven Days.* Accessed October 31, 2017. https://www .sevendaysvt.com/vermont/shumlin-says-vt-should-look-the-other-way-on-illegal-immigration-republicans-pounce/Content?oid=2179397.

Brown, Sandy, and Christy Getz. "Farmworker Food Insecurity and the Production of Hunger in California." In *Cultivating Food Justice: Race, Class, and Sustainability,* edited by Alison Hope Alkon and Julian Agyeman, 121–46. Cambridge, MA: MIT Press, 2011.

Cafiero, Carlo, Hugo R. Melgar-Quiñonez, Terri J. Ballard, and Anne W. Kepple. "Validity and Reliability of Food Security Measures." *Annals of the New York Academy of Sciences* 1331, no. 1 (2014): 230–48.

Campbell, Monica, and Tyche Hendricks. "NAFTA and Dumping Subsidized Corn on Mexico Has Driven 1.5 Million Farmers off the Land & Forced Millions to Migrate." *San Francisco Chronicle,* July 31, 2006.

Carney, Megan. "Compounding Crises of Economic Recession and Food Insecurity: A Comparative Study of Three Low-Income Communities in Santa Barbara County." *Agriculture and Human Values* 29, no. 2 (2012): 185–201.

Carney, Megan A. *The Unending Hunger: Tracing Women and Food Insecurity across Borders.* Oakland: University of California Press, 2015.

Cason, Katherine, Sergio Nieto-Montenegro, and America Chavez-Martinez. "Food Choices, Food Sufficiency Practices, and Nutrition Education Needs of Hispanic Migrant Workers in Pennsylvania." *Topics in Clinical Nutrition* 21, no. 2 (2006): 145–58.

Casper, Monica J., and Lisa Jean Moore. *Missing Bodies: The Politics of Visibility.* New York: NYU Press, 2009.

Chavez, Leo. *The Latino Threat: Constructing Immigrants, Citizens, and the Nation.* Stanford, CA: Stanford University Press, 2013.

Cisneros, J. David. "Contaminated Communities: The Metaphor of 'Immigrant as Pollutant' in Media Representations of Immigration." *Rhetoric & Public Affairs* 11, no. 4 (2008): 569–601.

Coates, Jennifer, Edward A. Frongillo, Beatrice Lorge Rogers, Patrick Webb, Parke E. Wilde, and Robert Houser. "Commonalities in the Experience of Household Food Insecurity across Cultures: What Are Measures Missing?" *The Journal of Nutrition* 136, no. 5 (2006): 1438S–48S.

Coates, Jennifer, Patrick Webb, and Robert Houser. *Measuring Food Insecurity: Going beyond Indicators of Income and Anthropometry.* Food and Nutrition Technical Assistance Project, Academy for Educational Development, 2003.

Coleman-Jensen, Alisha, Matthew P. Rabbitt, Christian A. Gregory, and Anita Singh. *Household Food Security in the United States in 2016.* ERR-237. Washington, DC: U.S. Department of Agriculture, Economic Research Service, 2017.

Decena, Carlos Ulises, and Margaret Gray. "The Border Next Door: New York Migraciones." *Social Text* 24, no. 3 (2006): 1–12.

De Genova, Nicholas. "Introduction: Latino and Asian Racial Formations at the Frontier of US Nationalism." In *Racial Transformations: Latinos and Asians Remaking the United States,* edited by Nicholas De Genova, 1–20. Durham, NC: Duke University Press, 2006.

———. "The Production of Culprits: From Deportability to Detainability in the Aftermath of 'Homeland Security.'" *Citizenship Studies* 11, no. 5 (2007): 421–48.

De Genova, Nicholas, and Nathalie Peutz. *The Deportation Regime: Sovereignty, Space, and the Freedom of Movement.* Durham, NC: Duke University Press, 2010.

De Genova, Nicholas P. "Migrant 'Illegality' and Deportability in Everyday Life." *Annual Review of Anthropology* 31 no. 1 (2002): 419–47.

Deitchler, Megan, Terri Ballard, Anne Swindale, and Jennifer Coates. "Validation of a Measure of Household Hunger for Cross-Cultural Use." 2010. https://www.fantaproject.org/sites/default/files/resources/HHS_Validation_Report_May2010_0.pdf

De León, Jason. *The Land of Open Graves: Living and Dying on the Migrant Trail.* Oakland: University of California Press, 2015.

Deleuze, Gilles, and Félix Guattari. *Anti-Œdipus: Capitalism and Schizophrenia.* Translated by Robert Hurley, Mark Seem and Helen R. Lane. New York: Viking Press, 1977.

Dhokarh, Rajanigandha, David A. Himmelgreen, Yu-Kuei Peng, Sofia Segura-Pérez, Amber Hromi-Fiedler, and Rafael Pérez-Escamilla. "Food Insecurity Is Associated with Acculturation and Social Networks in Puerto Rican Households." *Journal of Nutrition Education and Behavior* 43, no. 4 (2011): 288–94.

Dobbs, Taylor. "It's Law: Vermont Limits the Role of Local Cops in Federal Immigration Enforcement." *Seven Days,* March 28, 2017. http://digital.vpr.net/post/its-law-vermont-limits-role-local-cops-federal-immigration-enforcement.

Douphrate, David I., Lorann Stallones, Christina Lunner Kolstrup, Matthew W. Nonnenmann, Stefan Pinzke, G. Robert Hagevoort, Peter Lundqvist, Martina

Jakob, Huiyun Xiang, and Ling Xue. "Work-Related Injuries and Fatalities on Dairy Farm Operations—A Global Perspective." *Journal of Agromedicine* 18, no. 3 (2013): 256–64.

DuPuis, E. Melanie. *Nature's Perfect Food: How Milk Became America's Drink*. New York: NYU Press, 2002.

Elden, Stuart. "Missing the Point: Globalization, Deterritorialization and the Space of the World." *Transactions of the Institute of British Geographers* 30, no. 1 (2005): 8–19.

Esbenshade, Jill. "The 'Crisis' over Day Labor." *WorkingUSA* 3, no. 6 (2000): 27–70.

Essa, Jumanah S. "Nutrition, Health, and Food Security Practices, Concerns, and Perceived Barriers of Latino Farm/Industry Workers in Virginia." Master's thesis, Virginia Polytechnic Institute and State University, 2001.

Farmer, Paul. *Pathologies of Power: Health, Human Rights, and the New War on the Poor*. Oakland: University of California Press, 2004.

Food Chain Workers Alliance. "The Hands That Feed Us: Challenges and Opportunities for Workers along the Food Chain." Food Chain Workers, June 6, 2012. http://foodchainworkers. org.

Freidberg, Susanne. *Fresh*. Cambridge, MA: Harvard University Press, 2009.

Freire, Paulo. *Education for Critical Consciousness*. Vol. 1. New York: Bloomsbury Publishing, 1973.

Frymer, Paul. *Black and Blue: African Americans, the Labor Movement, and the Decline of the Democratic Party*. Princeton, NJ: Princeton University Press, 2008.

Galloway, Anne. "Young Man's Accidental Death on a Vermont Dairy Farm Points up Migrant-Worker Conundrum." *Vermont Digger,* December 27, 2009. https://vtdigger.org/2009/12/27/young-mans-accidental-death-on-a-vermont-dairy-farm-points-up-immigration-conundrum/#.Wh18ybQ-dok.

Garcia, Matt. *From the Jaws of Victory: The Triumph and Tragedy of Cesar Chavez and the Farm Worker Movement*. Berkeley: University of California Press, 2012.

Garcia, Matt, E. Melanie DuPuis, and Don Mitchell, eds. *Food across Borders*. New Brunswick, NJ: Rutgers University Press, 2017.

Giroux, Henry A. "Reading Hurricane Katrina: Race, Class, and the Biopolitics of Disposability." *College Literature* 33, no. 3 (2006): 171–96.

Goluboff, Risa Lauren. *The Lost Promise of Civil Rights*. Cambridge, MA: Harvard University Press, 2007.

Gray, Margaret. *Labor and the Locavore: The Making of a Comprehensive Food Ethic*. Berkeley: University of California Press, 2013.

Greenhouse, Steven. "Farm Labor Groups Make Progress on Wages and Working Conditions." *The New York Times,* July 3, 2015, Economy. https://www.nytimes.com/2015/07/04/business/economy/farm-labor-groups-make-progress-on-wages-and-working-conditions.html.

Guthman, Julie. "'If They Only Knew': The Unbearable Whiteness of Alternative Food." In *Cultivating Food Justice: Race, Class, and Sustainability,* edited by Alison Hope Alkon and Julian Agyeman, 263–81. Cambridge, MA: MIT Press, 2011.

———. *Agrarian Dreams: The Paradox of Organic Farming in California.* Oakland: University of California Press, 2014.

Hadley, Craig, Crystal L. Patil, and Djona Nahayo. "Difficulty in the Food Environment and the Experience of Food Insecurity among Refugees Resettled in the United States." *Ecology of Food and Nutrition* 49, no. 5 (2010): 390–407.

Harrison, Faye Venetia. "Ethnography as Politics." In *Decolonizing Anthropology: Moving Further toward an Anthropology for Liberation,* edited by Faye Harrison, 88–109. Washington DC: American Anthropological Association, 1991.

Harrison, Gail G., Ame Stormer, Dena R. Herman, and Donna M. Winham. "Development of a Spanish-Language Version of the US Household Food Security Survey Module." *The Journal of Nutrition* 133, no. 4 (2003): 1192–97.

Harrison, Jill Lindsey, and Sarah E. Lloyd. "New Jobs, New Workers, and New Inequalities: Explaining Employers' Roles in Occupational Segregation by Nativity and Race." *Social Problems* 60, no. 3 (2013): 281–301.

Harrison, Jill, Sarah Lloyd, and Trish O'Kane. "Overview of Immigrant Workers on Wisconsin Dairy Farms." Program on Agricultural Technology Studies, Madison, WI, 2009.

Harvey, David. *A Brief History of Neoliberalism.* New York: Oxford University Press, 2005.

Heintz, Paul. "Fear on the Farm: Trump's Immigration Crackdown Threatens Vermont's Dairy Industry." *Seven Days,* February 15, 2017. https://www.sevendaysvt.com/vermont/fear-on-the-farm-trumps-immigration-crackdown-threatens-vermonts-dairy-industry/Content?oid=4031604.

———. "Selling the Herd: A Milk Price Crisis Is Devastating Vermont's Dairy Farms." *Seven Days,* April 11, 2018. https://www.sevendaysvt.com/vermont/selling-the-herd-a-milk-price-crisis-is-devastating-vermonts-dairy-farms/Content?oid=14631009.

Hertz, Thomas. "USDA ERS—Farm Labor." USDA Economic Research Service, 2018. https://www.ers.usda.gov/topics/farm-economy/farm-labor/.

Hewitt, Ben. *The Town that Food Saved: How One Community Found Vitality in Local Food.* Emmaus, PA: Rodale, 2010.

Himmelgreen, David, Nancy Romero Daza, Elizabeth Cooper, and Dinorah Martinez. "'I Don't Make the Soups Anymore': Pre-to Post-Migration Dietary and Lifestyle Changes among Latinos Living in West-Central Florida." *Ecology of Food and Nutrition* 46, nos. 5–6 (2007): 427–44.

Hinrichs, C. Clare. "Consuming Images: Making and Marketing Vermont as Distinctive Rural Place." In *Creating the Countryside,* 259–78. Philadelphia: Temple University Press, 1996,

Holmes, Seth M. "Structural Vulnerability and Hierarchies of Ethnicity and Citizenship on the Farm." *Medical Anthropology* 30, no. 4 (2011): 425–49.

———. *Fresh Fruit, Broken Bodies: Migrant Farmworkers in the United States.* Berkeley: University of California Press, 2013.

Holt-Giménez, Eric. "From Food Crisis to Food Sovereignty: The Challenge of Social Movements." *Monthly Review* 61, no. 3 (2009):142–156.

Holt-Giménez, Eric, and Annie Shattuck. "Food Crises, Food Regimes and Food Movements: Rumblings of Reform or Tides of Transformation?" *The Journal of Peasant Studies* 38, no. 1 (2011): 109–44.

Jickling, Katie. "After Arrests, Attorney Says ICE Is Targeting Migrant Justice." *Seven Days,* March 21, 2017. https://www.sevendaysvt.com/OffMessage /archives/2017/03/21/after-arrests-attorney-says-ice-is-targeting-migrant-justice.

Johnson, Corey, Reece Jones, Anssi Paasi, Louise Amoore, Alison Mountz, Mark Salter, and Chris Rumford. "Interventions on Rethinking 'the Border' in Border Studies." *Political Geography* 30, no. 2 (2011): 61–69.

Jones, Andrew D., Francis M. Ngure, Gretel Pelto, and Sera L. Young. "What Are We Assessing When We Measure Food Security? A Compendium and Review of Current Metrics." *Advances in Nutrition: An International Review Journal* 4, no. 5 (2013): 481–505.

Kandel, William. *Profile of Hired Farmworkers, a 2008 Update.* ERR-60. Washington, DC: Economic Research Service, 2008. https://www.ers.usda.gov/publications /pub-details/?pubid=46041

Katz, Cindi. "All the World Is Staged: Intellectuals and the Projects of Ethnography." *Environment and Planning D: Society and Space* 10, no. 5 (1992): 495–510.

Katznelson, Ira. *When Affirmative Action Was White: An Untold History of Racial Inequality in Twentieth-Century America.* New York: WW Norton & Company, 2005.

Kearney, Michael, and Carole Nagengast. *Anthropological Perspectives on Transnational Communities in Rural California.* Davis, CA: California Institute for Rural Studies, 1989.

Keller, Julie C., Margaret Gray, and Jill Lindsey Harrison. "Milking Workers, Breaking Bodies: Health Inequality in the Dairy Industry." *New Labor Forum* 26 (2017): 36–44.

Kilanowski, Jill F., and Laura C. Moore. "Food Security and Dietary Intake in Midwest Migrant Farmworker Children." *Journal of Pediatric Nursing* 25, no. 5 (2010): 360–66.

Klindienst, Patricia. *The Earth Knows My Name: Food, Culture, and Sustainability in the Gardens of Ethnic Americans.* Boston: Beacon Press, 2006.

Kresge, Lisa, and Chelsea Eastman. *Increasing Food Security among Agricultural Workers in California's Salinas Valley.* Davis, CA: California Institute for Rural Studies, 2010.

Latham, Robert. "The Governance of Visibility: Bodies, Information, and the Politics of Anonymity across the US-Mexico Borderlands." *Alternatives* 39, no. 1 (2014): 17–36.

Ledbetter, Stuart. "Vt. Gov. Wants Police Directive on Migrant Workers." NBC5 News Archive, September 26, 2011. http://www.mynbc5.com/article/vt-gov-wants-police-directive-on-migrant-workers/3300307#ixzz1Y8aqfOMm.

Levitt, Peggy, and Nina Glick Schiller. "Conceptualizing Simultaneity: A Transnational Social Field Perspective on Society." *International Migration Review* 38, no. 3 (2004): 1002–39.

Licona, Adela C., and Marta Maria Maldonado. "The Social Production of Latin@ Visibilities and Invisibilities: Geographies of Power in Small Town America." *Antipode* 46, no. 2 (2014): 517–36.

Madison, D. Soyini. *Critical Ethnography: Method, Ethics, and Performance.* Thousand Oaks, CA: SAGE Publications, 2005.

Maloney, Thomas R., and David C. Grusenmeyer. *Survey of Hispanic Dairy Workers in New York State.* Department of Applied Economics and Management, College of Agriculture and Life Sciences, Cornell University, Ithaca, NY, 2005.

Mares, Teresa Marie, and Devon G. Peña. "Environmental and Food Justice: Toward Local, Slow, and Deep Food Systems." In *Cultivating Food Justice: Race, Class, and Sustainability,* edited by Alison Hope Alkon and Julian Agyeman, 197–220. Cambridge, MA: MIT Press, 2011.

Mares, Teresa Marie, Naomi Wolcott-MacCausland, and Jessie Mazar. "Eating Far From Home: Latino/a Workers and Food Sovereignty in Rural Vermont." In *Food Across Borders,* edited by Matt Garcia, E. Melanie DuPuis, and Don Mitchell, 181–200. New Brunswick, NJ: Rutgers University Press, 2017.

Mason, Katherine. "Responsible Bodies: Self-Care and State Power in the US Women, Infants, and Children Program." *Social Politics* 23, no. 1 (2015): 70–93.

Mazar, Jessie. "Resistance and Resilience: Latinx Migrant Farmworkers in the Northern Borderlands." Master's thesis, University of Vermont and State Agricultural College, 2016.

McCandless, Susannah Ruth. "Conserving the Landscapes of Vermont: Shifting Terms of Access and Visibility." PhD diss., Clark University, 2010.

McDonald, James H. "NAFTA and the Milking of Dairy Farmers in Central Mexico." *Culture, Agriculture, Food and Environment* 15, nos. 51-52 (1995): 13–18.

McMichael, Philip. "A Food Regime Genealogy." *The Journal of Peasant Studies* 36, no. 1 (2009): 139–69.

Messer, Ellen. "Anthropological Perspectives on Diet." *Annual Review of Anthropology* 13, no. 1 (1984): 205–49.

Migrant Justice. "About Migrant Justice." Migrant Justice / Justicia Migrante. Accessed September 6, 2018. https://migrantjustice.net/about.

———. "Farmworkers Call on Ben & Jerry's to Stand Up for Dairy Workers' Rights in Supply Chain!" Migrant Justice / Justicia Migrante, April 29, 2015. https://migrantjustice.net/blogs/anonymous/farmworkers-call-on-ben-jerrys-to-stand-up-for-dairy-workers-rights-in-supply-chain.

———. "Human Rights Riders and Farmworkers Deliver 'Cabot "Sour Cream" Award' to Mack Farm in Charlotte for Continued Wage Theft." Migrant Justice / Justicia Migrante, August 7, 2012. https://migrantjustice.net/node/185.

———. "Milk With Dignity Campaign." Brochure, May 2015. http://migrantjustice.net/sites/default/files/MilkWithDignityCampaignMay2015_1.pdf.

———. "Tragic Death of Migrant Farmworker José Obeth Santiz Cruz Inspires Vermonters to Build Bridges of Friendship and Solidarity with the Worker's Tojolabal Mayan Community and Travel to Chiapas, Mexico." Migrant Justice / Justicia Migrante, January 8, 2010. https://vtmfsp.org/node/19.

Minkoff-Zern, Laura-Anne. "Knowing 'Good Food': Immigrant Knowledge and the Racial Politics of Farmworker Food Insecurity." *Antipode* 46, no. 5 (2014): 1190–1204.

——. "Farmworker-Led Food Movements Then and Now: United Farm Workers, The Coalition of Immokalee Workers, and the Potential for Farm Labor Justice." In *The New Food Activism: Opposition, Cooperation, and Collective Action,* edited by Alison Hope Alkon and Julie Guthman, 157–78. Oakland: University of California Press, 2017.

Mintz, Sidney Wilfred. *Sweetness and Power: The Place of Sugar in Modern History.* New York: Penguin, 1986.

Mitchell, Don. *The Lie of the Land: Migrant Workers and the California Landscape.* Minneapolis: University of Minnesota Press, 1996.

Molina, Natalia. *Fit to Be Citizens?: Public Health and Race in Los Angeles, 1879–1939,* vol. 20. Berkeley: University of California Press, 2006.

Moos, Katherine. *Documenting Vulnerability: Food Insecurity among Indigenous Mexican Migrants in California's Central Valley.* Washington, DC: Congressional Hunger Center, 2008.

Nader, Laura. "Up the Anthropologist: Perspectives Gained from Studying Up." In *Reinventing Anthropology,* edited by Dell Hymes, 284–311. New York: Vintage Books, 1972.

National Agriculture Workers Survey. Chapter 3: "Income and Poverty." 2010. https://www.doleta.gov/agworker/report/ch3.cfm.

National Center for Farmworker Health. "Agricultural Worker Factsheet." http://www.ncfh.org/uploads/3/8/6/8/38685499/facts_about_ag_workers_2017.pdf.

National Research Council. *Food Insecurity and Hunger in the United States: An Assessment of the Measure.* Washington, DC: National Academies Press, 2006.

Nelson, Lise. "Racialized Landscapes: Whiteness and the Struggle over Farmworker Housing in Woodburn, Oregon." *Cultural Geographies* 15, no. 1 (2008): 41–62.

Nicholson, Melanie. "Without Their Children: Rethinking Motherhood among Transnational Migrant Women." *Social Text* 24, no. 3 (2006): 13–33.

Paasi, Anssi. "Border Studies Reanimated: Going beyond the Territorial/Relational Divide." *Environment and Planning A* 44, no. 10 (2012): 2303–9.

——. "Bounded Spaces in a 'Borderless World': Border Studies, Power and the Anatomy of Territory." *Journal of Power* 2, no. 2 (2009): 213–34.

——. "The Shifting Landscape of Border Studies and the Challenge of Relational Thinking." In *The New European Frontiers: Social and Spatial (Re) Integration Issues in Multicultural and Border Regions,* edited by Milan Bufon, Julian Minghi, and Anssi Paasi, 361–79. Newcastle upon Tyne, UK: Cambridge Scholars Publishing, 2014.

Palerm, Juan Vicente. "Immigrant and Migrant Farm Workers in the Santa Maria Valley, California." In *Transnational Latina/o Communities: Politics, Processes, and Cultures,* edited by Carlos G. Vélez-Ibáñez and Ann Sampaio, 247–72. Lanham: Rowman & Littlefield Publishers, 2002.

Park, Robert E. "Human Migration and the Marginal Man." *American Journal of Sociology* 33, no. 6 (1928): 881–93.

Parra, Pilar-Alicia and Max J. Pfeffer. "New Immigrants in Rural Communities: The Challenges of Integration." Paper presented at the 130th Annual Meeting of APHA, Philadelphia, November 9–13, 2002.

Parsons, Bob. "Vermont's Dairy Sector: Is There a Sustainable Future for the 800 Lb. Gorilla?" Opportunities for Agriculture Working Paper Series, vol. 1, no. 4. Burlington: University of Vermont Center for Rural Studies, 2010.

Patel, Raj. *Stuffed and Starved: Markets, Power and the Hidden Battle for the World Food System.* Brooklyn, NY: Melville House, 2008.

Peña, Devon G. *The Terror of the Machine: Technology, Work, Gender, and Ecology on the US-Mexico Border.* Austin: University of Texas Press, 1997.

Quandt, Sara A., Thomas A. Arcury, Julie Early, Janeth Tapia, and Jessie D. Davis. "Household Food Security among Migrant and Seasonal Latino Farmworkers in North Carolina." *Public Health Reports* 119, no. 6 (2004): 568–76.

Quesada, James, Laurie Kain Hart, and Philippe Bourgois. "Structural Vulnerability and Health: Latino Migrant Laborers in the United States." *Medical Anthropology* 30, no. 4 (2011): 339–62.

Rabinow, Paul. *Reflections on Fieldwork in Morocco.* Berkeley: University of California Press, 1977.

Radel, Claudia, Birgit Schmook, and Susannah McCandless. . "Environment, Transnational Labor Migration, and Gender: Case Studies from Southern Yucatan, Mexico and Vermont, USA." *Population and Environment* 32, nos. 2–3 (2010): 177–97.

Ready, Elspeth. "Challenges in the Assessment of Inuit Food Security." *Arctic* 69, no. 3 (2016): 266–80.

Relinger, Rick. "NAFTA and US Corn Subsidies: Explaining the Displacement of Mexico's Corn Farmers." *Prospect Journal of International Affairs at UCSD.* April 19, 2010. https://prospectjournal.org/2010/04/19/nafta-and-u-s-corn-subsidies-explaining-the-displacement-of-mexicos-corn-farmers-2/

Sanchez, Teresa Figueroa. "Californian Strawberries: Mexican Immigrant Women Sharecroppers, Labor, and Discipline." *Anthropology of Work Review* 34, no. 1 (2013): 15–26.

Sano, Yoshie, Steven Garasky, Kimberly A. Greder, Christine C. Cook, and Dawn E. Browder. "Understanding Food Insecurity among Latino Immigrant Families in Rural America." *Journal of Family and Economic Issues* 32, no. 1 (2011): 111–23.

Scheper-Hughes, Nancy. *Death Without Weeping: The Violence of Everyday Life in Brazil.* Berkeley: University of California Press, 1992.

Sen, Amartya. *Poverty and Famines: An Essay on Entitlement and Deprivation.* New York: Oxford University Press, 1981.

Sexsmith, Kathleen. "'But We Can't Call 911': Undocumented Immigrant Farmworkers and Access to Social Protection in New York." *Oxford Development Studies* 45, no. 1 (2017): 96–111.

Shields, Dennis A. *Consolidation and Concentration in the US Dairy Industry.* Congressional Research Service Report 41224, 2010.

Sifuentez, Mario Jimenez. *Of Fields and Forests: Mexican Labor in the Pacific Northwest.* New Brunswick, NJ: Rutgers University Press, 2016.

Sneyd, Ross. "Total Number of Dairy Farms In Vt. Falls below 1,000." VPR Archive, July 8, 2011. http://vprarchive.vpr.net/vpr-news/total-number-of-dairy-farms-in-vt-falls-below-1000/.

Sobal, Jeffrey. "Men's Foodwork in Food Systems: Social Representations of Masculinities and Cooking at Home." In *Food, Masculinities, and Home: Interdisciplinary Perspectives,* edited by Michelle Szabo and Shelley Koch, 125–43. New York: Bloomsbury Press, 2016.

Southern Poverty Law Center. "Injustice on Our Plates: Immigrant Women in the U.S. Food Industry." 2010. https://www.splcenter.org/sites/default/files/d6_legacy_files/downloads/publication/Injustice_on_Our_Plates.pdf.

Thomson, Julie R. "Farmworker Rights Leaders Plan to Protest on Ben & Jerry's Free Cone Day." *Huffington Post,* April 4, 2017. https://www.huffpost.com/entry/ben-and-jerrys-protest_n_58e273a7e4b0c777f78934fc.

Trauger, Amy. *We Want Land to Live: Making Political Space for Food Sovereignty.* Athens: University of Georgia Press, 2017.

True, Morgan. "Migrant Justice: Bail Granted for Activist Facing Deportation." *VTDigger,* May 4, 2016. https://vtdigger.org/2016/05/04/migrant-justice-group-bail-granted-for-activist-facing-deportation/.

USDA Food and Nutrition Service. "Women, Infants, and Children (WIC)." Accessed November 14, 2017. https://www.fns.usda.gov/wic/women-infants-and-children-wic.

Vermont Dairy Promotion Council. *Milk Matters: The Role of Dairy in Vermont.* 2015. http://vermontdairy.com/wp-content/uploads/2015/12/VTD_MilkMatters-Brochure_OUT-pages.pdf.

Vermont Department of Health. "Apply to WIC." Vermont Department of Health, Division of Children, Youth & Families. April 6, 2018. http://www.healthvermont.gov/children-youth-families/wic/apply.

Via Campesina. "Declaration of Nyéléni." February 27, 2007. Final edited version March 27, 2007. https://nyeleni.org/spip.php?article290.

Villarejo, Don, David Lighthall, Daniel Williams III, Ann Souter, Richard Mines, Bonnie Bade, Steve Samuels, and Stephen A. McCurdy. *Suffering in Silence: A Report on the Health of California's Agricultural Workers.* Davis: California Institute for Rural Studies, 2000.

Wainer, Andrew. "Immigrants in the U.S. Food System." *The 2014 Hunger Report* (blog). Accessed January 18, 2018. http://hungerreport.org/featured/immigrants-us-food-system/.

Washington Post Staff. "Full Text: Donald Trump Announces a Presidential Bid." *Washington Post,* June 16, 2015. https://www.washingtonpost.com/news/post-politics/wp/2015/06/16/full-text-donald-trump-announces-a-presidential-bid/.

Webb, Patrick, Jennifer Coates, Edward A. Frongillo, Beatrice Lorge Rogers, Anne Swindale, and Paula Bilinsky. "Measuring Household Food Insecurity: Why It's So Important and yet So Difficult to Do." *The Journal of Nutrition* 136, no. 5 (2006): 1404S–8S.

Weigel, M. Margaret, Rodrigo X. Armijos, Yolanda Posada Hall, Yolanda Ramirez, and Rubi Orozco. "The Household Food Insecurity and Health Outcomes of US–Mexico Border Migrant and Seasonal Farmworkers." *Journal of Immigrant and Minority Health* 9, no. 3 (2007): 157–69.

Winders, Jamie. "Seeing Immigrants: Institutional Visibility and Immigrant Incorporation in New Immigrant Destinations." *The ANNALS of the American Academy of Political and Social Science* 641, no. 1 (2012): 58–78.

Wirth, Cathy, Ron Strochlic, and Christy Getz. *Hunger in the Fields: Food Insecurity among Farmworkers in Fresno County.* California Institute for Rural Studies 13, 2007.

Wolcott-MacCausland, Naomi. "Health Access Negotiations and Decisions Among Latino/a Dairy Workers in Vermont." Master's thesis, University of Vermont, 2014.

———. *Vermont Dairy Farms and Bridges to Health.* Programmatic Report. Saint Albans: University of Vermont Extension, 2017.

———. "BTH Data." Unpublished manuscript, September 21, 2017.

Worker-Driven Social Responsibility Network. "Endorsers." Accessed December 14, 2017. https://wsr-network.org/about-us/endorsers/.

———. "Mission." Accessed December 14, 2017. https://wsr-network.org/about-us /mission/.

———. "What Is WSR?" Accessed December 14, 2017. https://wsr-network.org /what-is-wsr/.

INDEX

Familias Unidas por la Justicia, 172
Farmer, Paul, 33–34
farmers market coupons, 128
farmworker-led resistance: overview, 3,
9–10, 16, 28; on bias policing, 127,
154–57; on driver's privilege cards,
157–58; in food justice movement,
170–74; Milk with Dignity campaign,
10, 147, 158–63; targeted arrests from,
47, 155–56, 163–65, 182; transformative
power of, 188–91; on wage theft, 153–54.
See also *specific organizations*
farmworkers: Bracero program for, 16;
catering business of, 80–82, 83, 169; film
about, 152–53; H-2A visas for, 16, 20,
129, 198n39; Holmes's study on, 34, 41;
interview guide for, 193–94; legal protections for, 19; population overview of,
12, 15–17, 41; working conditions and
abuse of, 17–20, 42, 49, 70, 144, 189. *See
also* dairy workers; (in)visibility of
farmworkers
fatalities, 8, 18, 41, 151–52, 199n55. *See also*
disease and poor health
fear. *See* deportation fear; *encerrado*
Florida, 19. *See also* Coalition of Immokalee Workers (CIW)
food access. *See* food (in)security
Food Across Borders (publication), 4
food and cuisine of Mexico, 55, 69, 72–73,
77–78, 91
Food Chains (film), 159–60
Food Chain Workers Alliance (FCWA), 17,
20, 171
food (in)security: of Alma, 67, 71–74; of
Andrés, 74–77; of César, 100–102; of
children, 23, 63–65, 136; of Emmanuel,
85–88, 97–100; of Josefina, 80–82, 83; of
Martín, 77–80; of Natalia, 67, 68–71;
service providers on, 134–35; studies and
statistics on, 22–24, 57–67, 82–84. *See
also* poverty; service providers
food justice movement, 170–74, 190–91
food sovereignty, 88, 94–96, 185–88. *See
also* gardens; Huertas project
food system, 2–4, 11–20. *See also* dairy
industry; farmworkers
forced labor, 19, 174. *See also* farmworkers

Freire, Paolo, 167
Fresh Fruit, Broken Bodies (Holmes), 34
Fresno Farmworker Security Assessment,
60

Gabriel, 78–79, 140–41
Gabriela, 29, 40, 44, 48–52, 67
gardens: of Alma, 72, 74, 102–4; of Andrés,
188; of César, 100–102; of Emmanuel,
85–88, 97–100; of Gloria, 107–9; of
Josefina, 81; in Mexico, 69, 72–73; of
Natalia, 71; of Sofía, 104–7. *See also*
food sovereignty; Huertas project
Georgia, 19. *See also* Coalition of Immoka-
lee Workers (CIW)
Giroux, Henry A., 7
Gloria, 85, 107–9
grape industry, 3, 172, 173, 188
Gray, Margaret, 42, 69–70
Guatemalan farmworkers, 16, 41, 177
Guthman, Julie, 113, 171

H-2A Temporary Agricultural Worker
program, 16, 20, 129, 198n39
Harrison, Faye, 25, 180
Head Start program, 133
health. *See* disease and poor health
health care, access to, 21–22, 120, 126,
128–37, 169. *See also* social services
health insurance, 18, 131
Hector, 1, 2, 7, 8
Hernandez, Yesenia, 162, 165
Hinrichs, Clare, 39
Holmes, Seth, 33, 34, 41
Holt-Giménez, Eric, 95, 170, 171, 187
home-based businesses, 80–82, 83, 169
home-delivery services. *See* service providers
Honduran farmworkers, 16
household, as survey category, 23, 24, 58
Household Food Security Survey Mode
(USDA), 22–24, 58, 62–67
housing conditions, 18, 30–31, 39, 125, 133,
158–59, 168. See also *encerrado;* working
conditions
HP Hood, 12, 198n24
Huertas project: author's work in, 85, 89;
Emily's experience with, 110–14; har-
vest parties with, 56; kitchen gardening

Vermont Bankers Association, 157
Vermont Criminal Justice Training Council, 156–57
Vermont Dairy Promotion Council, 12–13, 168
Vermont Migrant Education Program, 40, 152
Vermont Migrant Farmworker Solidarity Project (VMFSP), 37, 41, 149, 151–53. *See also* Migrant Justice
Vermont Refugee Resettlement Program (VRRP), 137
Vermont S.184 (Act 193), 156
Vermont S.238, 157–58
Vermont Workers' Center, 154, 169, 171
La Via Campesina, 94–95
visas. *See* H-2A Temporary Agricultural Worker program
visibility. *See* (in)visibility of farmworkers

wage theft, 17, 19, 68, 70, 153–54. *See also* labor abuse
Washington, 41, 166, 189
whey production, 13
WIC (Women, Infants and Children) program, 66, 70, 74, 81, 120, 121–28, 133
Winders, Jamie, 120–21
Wisconsin, 15, 20, 189

Wolcott-MacCausland, Naomi: on generosity of gardeners, 85; on poor health and working conditions, 144; as research assistant, 23, 24, 64, 77, 113; work with BTH, 89, 132–36
women: border studies on, 36; division of labor in families, 44, 71, 78, 99; experiences of migrant mothers, 47–52, 57; unique experiences of food (in)security by, 68–69; working conditions of, 18; work opportunities for, 49, 80. *See also* children; WIC (Women, Infants and Children) program; *specific names*
worker-driven social responsibility (WSR) model, 10, 159–60, 172–73. *See also* farmworker-led resistance
Worker-Driven Social Responsibility (WSR) Network, 173–74, 189
workers' compensation, 18, 19
working conditions: long hours, 17, 49, 71, 75, 97, 189; paternalism and, 42–43, 69–70, 129, 141; poor health and disease due to, 18–19, 21, 83, 127–28, 144; sexual violence, 18; statistics on, 42. See also *encerrado;* housing conditions; labor abuse

Yankee values, 13, 39
yogurt production, 13